Austria

A Study of the Educational System of Austria and a Guide to the Academic Placement of Students in Educational Institutions of the United States

Karen Hammerlund Lukas

International Student Admissions Officer
University of Minnesota

1987

A Service of the International Education Activities Group of the American
Association of Collegiate Registrars and Admissions Officers
Washington, DC

Placement Recommendations and U.S. Grade Equivalents Approved by the National
Council on the Evaluation of Foreign Educational Credentials

Library of Congress Cataloging-in-Publication Data

Lukas, Karen Hammerlund.
  Austria: a study of the educational system of Austria and a guide to the
academic placement of students in educational institutions of the United
States.

(World education series)
  "A service of the International Education Activities Group of the
American Association of Collegiate Registrars and Admissions Officers."
  Bibliography: p.
  Includes index.
  1. Education—Austria.   2. School credits—Austria.   3. American
students—Austria.   I. Title.   II. Series.
LA672.L84 1987   370'.9436   87-980
ISBN 0-910054-89-4

Publication of the World Education Series is funded by grants from the Bureau
of Educational and Cultural Affairs of the United States Information Agency.

Contents

Tables

Preface

Many people in Austria and the United States have contributed to this volume by sharing their expertise and insights into Austrian and comparative education. Working with these people has been the most rewarding part of this project for me. To those who helped arrange contacts with educators, governmental officials, students, and others in Austria, and to those who patiently answered my endless questions and contributed to my understanding of Austrian education, I want to express my appreciation and gratitude. Although space does not permit me to list each person by name, I want to acknowledge the assistance of Professor William E. Wright, Director of the Center for Austrian Studies, University of Minnesota; Dr. Anton Porhansl and Ministerialrat Dr. Günter Frühwirth, former and current directors of the Austrian-American Educational Commission (Fulbright); Dr. Eva Turcu, Office of the Cultural Attaché, United States Embassy; the many ministry officials with whom I spoke at the Bundesministerium für Wissenschaft und Forschung (BMWF) and Bundesministerium für Unterricht, Kunst und Sport (BMUKS) and the English department staff and director, Dr. Gerhard Berger, at the Pädagogische Akademie der Diözese Graz/Seckau. I also want to thank the following who graciously agreed to read portions of the manuscript: Ministerialrat Dr. Helmut Aigner, BMUKS; Univ.-Prof. Dr. Werner Lenz, Institute for Educational Sciences, Universität Graz; Univ.-Asst. Mag. Dr. Walter Grünzweig, American Studies Department, Universität Graz; Dr. Lutz Musner, BMWF; and Rat Mag. Johann Wimmer, BMUKS.

Among the many people who assisted me in the United States, I am particularly indebted to my monitor Karlene N. Dickey, Associate Dean for Graduate Studies, Stanford University, who tirelessly read and commented on each draft and provided direction and encouragement; my editor at AACRAO, Henny Wakefield, and her assistant, Miranda Knowles, who carefully and expertly attended to the overwhelming number of details involved in transforming a manuscript into a book; the World Education Series Committee members and chair, Kitty Villa, for their helpful comments; the University of Minnesota Admissions Office staff who filled in for me during my absences; James S. Frey, Executive Director, Educational Credential Evaluators, Inc., Milwaukee, whose probing questions and careful reading of the manuscript served to strengthen it; and, needless to say, the United States Information Agency for their financial support of the World Education Series. Last, but not least, I want to thank my family, including husband Don and daughters Lisa and Sonja, for their continued patience and assistance throughout this three-year project.

As I spoke with people during the course of this project who have studied abroad and, as a result, have acquired a multicultural understanding and perspective, I was reminded again of the importance of international exchanges. I wish to dedicate this book to many future exchanges of students and scholars between the United States and Austria.

Karen Lukas
Minneapolis, Minnesota
March 1987

AUSTRIA

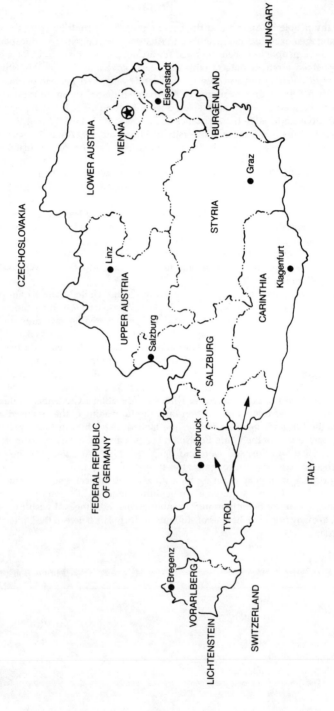

CZECHOSLOVAKIA

LOWER AUSTRIA

VIENNA

BURGENLAND

Eisenstadt

Graz

STYRIA

Linz

UPPER AUSTRIA

Salzburg

SALZBURG

CARINTHIA

Klagenfurt

HUNGARY

YUGOSLAVIA

FEDERAL REPUBLIC
OF GERMANY

Innsbruck

TYROL

ITALY

Bregenz

VORARLBERG

LICHTENSTEIN

SWITZERLAND

Chapter I

Introduction

Background Data

Official Name: Republic of Austria (Republik Österreich).

Location: South central Europe. Austria is a landlocked country that shares common borders with the following seven countries: Czechoslovakia, Federal Republic of Germany, Hungary, Italy, Liechtenstein, Switzerland, and Yugoslavia. Because of its location, Austria is sometimes called the "Alpine Republic." Located away from the large European industrial concentrations, Austria has a relatively low population density by European standards, 90 people per square kilometer, which is lower than that of all its neighboring countries except for Yugoslavia. Austria's location is a crossroads, both north to south and east to west, and a meeting point for three cultures, the Romanic, Germanic and Slavic cultures. Its location has had a significant impact on its history, and its borders have changed often in the course of history.

Size: 32,367 square miles (83,855 square kilometers) which is slightly larger than the state of South Carolina and slightly smaller than the state of Maine.

Population: 7,555,338 (1981 census) including 145,347 foreign workers of which the largest group (approximately 60%) comes from Yugoslavia and the second largest group from Turkey. Vienna (Wien) has a population of 1,515,666 which is approximately one-fifth of the total population.

Government: A democratic federal republic which according to federal law is permanently neutral and militarily nonaligned. Although the President (*Bundespräsident*) is the head of state, primary political influence rests with the Federal Chancellor (*Bundeskanzler*) who along with the vice-chancellor and 13 cabinet ministers conducts the primary affairs of government. The bicameral legislature consists of the National Council (Nationalrat) whose 183 members are elected by the nation at large every four years and the Federal Council (Bundesrat) whose current 63 members are chosen by the provincial parliaments.

Provinces—Capital City: Burgenland—Eisenstadt; Carinthia (Kärnten)—Klagenfurt; Lower Austria (Niederösterreich)—No capital city (administrative headquarters located outside the province in Vienna [Wien]); Salzburg—Salzburg; Styria (Steiermark)—Graz; Tyrol (Tirol)—Innsbruck; Upper Austria (Oberösterreich)—Linz; Vienna—Vienna; Vorarlberg—Bregenz. Vienna (Wien) is a city, a province, the provincial capital of Vienna, administrative headquarters for Lower Austria, and the federal capital.

Languages: 98% of the inhabitants speak German; the remainder speak Croatian, Czech, Hungarian, Slovak, and Slovene.

Religion: 84% of the inhabitants are Roman Catholic, 6% Protestant, 6% nondenominational, and 4% other.

Leading Industries: Iron ore mining and steel production; processing industries such as arts and crafts, chemicals, electronics, glass and porcelain, and textiles; and tourism.

Employment: In 1983, agriculture and forestry accounted for 7.4% of the labor force; industry and manufacturing, 32.3%; services, 35.8%; pensioners, 22.6%; and other, 1.9%. The unemployment rate was 4.5% in 1983.

Literacy Rate: 95%.

Selected Historical Events

976 A.D.	Leopold von Babenberg became Margrave of Austria, thus beginning Babenberg dynasty rule which lasted 270 years. In 996, the name Ostarrichi, from which the current name for Austria—Österreich— originated, was first documented. Austria was part of the Holy Roman Empire.
1273	Rudolf von Habsburg was chosen Holy Roman Emperor. Thus began the 640-year rule of the Habsburg dynasty.
1365	University of Vienna was established by Rudolf IV.
1740	Maria Theresia became empress and ruled until 1780. During her reign, six years of compulsory primary education were established (1774) but not implemented uniformly. Universities also were reorganized; control over them shifted increasingly from church to state.
1806	The Habsburgs lost the title of Holy Roman Emperor but assumed the title of Hereditary Emperor of Austria.
1867	Austria-Hungary was formed.
1869	Compulsory primary education was raised to eight years.
1914-18	World War I, after which the multinational Austro-Hungarian monarchy ruled by the Habsburgs was dissolved and the First Austrian Republic was created.
1938	The annexation of Austria by Germany (the *Anschluss*) occurred.
1939-45	World War II, after which the constitution of the First Austrian Republic was re-established and Allied occupation of Austria began.
1955	The Second Austrian Republic became a sovereign, independent and democratic country; and Allied occupation ended.

Characteristics of the Austrian Educational System

The Austrian educational system has been shaped and reshaped for centuries by politics, geography, religion, history, economics, and industrial development. The product of these forces and others, the modern Austrian educational system, has emerged with a new structure as a result of twentieth century educational reforms but has retained the fundamental values and traditions of the Austrian people. While preserving and reflecting these cultural traditions, the educational system provides the means by which Austrian heritage is transmitted to future generations. Austria's educational system serves the goals set for it by the Austrian people.

When describing the Austrian educational system, natives and foreigners may view the salience of certain characteristics differently. For example, Austrians are proud of their rich fine arts heritage which they preserve and protect through state support of the arts and the fine arts colleges. But U.S. educators may be surprised to count six of 18 university-level institutions devoted exclusively to the fine arts in a country the size of Maine with 7 1/2 million people. Although the six fine arts colleges enroll only 3% of the higher education student population, their existence attests to the priority Austrians accord the fine arts. Other characteristics of the Austrian educational system that distinguish it particularly from the U.S. educational system are described below.

Legal and Administrative Bases for the Educational System

The Austrian educational system is a federal system of education that is regulated by federal ministries and subject to a comprehensive set of federal laws. Consequently, the structure and operation of all schools are highly uniform throughout the country, and changes in the educational system occur only through the political process.

Whether education should be federally or provincially controlled was an open question in Austria until quite recently. Although the constitution of the First Austrian Republic was re-established after World War II and an amended constitution for the Second Austrian Republic was established in 1955, ideological differences between political parties prevented a resolution of this question until 1962. Educational legislation passed in that year assigns jurisdiction for education to the federal government and equalizes educational law with that of constitutional law. As such, educational legislation requires a 50% quorum plus a two-thirds majority vote in the National Council for passage. In practice, due to the relatively equal political strength of the two major political parties, the Austrian People's Party (Österreichische Volkspartei, ÖVP) and the Socialist Party of Austria (Sozialistische Partei Österreichs, SPÖ), passage of educational legislation requires the support of both parties. For this reason, educational legislation often is a result of compromise. In the decade following 1962, many educational laws were passed and the coalescing of political parties has been described as the "Grand Coalition." Educational laws passed during this period affect all parts of the educational system.

Compliance with educational laws is regulated at the federal level primarily by two of the 13 federal ministries, though several other ministries also become involved. The Science and Research Ministry (Bundesministerium für Wissenschaft und Forschung) has responsibility for overseeing the operation of all universities and fine arts colleges. And the Education, Arts and Sports Ministry (Bundesministerium für Unterricht, Kunst und Sport) oversees the operation of primary, secondary, and nonuniversity postsecondary institutions. General secondary schools (*Gymnasien*) and nonuniversity postsecondary institutions are regulated directly by this ministry while most other primary and secondary schools are regulated indirectly by the ministry through provincial school councils (*Landesschulräte*) and the further subordinated municipal school councils (*Bezirksschulräte*). Appointed by the provincial governor, the executive director of each province's school council in turn appoints school principals for lifetime tenure. Provincial and municipal school councils have advisory boards consisting of public interest groups which are sanctioned by federal law and which represent parents, teachers, churches, and other provincial interests such as trade, labor, or farmers.

Although the Education, Arts and Sports Ministry handles the pedagogical affairs for agriculture and forestry schools and the military academy, funding and staffing for these schools are handled by the Agriculture and Forestry Ministry (Bundesministerium für Land- und Forstwirtschaft) and the Defense Ministry (Bundesministerium für Landesverteidigung), respectively. In vocational schools, the Education, Arts and Sports Ministry regulates the general and theoretical education while the Trade, Commerce and Industry Ministry (Bundesministerium für Handel, Gewerbe und Industrie) regulates the accompanying apprenticeship training. Paramedical training which is considered to occur outside the regular educational system is regulated by the Health and Environmental Protection Ministry (Bundesministerium für Gesundheit und Umweltschutz) but is administered at the provincial level. The Foreign Affairs Ministry (Bundesministerium für Auswärtige Angelegenheit) oversees the prestigious Diplomatic Academy in Vienna.

Educational Access and Funding

Austrians accord educational access a high priority. Access to public education is legally guaranteed, regardless of race, social standing, social class, language, religion, or sex. The goal of legislation passed over the past 25 years has been to further increase educational access by removing social, economic, and regional barriers. The result has been a dramatic increase in numbers of students (particularly females) now attending universities (see Chapter VI). All schools have been legally coeducational since 1975, although many were coeducational before then.

Cost is not a major impediment to educational access. Education is provided free of charge to citizens and permanent residents from preprimary through university levels, and the many foreign university students pay only a nominal tuition. Financial assistance for living expenses is provided to approximately 10% of the domestic university students by the government. Eligibility for financial aid is based upon the student's and family's income. The proportion of the total federal budget expended on education has increased from 8.3% in 1970 to 12.6% in 1983 despite a recession starting in 1979 which forced cuts in other federal spending.

Overcoming regional barriers has been another priority. While foreign tourists judge the magnificent Austrian countryside as ideal, Austrians interested in equal educational access view remote rural areas as problematic. The widely dispersed population in rural areas complicates the provision of cost-effective, yet diverse, educational opportunities. Because of the existence of these areas, the Austrian government provides cost-of-living grants to students who must live away from home in order to attend secondary school and transportation allowances for those who must travel great distances to school.

Education and Religion

Strict separation of church and state does not exist in Austria. The relationship between the Roman Catholic Church and the Austrian state has a long history and has played an important role in shaping education. The original schools were monastery schools and, though the nature of the Church-state relationship has changed through the centuries, the Habsburg rulers until 1918 were major patrons of the Church. After World War I, the Church's influence over state affairs (and thus education) was felt primarily through the Christian Social Party whose most influential member and sometime chancellor, Ignaz Seipel, was himself a priest. During this period, relations between the Church and the other major political party, the Social-Democrats, were strained. The Church maintained strong political ties until 1938. During the National Socialist period from 1938 to 1945, the Church was persecuted and many members of the clergy were active in the Austrian resistance movement. In 1945, the Austrian bishops decided to continue withdrawing from active politics, but this decision did not have full impact on cultural policy until after Allied occupation ended in 1955.

Concordats between the Austrian state and the Holy See affecting the modern educational system were signed in 1933, 1949, and 1962. The 1962 treaty maintained the 1949 provision that religious instruction be provided in all schools and realized the 1933 treaty provision that Catholic schools be given state subsidies when economic conditions improved. For the first time in history, the 1962 treaty provided for state subsidy of Catholic school personnel costs up to 60%. This was raised to 100% in 1971. Currently, approximately 84% of the population is Roman Catholic. Training for the priesthood occurs in the Faculty of Catholic Theology at the Universities of Vienna, Graz, Innsbruck, and Salzburg.

Other laws officially recognize most of the other major religions in the world, the largest of which in Austria is the Protestant religion with membership consisting of approximately 6% of the population. The Protestant Church (Evangelische Kirche), consisting of the Augsburg and Reformed Confessions, is guaranteed autonomy, annual state subsidies, and a Faculty of Protestant Theology at the University of Vienna with a minimum of six full professorships.

Religion is taught in all public and private primary and secondary schools during regular school hours. Government-subsidized instruction—usually lasting two hours per week—is provided by a member of each student's officially-recognized church or religious community. Parents of students under 14 years of age may request exemption from religious instruction for their children, and students over 14 years of age may request exemption in their own behalf. Approximately 10% of students over 14 years of age request exemption, but fewer exemptions are requested for younger children.

Public and Private Education

All Austrian universities and fine arts colleges are public institutions; but primary, secondary, and nonuniversity postsecondary institutions may be either public or private institutions. Major differences do not exist between public and private education. Religion is taught in public as well as private schools, and private schools offering an approved curriculum may obtain permission to grant state-recognized leaving certificates (the names of which are provided for each school type in subsequent chapters). This permission or accreditation is known as official recognition (*Öffentlichkeitsrecht*). Private schools with official recognition become subject to federal educational laws, though private schools are administered not by the state but by another organization—usually the Roman Catholic Church. The salaries of teachers in officially-recognized private schools are equal to those of public school teachers and are paid by the state.

Two-Track Secondary Education System

Austrian secondary education is divided into two tracks. After completion of primary school, 10-year-olds are channeled into either the vocational- or university-preparatory track. Primarily, parents and teachers decide which track a child will enter, and this decision has ramifications for a child's future occupation, income level and social status. Vocational schools prepare workers for skilled trades while university-preparatory schools prepare students for higher education and entry into professional careers. Children from working-class families are more likely to enroll in vocational schools while children from upper-class families are more likely to enroll in university-preparatory schools. Prior to 1962, this decision was irrevocable. Current laws permit students to transfer between tracks, but transfers are not commonly requested.

The dual-track system at the lower secondary level (ages 10 to 14) has been the focus of recent political debate. Members of the Socialist Party charge that the current dual-track system promotes unequal educational opportunities and perpetuates the existing social order from one generation to the next. They advocate a homogeneous grouping of students, as found in primary schools, for eight years (through age 14) and a separation of students into tracks only at the upper secondary level (ages 14 to 18 or 19). Representatives of the People's Party oppose legislation to change the dual-track system because they believe a comprehensive lower secondary school would compromise the quality of education in the existing university-preparatory track. Instead, they support the current system which permits qualified students to transfer between tracks.

The education of 10- to 14-year-olds and the concept of comprehensive lower secondary education have been debated since the days of the monarchy and the First Austrian Republic. On a trial basis, a 1971 law permitted creation of a few comprehensive lower secondary schools where the homogeneous grouping of students continued through the eighth grade (age 14). Legislation to convert comprehensive education from a trial to a permanent status failed to pass in 1985. The political support required of both parties was not achieved. Thus, the comprehensive lower secondary schools established on a trial basis are being phased out of the educational system starting in 1985.

Both political parties support the two-track upper secondary system. Since the nine years of compulsory education can be completed through an optional year-long prevocational program at the lower secondary level, attendance in upper secondary education is voluntary. As recently as 1971, half of the Austrian work force had only a compulsory education; but this proportion has been decreasing steadily. Almost all students (93% in 1984) now attend some form of upper secondary school. Upper secondary education, which students normally enter at the age of 14, is the beginning of serious academic or vocational study. By the end of secondary school, students have acquired either a skilled trade necessary for direct entry into the work force or a liberal arts education prerequisite for university admission.

Responsibility for conveying a liberal arts education in preparation for direct entry into a university discipline was formally shifted in 1848 from universities to university-preparatory secondary schools where that responsibility still remains today. At that time university-preparatory education was increased from 10 to 12 total years (including four years of primary education) which, in most cases, is still the norm today. The 1962 School Organization Act increased university-preparatory education from 12 to 13 total years, but this provision of the law was never implemented. Although public opinion generally favored the law and other provisions of the law have been implemented, the provision to add the extra year proved extremely unpopular and a strongly endorsed (though nonbinding) plebiscite formed in opposition. As a result, implementation of this provision was postponed. With public opinion still strongly opposed, the extra year of university-preparatory education was formally dropped in 1985. A few nine-year schools (which combine with four years of primary education and total 13 years of university-preparatory education) exist but they offer specializations in subjects such as music or sports in addition to university-preparatory education.

Due to the highly developed upper secondary vocational track, the tertiary-level polytechnical schools found in other countries have not developed to any great extent in Austria. Most vocational education occurs in three general levels of upper secondary vocational schools. The top-level vocational schools provide vocational training as well as preparation for the maturity examination. The maturity (examination) certificate (*Reifeprüfungszeugnis, Reifezeugnis*) earned in the vocational track, like the same-name certificate earned in the university-preparatory track, permits students to enter university and nonuniversity postsecondary education. Vocational education has become increasingly popular as employment opportunities for university graduates have declined.

Structure of the Austrian Educational System

The Austrian educational system consists of preprimary, primary, and secondary sectors as well as higher education which is divided into university and nonuniversity postsecondary sectors. Table 1.1 provides a diagram of the educational system. In addition, state-subsidized and regulated day care centers (*Horte*) exist for children of compulsory school age during school vacations and after regular school hours. Day care centers have been established pri-

Table 1.1. The Austrian Educational System

Preschool	Primary	Lower Secondary	Upper Secondary	Postsecondary
Preschool	Primary School	Long-Form General Secondary Schools (*Allgemeinbildende Höhere Schulen, AHS*) (Lower and Upper Cycle)		University (*Universität*) Fine Arts College (*Kunsthochschule*)
		Language-Oriented General Secondary School (*Humanistisches Gymnasium, Neusprachliches Gymnasium, Realistisches Gymnasium*)		Teacher-Training Academy (*Pädagogische Akademie, Berufspädagogische Akademie, Pädagogisches Institut, Religionspädagogische Akademie*)
(*Säuglingskrippe, Kinderkrippe, Kindergarten, Sonderkindergarten*)	(*Grundschule, Volksschule*) (Lower Cycle)	Science-Oriented General Secondary School (*Naturwissenschaftliches Realgymnasium, Mathematisches Realgymnasium*)		Social Work Academy (*Akademie für Sozialarbeit*)
		Home Economics General Secondary School (*Wirtschaftskundliches Realgymnasium für Mädchen*)		Military Academy (*Militärakademie*)
			General Secondary Schools (Upper Cycle only) (*Oberstufenrealgymnasium, Aufbaugymnasium, Aufbaurealgymnasium, Gymnasium or Realgymnasium für Berufstätige*)	Medical Technology School (*Medizinische-technische Schule*) Vocational Institute (*Kolleg*)
		Lower Secondary School (*Hauptschule, Gesamtschule*)	Senior Vocational Schools (*Berufsbildende Höhere Schulen*): *Höhere Lehranstalt, Handelsakademie*	University or College Program or Course (*Hochschullehrgang, Universitätslehrgang, Hochschulkurs*)
			Nursing Schools (*Krankenpflegeschule, et al.*)	
			Teacher Training Schools (*Bildungsanstalt, et al.*)	

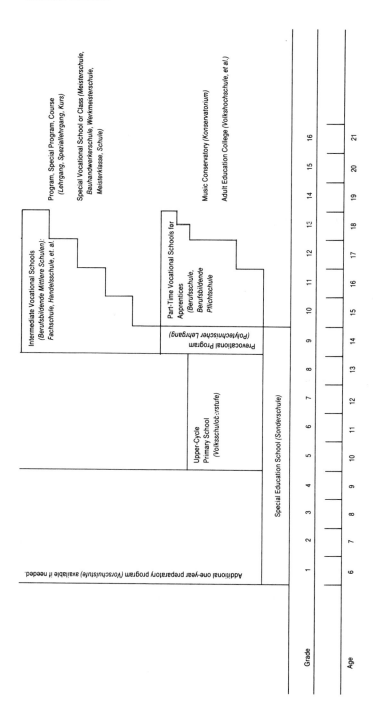

Intermediate Vocational Schools
(Berufsbildende Mittlere Schulen):
Fachschule, Handelsschule, et. al.

Program, Special Program, Course
(Lehrgang, Spezial/ehrgang, Kurs)

Special Vocational School or Class (Meisterschule,
Bauhandwerkerschule, Werkmeisterschule,
Meisterklasse, Schule)

Part-Time Vocational Schools for
Apprentices
(Berufsschule,
Berufsbildende
Pflichtschule

Music Conservatory (Konservatorium)

Adult Education College (Volkshochschule, et al.)

Prevocational Program
(Polytechnischer Lehrgang)

Upper-Cycle
Primary School
(Volksschuloberstufe)

Special Education School (Sonderschule)

Additional one-year preparatory program (Vorschulstufe) available if needed.

Grade

Age

marily in industrial areas for children whose parents both work outside the home. Teachers in day care centers are specially-trained educational assistants (*Erzieher*).

Preprimary Education

Preprimary schools are regulated and subsidized by provincial and municipal governments. The goal of preprimary education is to foster normal childhood development and readiness for primary school. Attendance is not compulsory. Preprimary education consists of infant schools (*Säuglingskrippen*) for children less than 1 year of age, nursery schools (*Kinderkrippen*) for children between the ages of 1 and 3, kindergartens (*Kindergärten*) for children between the ages of 3 and 6, and special kindergartens (*Sonderkindergärten*) for physically or mentally handicapped children between the ages of 3 and 6.

Primary and Secondary Education

Austrian primary and secondary education is organized such that segments corresponding to primary, lower secondary, and upper secondary are apparent. Chapter II describes compulsory education which consists of primary education (attended by all students) and the vocational track of lower secondary education. Chapter III describes the university-preparatory track of lower and upper secondary education. Chapter IV describes the three-tiered vocational track of upper secondary education. Upper secondary education also exists in social work (Chapter V), teacher training (Chapter VIII), and nurses' training (Chapter IX). The maturity certificate (*Reifeprüfungszeugnis, Reifezeugnis*) earned after completion of general secondary schools in the university-preparatory track and after completion of the highest level vocational schools provides the minimum qualification for entering higher education.

Higher Education

Austrian higher education is divided into a university and a nonuniversity sector, both of which normally require the maturity certificate for admission. The university sector, consisting of universities and fine arts colleges, provides the highest level of education in Austria and is described in Chapters VI and VII, respectively. Legislation passed since 1962 has created a nonuniversity postsecondary education system which consists of pedagogical academies (Chapter VIII) and social work academies (Chapter V). Though legally and administratively separate from the regular educational system, medical technology schools (Chapter IX) can be considered part of the nonuniversity postsecondary sector. Higher education for international students is described in Chapter X.

Chapter II

Compulsory Education

Introduction

Primary and vocational-track lower secondary schools are known as compulsory schools (*Pflichtschulen*) because they satisfy the minimum compulsory education requirement. The former eight-year compulsory education requirement established in 1869 was raised to nine years in 1962. Since primary education lasts four years and lower secondary education lasts an additional four years, a one-year prevocational program (*polytechnischer Lehrgang*) was created in 1962 to satisfy the additional required year of compulsory education. The percentage of employed people in the population having only the minimum compulsory education dropped from 51.2% in 1971 to 38.5% in 1981. This percentage continues to decline because fewer students (approximately 7% in 1984) are stopping their education after completing the minimum compulsory education requirement.

Primary Education

Primary schools exist as either four-year (lower cycle) or eight-year (lower and upper cycle) primary schools. All students attend a four-year primary school (known as a *Grundschule* or *Volksschule*), but only a few students still attend the eight-year primary school (known as a *Volksschule*). Eight-year primary schools historically satisfied the compulsory education requirement but are now being phased out of the educational system.

Four-Year Primary School (*Grundschule* or *Volksschule*)

Four-year primary schools provide compulsory education for children between the ages of 6 and 10. Children not mature enough at the age of 6 to enter the first grade attend a one-year preparatory program (*Vorschulstufe*). The primary school is characterized by a self-contained classroom, sometimes with supplementary instruction provided in subjects such as religion. In some schools a child may have the same classroom teacher for two and sometimes for all four years. Required subjects are art, German, handicrafts (for boys and girls separately or together), local history and geography, mathematics, music, physical education, reading, religion, traffic safety, and writing. In the third and fourth grades, children study a modern foreign language, usually English, for two half-hour classes per week. Bilingual instruction is provided in some schools for children who are members of a linguistic minority community.

Class size rarely exceeds 30 students and most classes contain between 10 and 25 students. The number of instructional hours per week ranges from 20 hours in the first grade to 28 hours in the fourth grade. Instructional hours may be distributed over five or six mornings per week at the discretion of educators in individual schools.

At midyear, students receive a report card (*Schulnachricht*) which is provided for information only and is signed by parents and returned to the school. Students receive a yearly certificate (*Jahreszeugnis*) after each year of study and a yearly and leaving certificate (*Jahres- und Abschlusszeugnis*) after the fourth year. The decision to place a child in either the vocational or university-preparatory track is made after a child completes four years of primary education at 10 years of age and is based upon academic performance, teacher recommendations, and parent preference.

Eight-Year Primary School (*Volksschule*)

Eight-year primary schools, consisting of four-year lower and upper cycles, are being phased out of the educational system. Although still existing in rural areas, only about 2% of the children in this age group still attended this type of school in 1984-85. Permission to attend the upper primary school (*Volksschuloberstufe*) is granted only in cases where attendance at a lower secondary school is not feasible due to its distance from the student's home. Primary schools have self-contained classrooms with one classroom teacher, a model that is being replaced at the upper primary level by lower secondary schools where instruction is provided by subject-specialized teachers.

Required subjects in the upper cycle are art, biology and ecology, descriptive geometry, domestic sciences for girls, geography and economics, German, handicrafts (for boys and girls together or separately), history and social studies, mathematics, one modern foreign language, music, physical education, physics and chemistry, and religion. As elective subjects, students may choose shorthand and typing. Class size ranges from 10 to 30, and the number of instructional hours per week ranges from 27 hours in the fifth grade to 29 hours in the eighth grade.

After passing an admission examination, students enrolled in upper primary schools are legally entitled to transfer to university-preparatory secondary schools on a year-for-year basis but few students request a transfer. Those who complete upper primary schools and receive a leaving certificate (*Abgangszeugnis, Abschlusszeugnis,* or *Jahres- und Abschlusszeugnis*) usually enter either a vocational school or the prevocational program.

Lower Secondary Education

The education of 10- to 14-year-old students has been the focus of recent political debate. Members of the Socialist Party (SPÖ) would like to extend the homogeneous grouping of students found in the elementary school through the eighth grade (age 14). Members of the other major party, the People's Party (ÖVP), wish to maintain the current "dual-track" secondary system where 10-year-olds are channeled into either the vocational or the university-preparatory track with opportunities to transfer between the two tracks.

Students in the vocational track enter a lower secondary school (*Hauptschule*), and students in the university-preparatory track enter the lower cycle of a general secondary school (*Gymnasium, Realgymnasium*) which is described in Chapter III. A comprehensive lower secondary school (*Gesamtschule*) where homogeneous student grouping continues through eighth grade was implemented on a trial basis in 1971 but is being phased out of the educational system starting in 1985. In its place, a compromise "new" lower secondary school is being implemented. After completing a lower secondary school, students may enroll in a vocational school, an upper-cycle general secondary school, or the prevocational program.

Lower Secondary School (*Hauptschule*)

Literally translated, a "*Hauptschule*" is a "main school," and the majority of 10-year-olds (approximately 65% in 1984-85) attend this type of school after completing primary school. Functionally translated, a "*Hauptschule*" is a "lower secondary school" (or sometimes, a "compulsory secondary general school") because it provides general education and prepares students to enter upper-secondary vocational schools. The functional translation "lower secondary school" will be used in this volume.

The class entering lower secondary school in 1985 entered the so-called "new" or revised lower secondary school which is a compromise between the two opposing political positions, i.e., the homogeneous grouping of all 10- to 14-year-olds into one school and the traditional streaming of 10-year-olds into a vocational or university-preparatory track. The compromise agreement retains the dual-track system, but in the vocational track a more homogeneous grouping of students is envisioned.

In the new lower secondary school, students are divided into two or three ability groups for the study of German, mathematics and a modern foreign language after an initial observation period lasting eight to 12 weeks. A student may be placed in the top group for one subject and a lower group for another. For the study of other subjects, students are not separated into ability groups. For the first time, all students (regardless of ability group) are required to study a modern foreign language (usually English). The maximum class size permitted by law in the new lower secondary school was reduced from 36 to 33 students, though the minimum class size remains 20 students. In ability groups, class size is between 15 and 30 students.

In the former lower secondary school, a first (*erste*) and second stream (*zweite Klassenzug*) existed within each grade level. Students in the first stream were expected to achieve at a higher academic level and followed a more accelerated curriculum than those in the second stream. Only students in the first stream were required to study a foreign language.

Ability grouping began in 1962 when legislation was passed allowing qualified students to transfer between the two tracks. Prior to 1962, transfer from lower secondary schools into the parallel university-preparatory schools on a year-for-year basis was impossible because the curriculum in each track was different. To facilitate transfer, the curriculum in German, mathematics and a modern foreign language for the higher group in both the new and former lower secondary schools is equal to that in parallel university-preparatory schools.

In addition to a modern foreign language, German, and mathematics, other required subjects are art, biology and ecology, descriptive geometry, domestic sciences for girls, geography and economics, handicrafts (for boys and girls together or separately), history and social studies, music, physical education, physics and chemistry, religion, and writing. As elective subjects, students may study Latin, shorthand, and typing. Instruction usually is provided by teachers specially trained in each subject, although teachers may teach outside their specialization. The number of instructional hours per week ranges from 30 hours in the fifth grade to 34 hours in the eighth grade.

Special forms of lower secondary schools or special classes within lower secondary schools exist where music or sports is emphasized. An aptitude test is required for admission to these schools or classes.

Students receive a yearly certificate (*Jahreszeugnis*) after each year of completed study and a yearly and leaving certificate (*Jahres- und Abschlusszeugnis*) after the final year of study.

Comprehensive Lower Secondary School (*Gesamtschule*)

A comprehensive lower secondary school (*Gesamtschule*, also called the *neue Mittelschule*) which extended the homogeneous student grouping found in elementary schools through the eighth grade was implemented on an experimental basis in 1971 but now is being phased out of the educational system. The last class, accepted in the fall of 1985, will finish in 1989. In 1984-85, approximately 10% of all students in this age group attended this school type.

To convert an experimental or pilot project into a permanent part of the educational system, a two-thirds majority vote must be achieved in Parliament. In practice, this requires agreement of at least the two major political parties. The political support required to establish comprehensive lower secondary education in Austria was not achieved. Proponents of the comprehensive school felt that attendance in a common school through the age of 14 would better enable students to achieve their highest academic potential. Opponents felt the comprehensive lower secondary school would dilute the quality of education available in general secondary schools.

The comprehensive lower secondary school tested various combinations of curricula from the lower secondary school (*Hauptschule*) and the lower-cycle general secondary school (*Langform der Allgemeinbildende Höhere Schule, Gymnasium, Realgymnasium*). Students receive a yearly certificate (*Jahreszeugnis*) after each year of completed study and a yearly and leaving certificate (*Jahres- und Abschlusszeugnis*) after the final year of study.

Prevocational Program (*Polytechnischer Lehrgang*)

After completing an upper primary or lower secondary school, students who intend to complete only the minimum nine-year compulsory education requirement or who want to prepare for an apprenticeship attend the one-year prevocational program (*polytechnischer Lehrgang*). This program often exists as an independent school; but when the number of students is too small to justify an independent school, the program is attached to another compulsory school.

The goal of the program is to provide a basic education while fostering practical living skills and preparing students to make a vocational choice. Required subjects are economics, German, health education, mathematics, physical education, practical living skills, practical orientation to vocational occupations, religion, and social studies and economics (including modern history). In addition, students must choose advanced instruction with one of the following emphases: (1) social studies and economics as related to practical living skills, (2) economics, (3) scientific basis for the modern economy and technical drawing, (4) housekeeping, and social studies and economics as related to practical living skills. Other required subjects from which students must choose are a modern foreign language, handicrafts (for boys and girls separately or together), housekeeping and child care, and other life- and vocational-preparation courses. For instruction in German and mathematics, students are divided into three achievement-level groups. By 1989, one modern language, usually English, also will be mandatory and will be taught in two or three achievement groups. Instruction is provided by subject-specialized teachers. Class size averages approximately 30 students but the legal maximum is 36 students. In achievement-level groups, class size ranges from 15 to 30 students.

Upon completion of the prevocational program, students receive a yearly and leaving certificate (*Jahres- und Abschlusszeugnis*) which is prerequisite for beginning an apprenticeship.

School for Physically or Mentally Handicapped Children (*Sonderschule*)

The nine years of special education correspond to the minimum compulsory education requirement. Special education schools (*Sonderschulen*) for physically or mentally handicapped children operate parallel to primary schools, lower secondary schools, and the prevocational programs. The curriculum is adapted to the child's handicap but follows as closely as possible the course of study prescribed for children of the same age in the regular school system. Special education schools may be independent institutions or may be attached to corresponding schools for other children. Usually, instruction is provided in a self-contained classroom.

Chapter III

General Secondary Education

Introduction

Parallel to vocational schools in the dual-stream secondary system are the general secondary schools (*Allgemeinbildende Höhere Schulen* or AHS, sometimes translated as grammar schools or top-level secondary general schools). General secondary schools comprise the university-preparatory stream of secondary education and are subdivided into various forms of the language-oriented school known as a *Gymnasium* or science-oriented (also home economics) school known as a *Realgymnasium*. Some are known as long-form general secondary schools (*Langform der* AHS) because they consist of a four-year lower cycle (*Unterstufe*) and four-year upper cycle (*Oberstufe*). Others consist only of an upper cycle. The lower cycle operates parallel to lower secondary schools (*Hauptschulen, Gesamtschulen*) and upper primary schools (*Volksschuloberstufe*) while the upper cycle operates parallel to the vocational schools. Although a few nine-year general secondary schools exist, most last eight years and comprise the fifth through twelfth years of education. The few general secondary schools that have nine-year curricula specialize in extra subject matter, e.g., music or sports. The placement of general secondary schools within the educational system is illustrated in Table 1.1 in Chapter I.

Attendance at a general secondary school carries a level of social prestige. Approximately one-quarter of all students in this age group attend a general secondary school. The curriculum is comprehensive and demanding. Although students initially choose which branch of general secondary school they attend, the curriculum in the chosen branch is fixed and few electives are possible. General secondary schools are the only Austrian schools that provide a "general academic" upper-secondary education. While vocational schools provide training at three levels of intensity, general secondary schools provide only a high-level or accelerated education. Upper secondary schools providing a nonaccelerated, general academic education do not exist in Austria.

General secondary schools are the primary providers of university-preparatory education and, as such, have been closely aligned throughout history with the educational prerequisites for university study. Until the mid-nineteenth century, university students were required to study two years of liberal arts and philosophy prior to entering one of the faculties. In 1848, philosophy was separated from the liberal arts and designated as a separate faculty while the two-year liberal arts requirement was tacked onto the general secondary school, thus increasing the length of general secondary education from six to eight years. As is still the case today, students attended four years of elementary school prior to entering general secondary schools. More than a century later, Austrians still consider the general secondary school to be the vehicle for conveying a general liberal arts education and for preparing students for direct entry into an academic university discipline. For direct entry into certain university disciplines, students must study particular subjects while in general secondary schools.

The maturity examination (*Reifeprüfung*) taken after completion of a general secondary school is rigorous. Passing this examination and obtaining the maturity examination certificate (*Reifeprüfungszeugnis*)—also called the maturity certificate (*Reifezeugnis*)—is the minimum requirement for entering universities and other postsecondary institutions. Austrians verbally refer to the maturity certificate as the *Maturazeugnis* (which is a combination of the Latin term for "maturity" and the German term for "certificate") or as simply the *Matura*. The German term, "*Reifeprüfungszeugnis*" or "*Reifezeugnis,*" always appears on the official written document (see sample documents in Appendix A). Before taking the maturity examination, students receive a yearly certificate (*Jahreszeugnis*) after each year of study in a general secondary school and a yearly and leaving certificate (*Jahres- und Abschlusszeugnis*) after the final year.

Schools that prepare students for the maturity examination may be either public or private. A private school legally permitted to use *Gymnasium* or *Realgymnasium* in its name has official recognition (*Öffentlichkeitsrecht*) from the Austrian government and is equivalent to comparable public schools. Public schools have the word "*Bund*" meaning "federal" or "public" in their name, e.g., *Bundesgymnasium* or *Bundesrealgymnasium*. Academic secondary schools with other names also may have official recognition from the Austrian government but do not have the exact curriculum and organizational structure required for using the name *Gymnasium* or *Realgymnasium* and may not grant the maturity certificate. An example of the latter type of school is the Vienna International School which is described along with similar schools in the section of this chapter entitled "Other Academic Secondary Schools."

Entry Requirements

Though the most common entry point into general secondary schools occurs after completion of elementary school, a system of "bridges and crossovers" exists for students to transfer between the vocational and university-preparatory tracks. Students may transfer to a general secondary school during enrollment in or after completion of a lower secondary school or an upper primary school. At each of these entry points, the law prescribes specific admission requirements. For admission to general secondary schools that emphasize art, music or sports, students must pass a special aptitude examination (*Eignungsprüfung*). The requirements for admission to general secondary schools at each entry point are described below.

- Entry after elementary school. Admission to a lower-cycle general secondary school requires grades of "very good" (*sehr gut*) or "good" (*gut*) in German, reading, and mathematics; and a grade of at least "satisfactory" (*befriedigend*) in all other required subjects during the fourth grade (see "Grading Scales" in this chapter). Prior to 1985, students who did not meet the specified admission requirements but who wished admission to a general secondary school could take an entrance examination (*Aufnahmeprüfung*) in German and mathematics. After 1985, an admission decision in borderline cases is decided in a conference of primary school officials familiar with the student's work. In general, students must show an achievement level that predicts a reasonable probability of success.

- Entry from lower secondary school. Students from the highest ability group in a lower secondary school who achieve grades of at least "satisfactory" (*befriedigend*) in all required subjects and grades of "very good" (*sehr gut*) or "good" (*gut*) in a modern foreign language, German, and mathematics may transfer at the end of any school year into the next higher class in a general secondary school. Students who wish to transfer to the general secondary school but who do not meet these requirements may take an entrance examination in those subjects for which the minimum grade was not obtained.
- Entry after completion of lower secondary school. Graduates of a lower secondary school who received grades of "satisfactory" (*befriedigend*) in the highest achievement-level group or grades not lower than "good" (*gut*) in the lower-level achievement group may enter an upper-cycle general secondary school. After 1989, any student who has studied in the highest achievement-level group in a lower secondary school and whose grades are not less than "satisfactory" in all compulsory subjects may transfer at the completion of lower secondary school into an upper-cycle general secondary school. Students who do not meet these requirements may take an entrance examination.

Long-Form General Secondary Schools

Approximately 23% of the 10- to 14-year-old population were enrolled in the lower cycle of long-form general secondary schools in 1984. Specific types of long-form general secondary schools are the language-oriented general secondary school (*Gymnasium*), science-oriented general secondary school (*Realgymnasium*), and the home economics general secondary school (*Wirtschaftskundliches Realgymnasium für Mädchen*). Individual schools may include one or more types, but all consist of a lower and upper cycle, lasting a total of eight years.

In all long-form general secondary schools, the following courses are required: art, biology and ecology, chemistry, two foreign languages (one of which must be a modern language), geography and economics, German, handicrafts or industrial arts (for boys and girls together or separately), history and social studies, mathematics, music, introduction to philosophy (in the upper cycle only), physical education, physics, and religion. Elective subjects common to all general secondary schools are descriptive geometry, foreign languages and Latin (in those schools where the language is not required), shorthand, and typing. Other electives (i.e., those listed in Table 3.1) may be available in individual schools. The course requirements specific to each type of long-form general secondary school are described below.

Language-Oriented General Secondary School (*Gymnasium*)

In addition to a modern language (usually English) for eight years, students are required to take Latin for the last six years. Further subject specialization occurs in each branch of the upper cycle.
- Classical Branch (*Humanistisches Gymnasium*) requires Greek (as a third foreign language) for four years.
- Modern Language Branch (*Neusprachliches Gymnasium*) requires another modern language (the third foreign language) for four years. See Table 3.1 for a complete list of subjects along with instructional hours.
- Science Branch (*Realistisches Gymnasium*) requires descriptive geometry in the upper cycle and additional mathematics, chemistry, and physics.

Two language-oriented general secondary schools provide additional training in languages. At the Public Slovenian General Secondary School in Klagenfurt (Bundesgymnasium für Slowenen in Klagenfurt) for Austrian students who are members of the Slovenian minority community, the Slovenian language is the language of instruction. At the Public General Secondary School of the Theresian Academy Foundation in Vienna IV (Öffentliches Gymnasium der Stiftung Theresianische Akademie in Wien IV), which is also known as the "Theresianum," the study of four foreign languages (English, French, Latin, and Russian) is required.

Science-Oriented General Secondary School (*Realgymnasium*)

In addition to a modern language (usually English) for eight years, students take geometrical drawing and additional mathematics during the lower cycle. Further subject specialization occurs in each branch of the upper cycle.
- Natural Sciences Branch (*Naturwissenschaftliches Realgymnasium*) requires Latin (as the second foreign language) for four years; additional mathematics; and either further descriptive geometry or further biology and ecology, chemistry, and physics.
- Mathematics Branch (*Mathematisches Realgymnasium*) requires a second modern language for four years; descriptive geometry for the last two years; and further mathematics, chemistry, and physics. See Table 3.1 for a complete list of subjects along with instructional hours.

A special type of science-oriented general secondary school, mathematics branch, is the Public Science-Oriented General Secondary School (Bundesrealgymnasium) in Reutte, Tyrol, which lasts an additional year (total education lasting 13 years) and offers four years' training in metallurgy in addition to the regular curriculum. Several schools which follow the course of study

Table 3.1. Required Subjects in the Modern Language Branch of General Secondary School (A) and Mathematics Branch of Science-Oriented General Secondary School (B)

| | | | Number of 50-Minute Lessons/Week (39–40 Weeks/Year) | | | | | | | | | | |
| Year: | 5 | 6 | 7 | | 8 | | 9 | | 10 | | 11 | | 12 | |
*Type of School:			A	B	A	B	A	B	A	B	A	B	A	B
Subject														
Art	2	2	2	2	2	2	2	2	2	2	†	†	†	†
Biology/Ecology	3	2	–	2	2	2	2	2	3	3	–	–	2	2
Chemistry	–	–	2	–	–	2	–	–	–	2	2	2	2	2
Descriptive Geometry	–	–	–	–	–	–	–	–	–	–	–	3	–	2
Electronic Data Proc.	–	–	–	–	–	–	2	2	–	–	–	–	–	–
Geography/Economics	2	2	2	2	2	2	2	2	3	3	2	2	1	1
Geometrical Drawing	–	–	–	2	–	2	–	–	–	–	–	–	–	–
German	5	5	4	4	4	4	3	3	3	3	3	3	3	3
History/Social Studies	–	3	2	2	2	2	2	2	2	2	2	2	3	3
Industrial Arts/Handicrafts	2	2	–	2	2	2	–	–	–	–	–	–	–	–
Latin	–	–	5	–	5	–	5	–	3	–	3	–	3	–
Mathematics	5	4	3	4	3	4	3	5	3	4	3	4	3	4
Modern Language—1st‡	5	4	3	3	3	3	3	3	3	3	3	3	3	3
Modern Language—2nd	–	–	–	–	–	–	5	5	3	3	3	3	3	3
Music	2	2	2	2	1	1	2	2	2	2	†	†	†	†
Philosophy	–	–	–	–	–	–	–	–	–	–	3	3	2	2
Physical Education	4	4	4	4	3	3	3	3	3	3	3	3	2	2
Physics	–	2	2	2	2	2	–	3	2	2	3	2	3	3
Religion	2	2	2	2	2	2	2	2	2	2	2	2	2	2
Total	32	34	33	33	33	33	36	36	34	34	34	34	34	34

Possible Elective Subjects: Croatian, English, French, Hungarian, Italian, Russian, Slovak, Slovenian, Spanish; Greek; Latin; Descriptive Geometry; Electronic Data Processing; Industrial Arts; Instrumental Music; Shorthand; Typing. (Subjects which are required in some general secondary schools may be electives in others.)

*School type A is the modern language branch of general secondary school and school type B is the mathematics branch of science-oriented general secondary school. The curriculum for all general secondary schools is identical for the first two years, which are known as the orientation phase.
†Students must choose 2 hours/week of either art or music.
‡Students usually choose English as their first modern language.

required in the science-oriented general secondary school also provide additional training in art, music (with or without instrumental music), or sports.

Home Economics General Secondary School (*Wirtschaftskundliches Realgymnasium für Mädchen*)

Although the legal German name for this school type is *Wirtschaftskundliches Realgymnasium für Mädchen* which translates literally as home economics general secondary school for girls, boys as well as girls may attend. Public schools have been legally coeducational since 1975. In addition to the first modern language (usually English), students take either another modern language or Latin for four years. Also required are handicrafts for one year; psychology/ education/philosophy for the last three years; and food science and home economics for the last two years.

General Secondary Schools Consisting Only of the Upper Cycle

Some forms of general secondary schools consist only of the upper cycle (*Oberstufe*) and serve special populations of students. The upper-cycle science-oriented general secondary school (*Oberstufenrealgymnasium*) is primarily designed for graduates of the lower secondary school (*Hauptschule*). The continuation language-oriented and science-oriented general secondary schools (*Aufbaugymnasium und Aufbaurealgymnasium*) are designed primarily for those who have completed eight years of primary school but also are open to adults of any age. Language-oriented and science-oriented general secondary schools for employed people (*Gymnasium und Realgymnasium für Berufstätige*) provide instruction during evening hours for working adults.

Upper-Cycle Science-Oriented General Secondary School
(*Oberstufenrealgymnasium*)

The upper-cycle science-oriented general secondary school (*Oberstufenrealgymnasium*) consists only of a four-year upper cycle and should not be confused with the upper cycle (*Oberstufe*) of the long-form science-oriented general secondary school (*Realgymnasium*). Students usually enter the upper-cycle science-oriented general secondary school after completion of a lower secondary school (*Hauptschule*). In 1985, there were 76 upper-cycle science-oriented general secondary schools. Prior to 1976, the upper-cycle science-oriented general secondary school was known as the fine arts general secondary school (*Musisch-pädagogisches Realgymnasium*).

Students may choose a specialized curriculum in the upper-cycle science-oriented general secondary school that emphasizes training in art or music, descriptive geometry, or sciences. Most schools of this type have at least two and usually all three of these curricula. Required courses common to all curricula are two foreign languages (the second of which may be another modern language or Latin), geography and economics, German, handicrafts (for one year), history and social studies, introduction to philosophy, physical education, psychology/education/philosophy (in the last two years), and religion. The following courses also are required but are emphasized in some curricula more heavily than in others: art, biology and ecology, chemistry, mathematics, music, and physics. Elective courses are available. The specialized curricula are as follows:

- Instrumental music specialization which requires art, general music, and instrumental music for four years.
- Descriptive geometry specialization which requires descriptive geometry and art or music for the last two years, and special emphasis in mathematics.
- Science specialization (with special emphasis in biology and ecology, chemistry, and physics) which requires additional mathematics and the respective sciences as well as art or music.

Sixteen special forms of general secondary schools exist for students with talent and interest in music or sports. One is a special form of upper-cycle science-oriented general secondary school for music study (*Oberstufenrealgymnasium für Studierende der Musik*) that lasts an additional year (total education of 13 years) and provides for simultaneous study in a university-level music college or a recognized music conservatory (*Konservatorium*). Music theory courses replace the music courses required in the standard instrumental music curriculum.

Schools for students interested and talented in sports have a curriculum that is similar to that for instrumental music except that sports courses replace the music courses in the curriculum. As part of the final maturity examination (*Reifeprüfung*) for the maturity examination certificate (*Reifeprüfungszeugnis*), students take a practical examination (*praktische Vorprüfung*) in their respective sport. An experimental version of this school type is the Upper-Cycle Science-Oriented General Secondary School for Competitive Athletics (Oberstufenrealgymnasium für Leistungssportler) which lasts an extra year (total education of 13 years).

Continuation Language-Oriented and Science-Oriented General Secondary Schools (*Aufbaugymnasium und Aufbaurealgymnasium*)

Continuation general secondary schools exist primarily for graduates of the eight-year primary school who wish to continue their education and obtain the maturity certificate required for entry into higher education, but graduates of other eight-year programs also may attend. Age is not a consideration for admission. Attendees are often adults whose education was interrupted or those who had to repeat classes in another form of general secondary school and thus exceeded the legally-established study duration. The language-oriented (*Aufbaugymnasium*) and the science-oriented (*Aufbaurealgymnasium*) continuation general secondary school consists only of a four-year upper cycle. Six continuation general secondary schools existed in 1985.

The language-oriented continuation general secondary school corresponds to the upper cycle of the classical (*humanististisches Gymnasium*) or modern-language (*neusprachliches Gymnasium*) general secondary schools. Except for four years of Latin in place of the handicrafts requirement, the core curricula are identical. In addition to core courses, Greek or a second modern language is required for the last three years.

The science-oriented continuation general secondary school corresponds to the natural science general secondary school (*naturwissenschaftliches Realgymnasium*). The core curricula are identical. In addition, descriptive geometry is required for the last two years, and special emphasis is placed on the study of mathematics, chemistry, and physics.

An experimental version of the continuation science-oriented general secondary school is the private Continuation Science-Oriented General Secondary School for Skiers (Aufbaurealgymnasium für Schisportler) in Stams, Tyrol. The program lasts five rather than the usual four years.

Language-Oriented and Science-Oriented General Secondary Schools for Employed Persons (*Gymnasium und Realgymnasium für Berufstätige*)

General secondary schools for employed persons provide an opportunity for working adults (older than age 17) who have successfully completed the first eight years of compulsory education to satisfy requirements for the maturity certificate. Classes are held in the evening, and the program normally takes four and one-half years to complete.

An example is the part-time science-oriented general secondary school for active-duty military personnel which is attached to the Theresian Military Academy (Theresianische Militärakademie). After completing the program and obtaining the maturity certificate, students may enter the regular tertiary-level military program (which is described in Chapter IV).

Other Academic Secondary Schools

Although officially recognized by the Austrian government, several private academic secondary schools exist that have an organizational structure and curriculum different than that in general secondary schools. For this reason, these schools may not call themselves a *"Gymnasium"* or *"Realgymnasium"* and may not give the regular maturity examination. Rather, students who complete these types of schools and want to enter Austrian higher education may take the Austrian external maturity examination (see "Maturity Examination After General Secondary Schools" later in this chapter).

One example of this type of school is the Rudolf Steiner School (Rudolf Steiner Schule) which is known as the Waldorf School (*Waldorfschule*) because the school follows the noncompetitive Waldorf philosophy of education. Students are encouraged to develop at their own pace and are given a narrative description of their accomplishments rather than grades.

Other academic secondary schools are foreign schools that enroll children of foreign diplomatic and business officials as well as a few Austrian children.

Foreign schools officially recognized by the Austrian government are the
Vienna International School (VIS), the American International School (AIS),
and the French Lycée of Vienna (Lycée Français de Vienne). Foreign secondary
schools located in Austria but not officially recognized by the Austrian government are the Czechoslovakian, Iraqi, Japanese, Libyan-Arabic, and Soviet
schools where the educational patterns follow those in the home country.

The Vienna International School and the American International School
(both located in Vienna) are patterned after the 12-year U.S. school system.
Both have an accelerated academic program which leads to the award of the
International Baccalaureate and a regular academic program that satisfies the
minimum requirements for a U.S. high school diploma. (Note: Further information about the IB may be obtained from the International Baccalaureate
North America [IBNA] Office, 680 Fifth Avenue, New York, NY 10019; or
from the Office du Baccalauréat International, Palais Wilson, CH 1211, Geneva
14, Switzerland.) The French Lycée of Vienna, which is recognized through
an agreement between the governments of France and Austria, is a 12-year
school patterned after the French educational system where students may
earn the French Baccalaureate.

Graduates of foreign secondary schools who wish to enter Austrian postsecondary education may request that the Austrian government recognize
their foreign diploma as equivalent to the Austrian maturity certificate (a
process called *Nostrifikation*) or they may take the external Austrian maturity
examination which is described in the next section. In the recognition process,
officials at the Education, Arts and Sports Ministry compare the curriculum
completed at the foreign secondary school with that in a closely related Austrian general secondary school. If the curricula differ, a ministry official informs
the student of course deficiencies. Students may compensate for these deficiencies by taking external examinations (*Externistenprüfungen*) which are
reported on an external examination certificate (*Externistenprüfungszeugnis*).
Although not recognized by the Austrian government, private *Matura* schools
exist to assist students in preparing for these examinations (see description in
the next section). If the external examinations are passed or if the curricula of
the foreign school and a related Austrian general secondary school are deemed
equivalent, then a ministry official issues a letter stating that the foreign
secondary school diploma is recognized (*nostrifiziert*) as equivalent to the
maturity certificate. This statement qualifies the student to enter Austrian
postsecondary education.

Maturity Examination After General Secondary Schools

Students who complete a general secondary school and pass the maturity
examination (*Reifeprüfung*) receive a maturity (examination) certificate (*Reifeprüfungszeugnis* or *Reifezeugnis*). Students who complete a senior vocational
school take a different maturity examination (see "Maturity Examination After
Senior Vocational Schools" in Chapter IV) but receive the same-name maturity

certificate (*Reifeprüfungszeugnis* or *Reifezeugnis*) as those who complete a general secondary school. Students who complete their education at secondary schools that do not have official recognition as a general secondary school and, under certain conditions, those who have not completed secondary school may take the external maturity examination (*Externistenreifeprüfung*) and receive an external maturity examination certificate (*Externistenreifeprüfungszeugnis*). All of these maturity certificates satisfy the entry requirements for universities and other postsecondary institutions.

The maturity examination taken after completion of a general secondary school contains a written and an oral part. The written part consists of four subjects, two of which are always German and mathematics. In a language-oriented school (*Gymnasium*), the other two subjects are foreign languages. In a science-oriented school (*Realgymnasium*), the remaining two subjects are either two foreign languages or one foreign language plus biology and ecology, descriptive geometry, or physics.

For the written part of the maturity examination, the students' teachers write examination questions and submit them to the provincial school council (*Landesschulrat*). The council reviews the questions in order to assure that they are appropriate and that their level is consistent across schools. The council may approve the questions or veto and return them to the school. If the questions are acceptable, the council selects one of the two or three sets of questions provided for each subject and returns the selected set to the school in a sealed envelope. The seal is broken in each student's presence on examination day. Members of the examination commission (*Prüfungskommission*) who administer the examination to the students are the students' teachers, the school principal, and an inspector from the provincial school council (*Landesschulinspektor*) who serves as chair.

The oral part consists of three subjects chosen from subject groupings. The first group includes art, German, history and social studies, music, philosophy, psychology/education/philosophy, and religion; the second group is either required or elective foreign languages; and the third group consists of biology and ecology, chemistry, computer science, descriptive geometry, geography and economics, mathematics, and physics. Students in a language-oriented school are examined in two subjects chosen from the first and second groups and in a third subject chosen from either the second or third group. Students in a science-oriented school are examined in two subjects chosen from the second and third groups and in a third subject chosen from either the first or third group. Students in the home economics or instrumental music types of science-oriented schools are examined in two subjects chosen from the first and third groups and in one subject chosen from any one of the three groups.

The written examination is initially evaluated by the student's teachers and grades are suggested. Then the examination papers are submitted to the chairperson for final approval. The oral examination final grades are approved by the examination commission. If the chairperson does not approve the final grade, the full examination commission votes on it and the chairperson casts only a tie-breaking vote when necessary. Although this seldom occurs, a chairperson who feels a law has been broken may suspend the decision and pass the matter on to the full provincial school council for a final decision.

Students may take additional examinations (*Zusatzprüfungen*) in subjects not formally required in their general secondary school. For example, students who study Latin as an elective rather than required subject may take an additional examination in Latin. Additional examinations also are reported on the maturity certificate.

For the external maturity examination, the subject selection, testing and grading procedures are identical to those for the regular maturity examination but the examinees do not know their examiners. The examiners are teachers and a principal from a general secondary school, but the examinees usually have attended another type of academic secondary school. Under certain conditions, students older than 18 years of age who have not completed a general secondary school also may take an external maturity examination. Prior to taking the external maturity examination, a preliminary examination covering several subjects may be required and a certificate for passing a preliminary examination for the maturity examination (*Zeugnis über die Able-gung einer Vorprüfung zur Reifeprüfung*) is issued. Preliminary examinations may be taken one subject at a time, and an external examination certificate for each subject (*Externistenprüfungszeugnis* or *Externistenprüfungszeugnis über den Lehrstoff einzelner Unterrichtsgegenstände*) is issued. (The German name for the preliminary subject examination, *Externistenprüfungszeugnis*, should not be confused with the name for the final external maturity examination certificate, *Externistenreifeprüfungszeugnis*.) The number that take and pass the external maturity examination is small.

To prepare for the external maturity examination, students may choose to attend a private *Matura* school (*Maturaschule*) which is neither recognized nor subsidized by the Austrian government. *Matura* schools assist only in examination preparation and do not provide a regular academic secondary school curriculum.

Grading Scales

Two different grading scales exist and both of them appear on the maturity certificate. The subject grading scale (*Beurteilungsstufen* or *Notenreihe*) is used for examination subjects on the maturity certificate and also for subjects listed on the yearly certificate (*Jahreszeugnis*) which is provided after each year of primary and secondary education. The comprehensive grading scale (*Gesamt-beurteilung*) which appears on the maturity certificate combines subject grades according to legally-defined formulae. The subject grade is equivalent to a U.S. class grade; and, though not an average, the comprehensive grade serves a function similar to that of the U.S. grade point average.

A subject grade that has the same characteristics as a "D" grade in the United States does not exist in Austria. A "D" grade in the United States is averaged with better grades in order to obtain a satisfactory average grade. A student who receives all "D" grades would not have an overall satisfactory grade, but a student in Austria whose subject grades are all "sufficient" (*genügend*)—the lowest passing grade—does have a satisfactory comprehensive grade.

The subject grading scale is as follows:

Grades	Suggested U.S. Equivalent
sehr gut or 1 (very good)	A
gut or 2 (good)	B+/B
befriedigend or 3 (satisfactory)	B-/C+
genügend or 4 (sufficient)	C
nicht genügend or 5 (not sufficient, fail)	F

The comprehensive grade is calculated as follows:

Grades	Definition	% Receiving Each Grade, 1985
mit ausgezeichnetem Erfolg bestanden (passed with high distinction)	At least half of the subject grades are *sehr gut* and the rest are *gut*.	12%
mit gutem Erfolg bestanden (passed with distinction)	No individual grades are lower than *befriedigend* and at least an equal number of *sehr gut* and *befriedigend* grades exist.	14%
bestanden (passed)	All individual grades are *genügend* or above but conditions necessary for a higher comprehensive grade do not exist.	62%
nicht bestanden (not passed)	One or more individual grades of *nicht genügend* exist.	12%

Students who miss the maturity examination due to illness or fail the examination may resit the examination (under certain legally-defined conditions). The following represents the distribution of repeat examination grades in 1985: 0.2% passed with high distinction, 0.7% passed with distinction, 84% passed and 15% did not pass.

Chapter IV

Vocational Education

Introduction

Vocational education begins at the upper secondary level and operates parallel to the university-preparatory stream of general secondary education. Vocational schools provide the technical preparation necessary for direct entry into the skilled labor force. Some vocational schools also provide university-preparatory education and access to the maturity (examination) certificate (*Reifeprüfungszeugnis, Reifezeugnis*) which is required to enter postsecondary education.

Vocational training has always been closely linked to economic development. Since the first vocational school was established some 200 years ago, vocational education has been constantly changing and adjusting to the needs of business and industry. Due to the economic recovery and development since World War II that has been described as the "Austrian economic miracle," many recent changes in vocational training have occurred.

The bulk of vocational training occurs at the secondary level. The postsecondary polytechnic programs that have developed in other countries have not developed to any great extent in Austria. Although originally at the secondary level, the training of social workers and compulsory school teachers was expanded and elevated to a nonuniversity postsecondary level of education which was first created in 1968. (See descriptions of these systems in Chapters V and VIII.) The remainder of vocational training which represents the great bulk of it occurs in a highly developed network of vocational schools that are primarily at the upper secondary level, although some training extends beyond what is traditionally considered secondary education.

Students enter the regular forms of vocational education after eight or nine years of compulsory education and choose from among three general levels of training. At the lowest level is a system of vocational training, known as a "dual system," where part-time general education accompanies an apprenticeship. At the middle and top levels are clusters of fulltime intermediate and senior vocational schools. Both groups of schools provide vocational training, but only senior vocational schools also provide access to the maturity examination and to postsecondary education. Special programs exist for graduates of the lower-level and middle-level vocational schools who want to complete senior vocational school requirements and obtain the maturity examination certificate and for general secondary school graduates who want vocational training at the senior vocational school level. Special forms of advanced vocational training also exist. The partial list of secondary-level vocational schools in Appendix B illustrates the manner in which different types and levels of vocational training are organized within educational institutions.

Vocational Schools for Apprentices (*Berufsschulen, Berufsbildende Pflichtschulen*)

Those who enter an apprenticeship after completing nine years of compulsory education (at 15 years of age) also must enroll in a part-time vocational school (*Berufsschule* or *Berufsbildende Pflichtschule*). Apprenticeship training is regulated by either the Trade, Commerce and Industry Ministry or the Agriculture and Forestry Ministry. These ministries certified approximately 230 trades in 1985 for which an apprenticeship is necessary. The general and theoretical education in the vocational school is regulated by the Education, Arts and Sports Ministry.

Attendance at a vocational school is compulsory for the duration of the apprenticeship which usually lasts three years, though a few last two, three and one-half, or four years. Academic programs are arranged in weekly, block, or seasonal time configurations in order to complement apprentices' on-the-job training schedules in business or industry. In all cases, the number of instructional hours is equivalent to one school day per week. Instruction is provided by subject-specialized teachers. The number of students per class ranges from 30 to 36, though the actual number in certain practicums may be only 20 students. A vocational school may serve one or more different types of apprenticeships.

The academic curriculum requires theoretical subjects relevant to the apprenticeship as well as general education and the study of religion (subject to the provisions of the Religious Instruction Law). As elective subjects, students may choose physical education or a modern foreign language. Students may be divided into two achievement-level groups for the study of up to three compulsory subjects, or they may receive remedial instruction. The purpose of achievement groups is to provide students who have higher achievement levels with the opportunity to transfer into higher-level vocational training. Completion of the "achievement group with advanced educational offerings" (*Leistungsgruppe mit erweitertem/vertieftem Bildungsangebot*) is noted on the leaving certificate (*Abschlusszeugnis*), but completion of the lower achievement group is not mentioned on the leaving certificate.

A preparatory program (*Vorbereitungslehrgang*, formerly called *Überleitungslehrgang*) allows apprenticeship graduates to prepare for transfer into the first, second or third year (depending upon the specialty) of a senior vocational school. The preparatory program lasts one or two semesters, and students must transfer into a related field at the senior vocational level. Though started as an experimental program, the preparatory program legally became a part of the educational system in 1986.

Young farm workers over 16 years of age who attend no other school after completing compulsory education are required to attend a two-year part-time agriculture and forestry vocational school (*land- und forstwirtschaftliche Berufsschule*). In addition, a two-year part-time domestic science school (*hauswirtschaftliche Berufsschule*) exists only for residents in the province of Vorarlberg and is required for girls who complete the minimum compulsory education requirement but do not attend any other school. Though not technically providing apprenticeship training, the school is legally classified as a vocational school for apprentices.

For the academic part of the program, students receive a certificate after each year of study (*Jahreszeugnis*) and a leaving certificate (*Abschlusszeugnis*) that may be combined with the last yearly certificate (*Jahres- und Abschlusszeugnis*). For successful completion of apprenticeship requirements, students receive employment certification from the ministry responsible for the training. In most trades a final apprenticeship examination certificate (*Lehrabschlussprüfungszeugnis* or *Lehrbrief*) is issued by the Trade, Commerce and Industry Ministry, but in agriculture or forestry trades a final apprenticeship examination certificate (*Gehilfenprüfungszeugnis, Gehilfenbrief* or *Lehrlingsprüfungszeugnis*) is issued by the Agriculture and Forestry Ministry.

Intermediate and Senior Vocational Schools (*Berufsbildende Mittlere und Höhere Schulen*)

Intermediate vocational schools (*Berufsbildende Mittlere Schulen*, BMS) and senior vocational schools (*Berufsbildende Höhere Schulen*, BHS) are two groupings of fulltime vocational schools that provide the knowledge and skills necessary for direct entry into a skilled trade. Senior vocational schools also provide university-preparatory general education and access to postsecondary (including university) education. The apprenticeship requirement for employment in certain trades is satisfied through successful completion of a relevant intermediate or senior vocational school program.

Though intermediate vocational schools are at a lower level than senior vocational schools, entry into both occurs after eight years of education. Most students enter after completing a lower secondary school (*Hauptschule*). An entrance examination (*Aufnahmeprüfung* or *Aufnahmsuntersuchung*) also is required. With the exception of one five-year fashion school, the various intermediate vocational schools provide instruction lasting one to four years (total education of nine to 12 years); all senior vocational schools have five-year programs (total education of 13 years).

A yearly assessment of progress in all intermediate and senior vocational schools is reported on a yearly certificate (*Jahreszeugnis*), and the last year usually is reported on a yearly and leaving certificate (*Jahres- und Abschlusszeugnis*). Otherwise, the student receives yearly certificates after each year of study plus a leaving certificate. The curriculum studied is printed on the leaving certificate. Those who attend a senior vocational school and receive passing grades on all yearly certificates are eligible to take the maturity examination (*Reifeprüfung*) and receive the maturity certificate (*Reifeprüfungszeugnis, Reifezeugnis*) which is required for entry into postsecondary education.

Since some intermediate vocational schools require a final examination and others do not, two sets of final credentials exist for intermediate vocational school graduates. In the following descriptions of intermediate vocational schools, the schools that require a final examination and those that do not are identified. From intermediate vocational schools that require no final examination, the leaving certificate, whether reported along with the last yearly certificate or by itself, is the only certificate students receive. From intermediate vocational schools that require a final examination, a leaving certificate or yearly and leaving certificate also is awarded; but students are required to take an additional examination which, if passed, is reported on a leaving examination certificate (*Abschlussprüfungszeugnis*). Two or more failing grades on the leaving certificate will disqualify the student from taking the final examination until the failed examination or the school year has been successfully repeated. Although the leaving certificate with passing grades gives the student the same privileges as a final apprenticeship examination certificate in several related fields, few employers will hire workers without the leaving examination certificate from schools where a final examination is required.

Types of intermediate and senior vocational schools existing in 1985 are grouped by subject matter and listed in Table 4.1. Some intermediate vocational schools also exist for physically handicapped students. Often training in similar trades at both the intermediate and the senior level is provided in the same institution. These institutions organize distinct trades into different departments where instruction at different levels occurs. The level or kind of training offered at a particular institution may or may not be obvious by looking only at the name of the school. For example, the Public Business Academy and School (Bundeshandelsakademie und Bundeshandelsschule) in Neunkirchen obviously consists of both senior and intermediate level programs in business, but the Higher Technical Institute (Höhere technische Bundeslehranstalt) in Vienna has senior as well as intermediate vocational school programs in telecommunications/electrical engineering technology and electrical engineering/production technology, and a senior vocational school program in electronic data processing and organization. A partial list of secondary-level vocational schools in Appendix B illustrates the manner in which different types and levels of vocational training are organized within educational institutions.

Certain "key" words in the names of some schools have special significance. The word *Bund* meaning "public" or "federal" always appears in the name of public institutions. For example, the Higher Public Institution for Domestic Science (Höhere Bundeslehranstalt für wirtschaftliche Frauenberufe) in Klagenfurt is a public institution for domestic sciences while the Business School of the Lambach Foundation (Handelsschule des Stiftes Lambach) is a private business school. Officially recognized private intermediate and senior vocational schools provide the same curriculum and leaving certificate as equivalent public schools. Institutions with the word *Versuch* (meaning "test" or "inquiry") in their title are research as well as teaching institutions, e.g., Public Higher Technical Teaching and Research Institution (Höhere technische Bundes- Lehr- und Versuchsanstalt) in Bregenz.

Table 4.1. Types of Intermediate and Senior Vocational School Programs*
Grouped by Field, 1985†

AGRICULTURE AND FORESTRY

Intermediate Vocational Schools/IVS *(Berufsbildende Mittlere Schulen)*

4-year voc. school *(Fachschule)*, with specialization in hort. *(Gartenbau)*.
3-year voc. school *(Fachschule)*, with specializations in agri.
(Landwirtschaft), agri. & forest. technol. *(Land- und Forsttechnik)*, agri. & wine
produc. *(Landwirtschaft und Weinbau)*.
3-year agri. bus. school *(Landwirtschaftliche Handelsschule)*.
2-year voc. school *(Fachschule)*, with specializations in agri., rural domestic
sciences *(Ländliche Hauswirtschaft)*, wine produc. *(Weinbau und
Kellerwirtschaft)*.
1-year voc. school *(Fachschule)*, with specializations in agri., fruit growing
(Obstbau), rural domestic sciences.

Senior Vocational Schools/SVS *(Berufsbildende Höhere Schulen)*

Higher inst. for agri. technol. *(höhere Lehranstalt für Landtechnik); alpine agri.
(alpenländische Landwirtschaft)*; forest. *(Forstwirtschaft)*; gen. agri. *(allgemeine
Landwirtschaft)*; hort. *(Gartenbau)*; rural domestic sciences *(landwirtschaftliche
Frauenberufe)*.

BUSINESS

Intermediate Vocational Schools

4-year skiing bus. school *(Kaufmännische Lehranstalt für Skisportler)*.
3-year bus. school *(Handelsschule)*.
2–3 year school for data proces. *(Schule für Datenverarbeitungskaufleute)*.
2-year office & administration school *(Büro- und Verwaltungsschule)*.
1-year office school *(Büroschule)*.

Senior Vocational School

Bus. academy *(Handelsakademie)*.

DOMESTIC SCIENCES

Intermediate Vocational Schools

3-year voc. school for domestic sci. *(Fachschule für wirtschaftliche Frauenberufe)*.
2-year domestic sci./housekeeping school *(Hauswirtschaftsschule)*.
1-year housekeeping school *(Haushaltungsschule)*.

Senior Vocational School

Higher inst. for domestic sci. *(höhere Lehranstalt für wirtschaftliche
Frauenberufe)*.

INDUSTRIAL, TRADE AND ARTISAN SCHOOLS

Chemistry

Intermediate Vocational Schools

4-year voc. school for biochem. & biochem. technol. *(Fachschule für Biochemie
und biochemische Technologie)*; chem. indus. technol. *(chemische
Betriebstechnik)*; tanning chem. & leather technol. *(Gerbereichemie und
Ledertechnik; tech. chem. *(technische Chemie)*.

Senior Vocational School

Higher tech. inst. for silicate technol. & inorganic materials *(höhere technische Lehranstalt für Silikattechnik und anorganische Werkstoffe);* biochem & biochem. technol. *(Biochemie und biochemische Technologie);* chem. indus. technol. *(chemische Betriebstechnik);* tanning chem. & leather technol. *(Gebereichemie und Ledertechnik);* techn. chem. *(technische Chemie).*

Construction and Wood

Intermediate Vocational Schools

4-year arch. voc. school *(Baufachschule).*

4-year voc. school for arch. technol. *(Fachschule für Bautechnik);* artisan wood & stove carving *(gewerbliche Holz- und Steinbildhauerei);* cabinetmaking & interior decorating *(Tischlerei und Raumgestaltung);* carpentry *(Zimmerer);* lathe operation *(Drechslerei);* stone masonry *(Steinmetzerei);* wood & sawmill technol. *(Holzwirtschaft und Sägetechnik).*

3-year voc. school for painting & appl. technol. *(Fachschule für Malerei, Anstrich und verwandte Techniken).*

Senior Vocational Schools

Higher tech. inst. for above-ground bldg. constr. technol. *(höhere technische Lehranstalt für Bautechnik—Hochbau);* below-ground bldg. constr. technol. *(Bautechnik—Tiefbau);* constr. & environ. engr. technol. *(Bautechnik—Umwelttechnik);* furniture making & interior arch. *(Möbelbau und Innenausbau);* wood sci. *(Holzwirtschaft);* wood technol. *(Holztechnik).*

Data Processing

Senior Vocational School

Higher inst. for electron. data proces. & organiz. *(höhere Lehranstalt für elektronische Datenverarbeitung und Organisation).*

Electronics

Intermediate Vocational Schools

4-year voc. school for elec. engr. & produc. technol. *(Fachschule für Elektrotechnik und Leistungselektronik);* elec. engr. technol. *(Elektrotechnik);* telecommunica. & elec. engr. technol. *(elektrische Nachrichtentechnik und Elektronik).*

Senior Vocational Schools

Higher tech. inst. for electron. & biomed. technol. *(höhere technische Lehranstalt für Elektronic und biomedizinische Technik);* elec. engr. technol. *(Elektrotechnik);* electron. control & regulation technol. *(Elektrotechnik—Steuerungs- und Regeltechnik);* telecommunica. & elec. engr. technol. *(elektrische Nachrichtentechnik und Elektronik).*

Glass Blowing

Intermediate Vocational School

4-year glass blowing voc. school *(Glasfachschule).*

Graphics

Intermediate Vocational Schools

4-year voc. school for photogr. *(Fachschule für Photographie);* printing technol. *Reproduktions- und Drucktechnik).*

Senior Vocational School

Higher tech. inst. for printing technol. *(höhere technische Lehranstalt für Reproduktions- und Drucktechnik).*

Industrial Arts

Intermediate Vocational Schools

5-year fashion school *(Modeschule),* with specializations in fashion design & ladies' clothing constr. *(Modeentwurf und Damenkleidermachen),* knit fashions *(Strick- und Wirkmode),* leather design *(Modell-Lederwaren),* millinery design *(Modellmodisterei),* textile design *(Textilentwurf und -druck).*

4-year voc. school for appl. arts *(Fachschule für bildnerische Gestaltung),* with specializations in ceramic design *(Keramische Formgebung),* graphic design, interior design *(Dekorative Gestaltung),* metal formations *(Metallgestaltung),* plastic design *(plastische Formgebung),* textile design *(Textilentwurf und -druck).*

4-year voc. school for appl. painting *(Fachschule für angewandte Malerei);* ceramics *(Keramik und Ofenbau);* commercial art *(Gebrauchsgraphik);* metal handwork *(Metallhandwerk).*

3-year voc. school for textile technol. *(Fachschule für Textiltechnik),* with specialization in patternmaking *(Musterzeichnen).*

Senior Vocational Schools

Higher indus. inst. for indus. arts *(höhere gewerbliche Lehranstalt für Kunstgewerbe);* appl. arts *(bildnerische Gestaltung)* with many of the same specializations as for interm. voc. school of this type.

Higher tech. inst. for textile technol. *(höhere technische Lehranstalt für Textiltechnik).*

Industrial Technology

Intermediate Vocational School

4-year voc. school for indus. technol. *(Fachschule für Betriebstechnik).*

Senior Vocational School

Higher tech. inst. for mech. engr. & indus. technol. *(höhere technische Lehranstalt für Maschinenbau—Betriebstechnik).*

Mechanical Engineering Technology and Metalwork

Intermediate Vocational Schools

4-year voc. school for aircraft technol. *(Fachschule für Flugtechnik);* gunsmith technol. *(Büchsenmacher und Schäfter);* mechanics *(Mechaniker);* mech. engr. & automotive technol. *(Maschinenbau—Kraftfahrzeugbau);* mech. engr. technol. *(Maschinenbau);* metalworking *(Metallbearbeitung);* micromech. *(Mikromechaniker);* micromech. & microelectron. *(Mikromechanik und Mikroelektronik);* precision technol. *(Feinwerktechnik);* watch makers *(Uhrmacher).*

Senior Vocational Schools

Higher tech. inst. for mech. & aeronau. engr. technol. *(höhere technische Lehranstalt für Maschinenbau—Flugtechnik);* mech. & armaments technol. *(Maschinenbau—Waffentechnik);* mech. & automotive engr. technol. *(Maschinenbau—Kraftfahrzeugtechnik);* mech. & foundry technol.

(Maschinenbau—Giessereitechnik); mech. & materials technol.
(Maschinenbau—Werkstofftechnologie); mech. engr. technol. *(Maschinenbau);*
plastics & synthetics technol. *(Kunststofftechnik);* mech. engr. technol. &
installations/bldg. technol./energy plan. *(Maschinenbau—Installation,
Gebäudetechnik und Energieplanung);* mech. engr. technol. & installations/
heating/air conditioning technol. *(Maschinenbau—Installation, Heizungs- und
Klimatechnik);* precision technol. *(Feinwerktechnik);* mech. engr. technol. & tool
making *(Maschinenbau—Werkzeug- und Vorrichtungsbau);* mech. engr.
technol. & welding technol. *(Maschinenbau—Schweisstechnik).*

Mining and Metallurgy

Senior Vocational Schools

Higher tech. inst. for mech. & metall. engr. technol. *(höhere technische
Lehranstalt für Maschinenbau—Hüttentechnik).*

Textiles

Intermediate Vocational Schools

4-year voc. school for fashion & clothing technol. *(Fachschule für Mode und
Bekleidungstechnik);* textile handwork *(Textilhandwerk)* with specialization in
weaving *(Weberei).*
3-year weaving school *(Webereifachschule).*
3-year textile bus. voc. school *(Fachschule textilkaufmännischer Richtung).*
3-year voc. school for the clothing indus. *(Fachschule für Bekleidungsindustrie);*
textile indus. *(Textilindustrie);* textile technol. (Textiltechnik).

Senior Vocational Schools

Higher indus. inst. for fashion & clothing technol. *(höhere gewerbliche Lehranstalt
für Mode und Bekleidungstechnik).*
Higher tech. inst. for textile technol. *(höhere technische Lehranstalt für
Textiltechnik),* with specializations in knitting *(Wirkerei und Strickerei),* weaving/
spinning *(Weberei und Spinnerei),* textile chem. *(Textilchemie).*
Textile bus. higher indus. inst. *(höhere gewerbliche Lehranstalt
textilkaufmännischer Richtung).*

Tourist Business

Intermediate Vocational Schools

3-year hotel mgmt. school *(Hotelfachschule).*
3-year restaurant mgmt. school *(Gastgewerbefachschule).*
3-year tourism school *(Tourismusfachschule).*
2-year voc. school for tourist bus. *(Schule für den Fremdenverkehr).*

Senior Vocational Schools

Higher indus. inst. for tourist bus. *(höhere gewerbliche Lehranstalt für
Fremdenverkehrsberufe).*

---

*All senior vocational school programs are five years in length. Students enter IVS and SVS
programs after completing eight years of education.
†When a school type is identical to the preceding one, it is not repeated. For example, under
agriculture and forestry, the senior vocational school programs are *höhere Lehranstalt für
Landtechnik, höhere Lehranstalt für alpenländische Landwirtschaft,* etc.; but the second and
succeeding entries contain only the vocation and not the school type.

The law prescribes the curriculum for each intermediate and senior vocational school according to categories of schools (see below). Instruction in all intermediate and senior vocational schools is provided by subject-specialized instructors, and class size ranges from 30 to a maximum of 36 students.

Industrial, Trade, and Artisan Schools

Within the legal category of "industrial, trade, and artisan schools" are intermediate and senior vocational schools that offer the greatest variety of specializations but enroll only about one-third of all students in intermediate and senior vocational schools. Schools within this category provide technical-industrial training as well as training in the tourist and clothing industries.

An intermediate vocational school in this category usually is called a *Fachschule* and may exist as an independent institution or as a department within an institution. Most programs last three or four years, but one five-year intermediate-level Fashion School of the City of Vienna (Modeschule der Stadt Wien) also exists. In addition to vocational training in the relevant trade, the intermediate vocational school curriculum includes business management, citizenship, foreign language, geography, German, history, natural sciences, physical education, religion, and theoretical basis for the trade. See Table 4.2 for a list of subjects with instructional hours for the intermediate vocational school program in mechanical engineering technology.

Intermediate vocational school programs within this category conclude with a final examination and award of a leaving examination certificate (*Abschlussprüfungszeugnis*). A student who fails the final examination already has a leaving certificate (*Abschlusszeugnis)* or yearly and leaving certificate (*Jahres- und Abschlusszeugnis*) signifying completion of the last year of the study program. In this case, the leaving certificate functions as a final apprenticeship examination certificate (*Lehrabschlussprüfungszeugnis*), although many employers are reluctant to hire a worker who has failed the final examination in programs where it is required.

Senior vocational schools within this category usually are known as higher institutions (*höhere Lehranstalten*), higher technical institutions (*höhere technische Lehranstalten*), or higher industrial institutions (*höhere gewerbliche Lehranstalten*). In addition to vocational training, required academic subjects in the senior vocational school curriculum are chemistry, citizenship, descriptive geometry, electronic data processing, one modern foreign language, geography and economics, German, history and social sciences, mathematics, physical education, physics, religion, and theoretical foundations of the vocational trade. See Table 4.3 for a complete list of subjects plus instructional hours for the senior vocational school program in mechanical engineering technology.

After three years of work experience in the field, graduates of senior vocational schools in industrial and technical fields may receive certification from the Construction and Engineering Ministry or the Agriculture and Forestry Ministry to use the title "Engineer" (*Ingenieur*). The document certifying this title is known as the *Ingenieururkunde*.

Table 4.2. Course List for Mechanical Engineering Technology at the Intermediate Vocational Level

Compulsory Subjects	Year:	9	10	11	12
		Number of 50-Minute Lessons/Week			
Business Economics & Law		–	–	–	2
Business Technology & Mathematics		–	–	–	2
Chemistry & Applied Chemistry		2	–	–	–
Citizenship		–	–	–	2
Descriptive Geometry		3	2	–	–
Electro-Technology		–	–	3	–
Geography		1	1	1	–
German		3	2	2	2
History		1	1	1	–
Machine Elements		–	3	4	–
Mathematics & Applied Mathematics		5	3	–	–
Mechanical Technology		–	2	2	3
Mechanics		–	3	1	1
Physical Education		2	2	2	2
Physics & Applied Physics		3	2	–	–
Production Laboratory		–	–	–	2
Religion		2	2	2	2
Technical Drawing		4	3	3	3
Vocational Theory		–	–	3	3
Work Hygiene & Accident Prevention		–	–	–	1
Workshop		14	14	16	15
Total		40	40	40	40

Elective subjects are also available.

Table 4.3. Course List for Mechanical Engineering Technology at the Senior Vocational Level

Compulsory Subjects	Year:	9	10	11	12	13
		Number of 50-Minute Lessons/Week (41–42 Weeks/Year)				
Chemistry & Applied Chemistry		2	2	2	–	–
Citizenship		–	–	–	–	1
Descriptive Geometry		3	2	–	–	–
Design Practice		–	–	–	–	6
Economics & Law		–	–	–	2	1
Electronic Data Processing		–	–	–	2	–
Electro-Technology		–	–	–	2	3
Environ. Protec. & Accident Prevent.		–	–	–	–	1
Geography & Economics		2	1	1	–	–
German		3	2	2	2	2
History & Social Studies		–	1	1	2	–
Kinematics & Gears		–	1	–	–	–
Machine Elements		–	6	11	4	–
Manufacturing Technology		–	–	–	2	3

continued

Mathematics & Applied Mathematics	5	4	3	3	–
Measurement & Control Technology	–	–	–	–	2
Mechanical Technology	1	2	2	2	–
Mechanics	–	3	4	4	2
Modern Foreign Language	2	2	2	2	2
Physical Education	2	2	2	1	1
Physics & Applied Physics	3	2	2	1	–
Piston-Driven Machines	–	–	–	2	2
Production Laboratory	–	–	–	–	4
Production Technology	–	–	–	–	3
Religion	2	2	2	2	2
Technical Drawing	3	–	–	–	–
Thermal Installations	–	–	–	–	2
Turbines	–	–	–	3	4
Workshop	13	9	7	3	–
Workshop Laboratory	–	–	–	2	–
Total	41	41	41	41	41

Elective subjects are also available.

Business Schools

Slightly more than a third of all students in intermediate and senior vocational education enroll in schools legally categorized as business schools. At the intermediate level, the largest group are three-year business schools (*Handelsschulen*), but others lasting one to four years also exist (see Table 4.1, Business section). Required subjects are business management, citizenship, a modern foreign language, geography, general business, German, natural sciences, physical education, religion, theoretical foundations of business, and vocational practicums. No final examination is required, and graduates of intermediate business schools receive a leaving certificate (*Abschlusszeugnis*) which is often combined with the yearly certificate (*Jahres- und Abschlusszeugnis*).

Senior vocational schools within this category are known as business academies (*Handelsakademien*). See Table 4.4 for a detailed course list and instructional hours.

Domestic Science Schools

Domestic science schools enroll approximately one-fifth of the intermediate and senior vocational school population. The intermediate domestic science school is known as a *Fachschule für wirtschaftliche Frauenberufe* (lasting three years), *Hauswirtschaftsschule* (two years), or *Haushaltungsschule* (one year). Required subjects are biology, business management, citizenship, fine arts, foreign language, German, natural sciences, physical education, practicums, religion, theoretical domestic science subjects, and, for three-year programs,

Table 4.4. Course List for Senior-Vocational Level Business Academy

Compulsory Subjects	Year:	9	10	11	12	13
			Weekly Hours			
Accounting		4	3	3	3	3
Biology & Science of Consumer Goods		3	2	2	–	–
Business Mathematics		3	–	–	–	–
Business Management		3	3	3	3	3
Chemistry		–	2	2	–	–
Citizenship & Law		–	–	–	2	2
Data Processing		–	–	–	2	2
Economics & Sociology		–	–	–	–	3
English		3	2	3	2	3
Geography & Economics		3	2	2	–	–
German		3	2	3	3	2
History & Social Studies		–	3	2	2	–
Mathematics & Applied Mathematics		–	3	3	3	3
Physical Education		2	2	2	2	2
Physics		–	–	–	2	2
Religion		2	2	2	2	2
Second Modern Language		–	4	3	4	3
Special Business Topics		–	–	–	2	2
Stenography, Typing & Word Processing		5	2	2	–	–
Total		31	32	32	32	32

Elective subjects are also available.

history and geography. No final examination is required, and graduates receive a leaving certificate (*Abschlusszeugnis*) which may be combined with the last yearly certificate and is called a yearly and leaving certificate (*Jahres- und Abschlusszeugnis*).

A domestic science institution at the senior vocational level is known as a *höhere Lehranstalt für wirtschaftliche Frauenberufe*. Required subjects are art, chemistry, citizenship, two modern foreign languages, geography and economics, German, history and social studies, housekeeping and domestic sciences, mathematics, music, physical education, physics, religion, and theoretical and practical subjects. Compulsory practicums occur in hotels and catering enterprises.

Social Work Schools

The former senior vocational schools in social work were elevated in 1976 to tertiary-level social work academies. They are described in Chapter V along with intermediate vocational schools of social work and other special schools of social work.

Teacher Training Schools

Teacher training occurs in schools that are legally parallel to intermediate and senior vocational schools, postsecondary pedagogical academies, and universities, though training at the intermediate vocational level is being phased out of the educational system. Handicraft teachers, preschool teachers, educational assistants in day care centers or dormitories, and some physical education teachers and sports trainers are trained in schools at the upper secondary level. See descriptions of these programs in Chapter VIII.

Agriculture and Forestry Schools

Senior vocational schools in agriculture and forestry and one intermediate-level forestry school are federal schools; thus, pedagogical concerns are handled by the Education, Arts and Sports Ministry and funding and staffing concerns are handled by the Agriculture and Forestry Ministry. In other agriculture and forestry intermediate vocational schools, educational affairs are handled by the provinces.

The one- to four-year academic curricula in intermediate-level agriculture and forestry schools (known as *Fachschulen*) are fundamentally equivalent to those in parallel industrial or technical intermediate vocational schools and equivalent types of leaving (examination) certificates are issued. Programs in agriculture and forestry may be reduced by one year for those who enter after completion of an apprenticeship and the corresponding part-time agriculture and forestry school (*land- und forstwirtschaftliche Berufsschule*). The last year in an intermediate-level agriculture and forestry school may consist of two winter semesters with a practicum between them.

In senior-level agriculture and forestry schools (known as *höhere Lehranstalten*), required subjects are biology, chemistry, citizenship, descriptive geometry, fine arts, a modern foreign language, geography and economics, German, history and social studies, mathematics, physical education, physics, and religion, as well as technical agriculture and forestry subjects. Also required is a practicum lasting four-and-a-half months. Alternate forms of senior vocational schools in agriculture and forestry exist for those who have completed the nine-year compulsory education requirement and have been employed at least two years in the field. These students may complete the requirements for the five-year program in four years and receive the maturity certificate needed to enter postsecondary education.

Special Forms of Vocational Training

Regular access into a vocational career occurs through completion of an apprenticeship with its attendant part-time vocational school or through completion of an intermediate or senior vocational school program. Special forms of vocational training are reserved for adults who want to train for a vocational career or who want to upgrade or supplement their previous vocational training. Most programs of this type exist as separate departments within secondary-level vocational schools. The partial list of secondary-level vocational schools in Appendix B illustrates the manner in which different types and levels of vocational training are organized within educational institutions. Table 4.5 provides a partial list of special vocational training options available in selected fields. A description of the various types of special programs is provided below.

Continuation Program (*Aufbaulehrgang*)

Graduates of an intermediate vocational school (*Fachschule* or *Handelsschule*) may attend a continuation program (*Aufbaulehrgang*) and complete the requirements for the senior vocational school program in the same field. Those who have completed a preparatory program (*Vorbereitungslehrgang*) after an apprenticeship also may qualify for entry into continuation programs. Continuation programs normally last four to six semesters. In addition to higher-level employment qualifications, those who complete continuation programs, like those who complete senior vocational schools, may take the maturity examination, the passing of which is the requirement for entering postsecondary education. Continuation programs have been tried on an experimental basis since 1975, and a bill to make them a permanent part of the educational system was passed in 1986.

Vocational Institute (*Kolleg*)

"Vocational institute" is a functional translation of *Kolleg*, since a literal translation (college) would not correctly describe a *Kolleg*. Vocational institutes exist for graduates of general secondary schools who want vocational training, though graduates of senior vocational schools in other fields also may attend. The entry requirement is the maturity certificate (*Reifeprüfungszeugnis, Reifezeugnis*) which also is the entry requirement for postsecondary education. The exit credential is another maturity certificate which is verbally referred to as the "second" maturity certificate or "second *Matura*." The official exit credential is titled simply *"Reifeprüfungszeugnis"* but identifies the program as that of a vocational institute (*Kolleg*). (See "Maturity Examination After Senior Vocational Schools" below.)

Established as experimental programs in 1975, vocational institutes are now a legal part of the educational system. Prior to their establishment, students who attended general secondary schools were unable to obtain vocational training and those who attended a senior vocational school were able to obtain vocational training in only one field. Like other vocational training, vocational institute training addresses an economic need. While the economy has reached

Table 4.5. Selected Special Forms of Vocational Education Grouped by Field, 1985

TYPE OF PROGRAM	Description	Admission Criteria	Length	Final Certificate
CHEMISTRY				
Continuation Program (Aufbaulehrgang)	Cont. prog. in biochem. & biochem. technol.	Relev. compl. voc. training (Fachschule)	2.5 years	Reifeprüfungszeugnis (Maturity Certificate)
Vocational Institute (Kolleg)	Tech. chem.	Reifeprüfungszeugnis	2 years	Second Reifeprüfungszeugnis
Program (Lehrgang)	Advd. prog. for chem. technicians	Relev. compl. voc. training	2 years	Abschlusszeugnis (Leaving Certificate)
Master School (Werkmeisterschule, Meisterschule)	Part-time school in tech. chem., food technol.	Relev. compl. voc. training	2 years part-time	Abschlusszeugnis
CONSTRUCTION AND WOOD				
Employed Adults	Higher tech. instit. for constr. technol.	Relev. compl. voc. training	4–5 years	Reifeprüfungszeugnis
Craftsman School (Bauhandwerkerschule)	Craftsmen's school for carpenters, painters, stone masons	Relev. compl. voc. training	3 winter semesters	Abschlusszeugnis
Vocational Institute	Above- or below-ground constr. technol. & furniture constr./interior design	Reifeprüfungszeugnis	2 years	Second Reifeprüfungszeugnis
Master Class (Meisterklasse)	Master class for cabinetmakers	Relev. compl. voc. training	1 year	Abschlusszeugnis
Master School	Master school for arch. technol., cabinetmaking & interior design,	Relev. compl. voc. training	1–2 years	Abschlusszeugnis

Type	Description	Entry requirement	Duration	Certificate
School (*Schule*)	carpenters, painters, sculpture / School for furniture making	Min. 18 years of age	1 year	*Abschlusszeugnis*
Special Program (*Speziallehrgang*)	Special program for employed adults in surveying technol.	*Reifeprüfungszeugnis*	1 year	*Abschlusszeugnis*
DATA PROCESSING				
Vocational Institute	Electron. data proces. & organiz.	*Reifeprüfungszeugnis*	2 years	Second *Reifeprüfungszeugnis*
Program	Electron. data program.	17 years old	.5 year	*Lehrgangszeugnis*
School	School for electron. data proces.	17 years old	1 year, 1.5 years part-time	*Abschlusszeugnis*
Special Program	Prog. in automation technol., in electron. data proces. & organiz.	*Reifeprüfungszeugnis*	.5 year, 1 year part-time	*Abschlusszeugnis*
Special Program	Sr. voc. level prog. in organiz. & mgmt.	*Reifeprüfungszeugnis*	1 year, 2 years part-time	*Abschlusszeugnis*
TOURIST TRADE				
Continuation Program	Cont. prog. for grads. of *Fachschulen* for tourist bus. & for domestic sci.	Relev. compl. voc. training	3 years	*Reifeprüfungszeugnis*
Vocational Institute	Tourist trade	*Reifeprüfungszeugnis*	2 years	Second *Reifeprüfungszeugnis*
Program	Hotel & restaurant mgmt. for adults	18 years old	2 years	*Abschlusszeugnis*

a level of saturation for graduates in many university disciplines, the demand for engineering technicians and middle-level managers has remained fairly constant in vocations for which vocational institute programs have been developed.

Vocational institutes are attached to senior vocational schools as separate departments. The curriculum is identical to that in the corresponding senior vocational school; but since students have completed the academic requirements for the maturity certificate prior to admission, the required courses consist only of vocational subjects. See Table 4.6 for a list of courses plus instructional hours for a vocational institute program in electrical engineering technology. Except for the business vocational institute program which lasts one and one-half years, all other vocational institute programs last two years. In some cases, the equivalent program is spread over a longer time frame and is offered in the evenings to accommodate employed adults.

After three years of experience in the field, vocational institute graduates in technical fields, like their counterpart graduates from senior vocational schools, may receive certification to use the title "Engineer" (*Ingenieur*). The certificate issued by the appropriate federal ministry is called the *Ingenieururkunde*. Vocational institute programs substitute for the final apprenticeship examination certificate (*Lehrabschlussprüfungszeugnis, Lehrbrief*) issued by the Trade, Commerce and Industry Ministry. No vocational institute programs exist in agriculture or forestry.

Table 4.6. Vocational Institute Program in Electrical Engineering Technology

Compulsory Subjects	Semester:	Number of 50-Minute Lessons/Semester (41–42 Weeks/Year)			
		I	II	III	IV
Applied Mathematics		2	2	–	–
Design Practice		–	–	5	5
Economics & Law		–	–	3	3
Electr. Machines & Electr. Power		–	2	7	7
Electrical Systems		–	4	6	6
Electr. Telecommunica. & Electron.		–	3	5	5
Electronic Data Processing		2	2	–	–
Environ. Protec. & Accident Preven.		2	–	–	–
Intro. to Electr. Engr. Technol.		6	6	–	–
Laboratory		–	4	8	8
Machine Elements & Use		–	4	2	2
Measurement & Control Technology		4	6	4	4
Mechanical Technology		3	3	–	–
Mechanics		5	–	–	–
Technical Drawing		4	–	–	–
Workshop		12	4	–	–
	Total	40	40	40	40

Elective subjects are also available.

Higher Technical Institution for Reproduction and Printing Technology

Only one higher technical institution for reproduction and printing technology (*höhere Lehranstalt für Reproduktions- und Drucktechnik*) program exists, and it is a department within the Public Higher Teaching and Research Institution for Graphic Arts (Höhere Graphische Bundes- Lehr- und Versuchsanstalt in Vienna). Although similar to other senior vocational schools in most respects, the higher technical institution for reproduction and printing technology has one unique characteristic. Students who have completed eight years of education as well as intermediate and senior vocational school graduates may enter. Those who have no maturity certificate upon entry may receive one upon successful completion of the program, and those who have the maturity certificate upon entry receive a second maturity certificate upon successful completion. Graduates may obtain certification to use the title "Engineer" (*Ingenieur*) after three years of experience in the field in the same manner as senior vocational school or vocational institute (*Kolleg*) graduates.

Students who enter the program after completing eight years of education enter the regular five-year senior vocational school curriculum. Those who have completed an intermediate or senior vocational school program enter the third year of the program. The number of students in this field is too low to justify creation of either a vocational institute (*Kolleg*) for those who already have the maturity certificate or a continuation program (*Aufbaulehrgang*) for those who have completed an intermediate vocational school. Instead, the third year curriculum is varied so that those who do not have the maturity certificate take the courses required for the maturity examination and those who already have the maturity certificate do not repeat courses.

Courses, Programs and Special Programs

Most courses (*Kurs*) or programs (*Lehrgang*) are attached to senior vocational schools and provide supplementary or advanced vocational training to graduates of intermediate or senior vocational schools. Special programs (*Spezial-lehrgang*) are developed on an *ad hoc* basis while programs and courses are developed in response to an on-going need. The requirements for admission vary by program. Like vocational institutes, some programs require the maturity certificate for admission; but unlike vocational institutes, programs lasting longer than one year conclude with a leaving certificate (*Abschlusszeugnis*) rather than a second maturity certificate. Programs lasting less than one year conclude with a program certificate (*Lehrgangszeugnis*), and courses conclude with a course certificate (*Kurszeugnis*).

Special Vocational Schools/Classes

Various special vocational schools or classes exist for those who have completed vocational school training and wish specialized or upgraded vocational training. These schools serve a variety of goals, i.e., vocational enrichment, promotional opportunities, preparation for a new vocation, or preparation for master craftsman examinations (*Meisterprüfungen*). Such special vocational schools or classes are called craftsman or master schools (*Meisterschulen, Bauhandwerkerschulen,* or *Werkmeisterschulen*), master classes (*Meisterklassen*) or, simply, schools (*Schulen*). Addressing goals similar to those of special vocational schools are intermediate and senior vocational schools for working adults where an equivalent program is offered in the evenings over a longer period of time in order to accommodate adults' working schedules.

Those who successfully complete programs in special vocational schools receive a leaving certificate (*Abschlusszeugnis*). The results of master craftsman examinations, which are higher-level employment certification examinations, are also reported on a leaving certificate. Students who complete intermediate or senior vocational schools for working adults receive the same credential as those attending the fulltime program. (See descriptions in earlier sections.)

These special vocational options may exist as separate departments within existing senior vocational schools or as independent institutions. Some, but not all, master schools are operated at the provincial level by the Chamber of Trades and Crafts (Wirtschaftsförderungsinstitut, WIFI) or the Federation of Trade Unions (Berufsförderungsinstitut, BFI), both of which are adult education institutions (see "Adult Education" later in this chapter).

Maturity Examination After Senior Vocational Schools

The maturity (examination) certificate (*Reifeprüfungszeugnis* or *Reifezeugnis*) earned after completion of a senior vocational school has the same official name as that earned after completion of a general secondary school (see sample documents in Appendix A) and satisfies the entry requirements for universities and other postsecondary institutions. Austrians verbally refer to the maturity certificate from technical and industrial senior vocational schools as the technical *Matura* (which is Latin for "maturity"), but they refer to the maturity certificate from other senior vocational schools (and general secondary schools) as simply the *Matura*. The maturity certificate from senior vocational schools meets the university direct-entry requirements for majors that require additional mathematics. Since students do not study Greek, Latin or philosophy in a senior vocational school, they may not directly enter university majors for which these are prerequisite subjects. Biology and ecology, and descriptive geometry are studied in some but not all senior vocational schools. The examination subjects are both vocational and academic. As a rule, four written and three oral examinations are required, but in certain types of vocational schools one examination subject may carry the same weight as two or three examinations for other types of vocational schools. The examination subjects vary according to the legal classification of the school.

The official leaving certificate from a vocational institute (*Kolleg*) also is a maturity examination certificate (*Reifeprüfungszeugnis*), but verbally it is referred to as the "second *Matura*" because the first maturity certificate was required for admission to the vocational institute program. The examination subjects for this maturity examination are the same technical ones required for the corresponding senior vocational school, but academic examination subjects are waived because they were covered in the first maturity examination.

The maturity examination grading scale described in Chapter III, "Grading Scales," applies to all maturity examinations. The following percentages of students who took the maturity examination after senior vocational schools in 1985 received each comprehensive grade: 11% passed with high distinction (*mit ausgezeichnetem Erfolg bestanden*), 15% passed with distinction (*mit gutem Erfolg bestanden*), 62% passed (*bestanden*), and 12% did not pass (*nicht bestanden*), though most have a right to resit the examination.

Examination subjects for schools within each legal category are described below.

- Industrial, Technical and Artisan Schools. In technical fields, the written part consists of an examination in German and a comprehensive technical design examination taken over 40 hours (five days), while the oral part consists of one humanities and three technical subjects. In the tourist field, written examinations are required in German, a modern language, management, and mathematics, and oral examinations are required in cultural and political education (humanities), economics or tourist business subjects, and a second modern language.
- Business Schools. In business academies, written examinations are required in accounting, German, a modern language, and mathematics while oral examinations are required in the second modern language, management, and any other required subject except physical education. Because Latin is an optional subject in business academies, an additional examination (*Zusatzprüfung*) may be taken in Latin.
- Domestic Science Schools. For senior domestic science schools, the written examination includes economics, German, a modern language, and science. The oral examination includes a second modern language as well as the student's choice of economics, humanities, or sciences.
- Agriculture and Forestry Schools. Except for the rural domestic science training institution (*höhere Lehranstalten für landwirtschaftliche Frauenberufe*), the same examination subjects are required for all agriculture and forestry schools. Written subjects are accounting and management, agriculture and forestry, and German; and oral subjects are accounting and management, farming subjects, and humanities. In the rural domestic science branch, the written subjects are domestic sciences, German, nutrition, and textiles; and the oral subjects are accounting and management, animal husbandry or gardening, and domestic sciences.

Additional Forms of Vocational Education

Though legally separate from the regular vocational education system, military training, a private secretarial school, and adult education serve goals that are similar to those of some vocational schools.

Theresian Military Academy

The only military-training school in Austria is the Theresian Military Academy (Theresianische Militärakademie) located in Wiener Neustadt. Tertiary-level military officer training often is described along with secondary-level vocational education but is not legally a part of the regular vocational training system. Jurisdiction for funding and staffing belongs to the Defense Ministry, while the educational program is handled by the Education, Arts and Sports Ministry.

Admission to the postsecondary program occurs only through military service. In addition to the maturity certificate (*Reifeprüfungszeugnis, Reifezeugnis*), completion of the obligatory six-month basic military service is required for admission. Those who wish to attend the military academy must re-enlist for a six-month preparatory program and pass an aptitude test prior to admission to the regular six-semester (three year) program. The coursework is primarily military training and physical education, but students also study Austrian and international law, foreign languages, military geography, military history, national economy, political science, psychology, and sociology.

Successful completion of the program leads to a commission as a second lieutenant. No academic certificate, degree, or grades are issued. Instead, those who complete the requirements receive a document in the form of a letter from the Defense Minister indicating their appointment as a second lieutenant. This document is similar to that received by civil servants upon their appointment or promotion.

In addition to the postsecondary military officer training program, the military academy has a part-time science-oriented general secondary school for active-duty military personnel who wish to earn the maturity certificate (see description in Chapter III).

European Secretary Academy

Established in 1968, the European Secretary Academy (Europäische Sekretärinnenakademie) is a private school that has never requested official recognition (*Öffentlichkeitsrecht*) from the Austrian government. Although the school cannot issue certificates equivalent to any issued by recognized schools in Austria, the trilingual Diploma for the European Secretary/*Diplom der Europasekretärin*/*Diplôme de Secrétaire Européene* is recognized as a secretarial qualification in 15 European countries, including Austria.

The two-year European secretary program requires the maturity certificate for admission as well as previous study of English, French, and German. The program includes academic training in economics, government, and languages in addition to secretarial training and concludes with the award of the European Secretary Diploma which is taken before an international professional examining board.

Shorter programs also are available for those who have completed at least ten years of education, but these programs do not conclude with Austrian-recognized or internationally-recognized leaving certificates.

Adult Education

An estimated 10% of the Austrian population participates in some form of adult education each year. Approximately 8,500 adult education centers and 2,000 public libraries provide adult education programs. Originally, adult education was established by various private organizations rather than by the federal government, and for this reason a great deal of diversity exists. Now the federal, provincial, and municipal governments also provide and subsidize some forms of adult education.

The goals of adult education are as varied as the students but range from vocational or personal enrichment to vocational upgrading. Through attendance in adult education programs, workers may qualify for increased salaries or promotions.

Officially-recognized academic certificates are not issued by adult education programs, although students and/or their employers may receive a certificate of attendance (*Kursbestätigung, Besuchsbestätigung*). Students also may prepare for publically-recognized examinations through attendance in adult education classes. An external examination process exists for all such examinations.

Although others exist, the following are well-established organizations providing adult education:

- Agricultural Advanced Education Institute (Ländliche Fortbildungsinstitut) provides continuing and advanced agricultural training to adults in rural areas.
- Association of Austrian Adult Education Colleges (Verband Österreichischer Volkshochschulen) supports and finances the many adult education colleges (*Volkshochschulen*). Providing the largest amount of adult education in Austria, adult education colleges offer personal and vocational enrichment courses in all branches of the arts and sciences.
- Association of Austrian Educational Foundations (Ring Österreichischer Bildungswerke) encompasses Catholic and Protestant adult education institutions as well as other adult education institutions and provides education in religion, social and moral issues, art and music.
- Association of Public Libraries in Austria (Verband Österreichischer Volksbüchereien) provides education on library use and leisure-time activities.
- Austrian Institute for Political Education (Österreichisches Institut für Politische Bildung) exists to promote the political education of adults.
- Federal Administration Academy (Verwaltungsakademie des Bundes) provides a form of adult education but exists only for government civil servants from the lowest to the highest occupational categories. Attendance is necessary for gaining civil servant tenure.
- Institute of Trades and Crafts (Wirtschaftsförderungsinstitut, WIFI) is a large organization offering vocational training and retraining to persons employed in the commercial or trade sectors of the economy.
- Institute of Trade Unions (Berufsförderungsinstitut, BFI) provides advanced vocational training for vocationally skilled and semiskilled employees.

Chapter V

Social Work Education

Introduction

Since training in social work is considered to be part of the vocational education system, social work does not exist as a course of study in Austrian universities. Social work training occurs at the upper secondary level and at the nonuniversity postsecondary level. Secondary-level social work schools are equivalent to variable-length intermediate vocational schools but may have age as well as academic admission requirements. The former senior vocational schools in social work were redefined in 1976 and converted into postsecondary social work academies which require the maturity certificate (*Reifeprüfungszeugnis, Reifezeugnis*) for admission. Training in marriage and family counseling is legally organized according to a program (*Lehrgang*) format, and the maturity certificate is normally required for admission.

Intermediate Vocational Schools In Social Work

Intermediate vocational schools for social work exist at the upper secondary level as separate institutions or as departments within larger institutions. In two instances, social work schools exist as departments within domestic science vocational schools (*höhere Lehranstalt für wirtschaftliche Frauenberufe*). Appendix B (Social Work Schools section) provides a partial list of secondary-level social work schools and illustrates the manner in which different types and levels of training are organized within educational institutions.

In addition to academic requirements, admission to social work schools sometimes requires a minimum age. Due to the emotional and intellectual maturity required for employment in social work occupations, the Education, Arts and Sports Ministry reserves the right to require a mature age, additional study in another school type, or completion of a practicum prior to admission. No final examination is required and graduates of intermediate-level social work schools receive a leaving certificate (*Abschlusszeugnis*) which may be combined with the final yearly certificate (*Jahres- und Abschlusszeugnis*).

Schools of general social work that last two years are called *Schulen für Sozialdienste* and those that last three years are called *Fachschulen für Sozialberufe*. In the three-year school, students choose between a general or a medical social work emphasis. Admission to either school requires completion of eight years of education; thus, the minimum total study duration is 10 years for the two-year program and 11 years for the three-year program. The three-year curriculum includes art, biology and ecology, chemistry, citizenship, a modern foreign language, geography and economics, German, history and social studies, law, music, physical education, physics, psychology, religion, and sociology as well as vocational courses in social work. The two-year curriculum is an abbreviated version of this one.

The following are specialized schools of social work at the intermediate vocational school level:

- Child-Care School (*Kinderpflegeschule*, formerly *Kinderpflegerinnenschule*) provides three-year programs to train child-care workers in preschools. The minimum admission requirement is completion of the nine-year compulsory education requirement. The total study program lasts a minimum of 12 years.

- Family Helper School (*Familienhelferinnenschule*) provides two-year programs and trains those who replace or assist a family's caretaker or who assist in family emergencies. The admission requirement is a minimum age of 17 years, completion of the nine-year compulsory education requirement, and one year of relevant experience. The total study program lasts a minimum of 11 years.

- Social Work School for Those Who Work with Physically Handicapped Persons (*Fachschule für Sozialberufe—Behindertenarbeit*) provides a training program lasting three years. The minimum admission requirement is 17 years of age and completion of the nine-year compulsory education requirement.

- School for Geriatric Social Workers (*Fachschule für Altendienste*) lasts one year. The minimum admission requirement is 19 years of age and completion of the nine-year compulsory education requirement.

Social Work Academies

A 1976 law redefined senior vocational schools in social work (*Lehranstalten für gehobene Sozialberufe*) and created academies for social work (*Akademien für Sozialarbeit*) to provide the highest-level social work training in the country. The nine social work academies in Austria are considered to be part of a nonuniversity postsecondary system of education. The current two-year program expanded to three years for students entering in the fall of 1986 and graduating in 1989. Two of the nine social work academies offer the equivalent program on a part-time basis over a longer time period for working adults.

In addition to an aptitude test, the usual entry requirement is the maturity certificate (*Reifeprüfungszeugnis, Reifezeugnis*). Those who have a particular aptitude for the field of social work as evidenced by an aptitude test but who do not have the maturity certificate may qualify for admission by taking a one-year preparatory program (*Vorbereitungslehrgang*). To be eligible for the preparatory program, the student must be at least 17 years of age, have completed nine years of compulsory education (though applicants usually have completed vocational training in social work at a lower level) and have at least nine months' experience in a social work practicum or six months' fulltime employment as a social worker aide. An estimated 10% to 15% of the students who enter a social work academy do not have the maturity certificate.

The one-year preparatory program for those who do not have the maturity certificate contains the following compulsory courses: art, biology and ecology, citizenship, one modern foreign language, geography and economics, German, history and social studies, mathematics, music, introduction to philosophy, physical education, physics and chemistry, religion, and skills in modern living. After completion of the preparatory program, students receive a yearly certificate (*Jahreszeugnis*).

The curriculum for the regular two-year social work program is outlined in Table 5.1. After successful completion of all coursework and practicums, students take a comprehensive diploma examination (*Diplomprüfung*) which consists of a written and an oral part. Those who pass the diploma examination receive a diploma (*Diplom*). Individual class grades are reported in a study book (*Studienbuch*).

Marriage and Family Counseling Schools

The training of marriage and family counselors is legally organized according to the program (*Lehrgang*) format; but unlike most other programs, marriage and family counseling programs exist as separate schools known as *Schule für Ehe- und Familienberater, Lehranstalt für Familientherapie,* or *Lehranstalt für Ehe- und Familienberater.* All are private and most are run by the Roman Catholic Church.

In addition to an aptitude test, those admitted must be between 27 and 40 years of age and, as a rule, must have the maturity certificate (*Reifeprüfungszeugnis, Reifezeugnis*) which also is required for admission to other postsecondary education. Although the program duration is seven semesters (3 1/2 years), the program is essentially part-time with instruction provided only three or four days per week. The curriculum is strongly specialized and includes a practicum lasting 120 hours. For a course list and instructional hours, see Table 5.2. No comprehensive final examination is required, and those who complete the program receive a leaving certificate (*Abschlusszeugnis*).

Schools of Social Work and Theology

The following schools provide training in social work and theology. Graduates of these schools receive a leaving certificate (*Abschlusszeugnis*).

- School for Protestant Deacons (*Diakonenschule*) exists as a department within a larger association for Protestant Deacon Work (Verein Evangelisches Diakoniewerk) in Feldkirchen and offers a two-year study program. In addition to an aptitude test, those admitted to the program must be 19 years old and must have completed an intermediate vocational school in social work or teacher training.

Table 5.1. Course List for Two-Year Social Work Academy Program

Compulsory Subjects*	Number of 50-Minute Lessons/Week			
Semester:	I	II	III	IV
Human and Social Sciences				
Economics & Social Politics	2	2	–	–
Law	3	3	2	2
Medical Sociology	3	3	2	2
Pedagogy	2	2	1	–
Political Science	–	–	1	–
Psychology	2	2	2	2
Religion	2	2	2	2
Social Philosophy	–	–	2	–
Sociology	2	2	–	–
Methods of Social Work	8	9	12	14
Supplement. Topics in Soc. Work	2	2	3	3
Elective Courses	4	4	2	2
Total	30	31	29	27

*Two 8-week practicums are completed in addition to the coursework.

Table 5.2. Course List for Schools for Marriage and Family Counseling

Subject	# Periods*	Subject	# Periods*
Intro. to Relev. Legal Fields	10	Self-Experience in Groups	80
Intro to Relev. Medical Fields	20	Social Institutions	8
Methodol. of Family & Group Work; Methodol. of Adult Educ.	156	Social Philosophy & Sociology	24
Professional Ethics	16	Total	464
Psychiatry	10	Compuls. Prac. Experience	120
Psychology	116	Grand Total	584
Relig. Fndns. of Marriage & Family	24		

*Forty 45-minute periods are equivalent to one weekly period over a year.

- School for Pastoral Professions (Lehranstalt für pastorale Berufe) exists in Vienna. Admission to the program requires the maturity certificate (*Reifeprüfungszeugnis, Reifezeugnis*) plus one year of practical experience in social work. The program extends to four years, but the third year consists only of practical pastoral work. The first, second, and fourth years consist of coursework. Approximately one-third of the program consists of coursework in theology and the remainder is coursework in auxiliary social sciences, education, and counseling.

Chapter VI

University Education

Introduction to Higher Education

University-level higher education occurs in 18 institutions which are considered equal in quality and level within the educational system. Twelve of the institutions are called an *Universität*, five are a *Hochschule*, and one is an *Akademie* or academy (though it is legally equivalent to a *Hochschule*). The terms *Universität* and *Hochschule* both can be translated into English as "university," although institutions called *Universitäten* have a broader academic focus than institutions called *Hochschulen*. For this reason, *Universität* will be translated as "university" and *Hochschule* will be translated as "college." As a generic term, *Akademie* cannot be translated as "university" or "college" because academies also exist at the secondary and nonuniversity postsecondary levels.

The universities consist of three "classical" universities, two technical universities, four special-purpose universities, and three "new" universities. The colleges (including the one academy) are all fine arts colleges (*Kunsthochschulen*). There are three music colleges, two art colleges, and one art academy (with equivalent "college" status). All are public institutions.

In the phrase *wissenschaftliche Hochschulen und Universitäten*, the adjective *wissenschaftlich* provides a succinct description of the goals of university-level institutions. *Wissenschaftlich* has no one-word equivalent in English but rather combines the meanings associated with "scientific" and "scholarly." Thus, the primary goals of universities and colleges are the advancement of science and scholarship through research and the preparation of the next generation of scientists and scholars. Study programs are designed to foster independent, critical, and creative thinking as opposed to rote learning and are organized so that independent study and individual initiative are required for academic success. Another goal of universities and colleges is the provision of continuing education to correspond with new scientific developments. To this end, programs and courses exist within universities and colleges for students who already have a degree or who do not seek a degree. In addition to these goals, art and music colleges strive to nourish artistic talents to their highest level while imparting a comprehensive, professional education.

In 1984, universities enrolled 89% of all students in postsecondary education while art and music colleges enrolled 3%. Nonuniversity postsecondary institutions (e.g., pedagogical academies, social work academies, and medical technology schools) enrolled the remaining students. In 1983, approximately 13% of the 18- to 25-year-old population was enrolled in universities and colleges, but of those who begin university studies only about half actually complete a degree program. Less than 4% of the current Austrian labor force consists of university graduates.

Due to the differences between universities and fine arts colleges, universities will be described in this chapter and fine arts colleges in Chapter VII. Since some similarities also exist, the reader will be referred to this chapter for descriptions that apply to both colleges and universities.

Brief Historical Review

Austrian universities were established in three phases that generally correspond with developments in science and technology. Founded during the earliest phase were the University of Vienna (Universität Wien) in 1365, University of Graz (Universität Graz or Karl-Franzens-Universität Graz) in 1585, University of Salzburg (Universität Salzburg) in 1623, and University of Innsbruck (Universität Innsbruck) in 1669. These earliest universities were organized in the same faculty-divided fashion as the earlier-established University of Paris in France. The original or "classical" faculties are those for theology, law, and medicine. Only the Universities of Vienna, Graz and Innsbruck have the classical faculties and, thus, are known as "complete" universities. Though originally planned as a "complete" university, the University of Salzburg was closed in 1810 (but reopened in 1962).

The early European universities developed during the Middle Ages out of a growing need for scientific knowledge that the existing monastery schools were unable to provide. Universities were formed through a union of private schools and scholars from different regions and through decrees issued by governmental leaders and the Pope. The University of Vienna was the second university established in central Europe after Charles University of Prague which was founded in 1348. After the Jesuits were organized in 1540, they exerted an important influence on the early universities, and ultimately assumed control of the newly formed University of Graz in 1656. After the Jesuit order was disbanded in 1773, higher education increasingly became a concern of the state, although the church continued to exert an important influence.

Until the mid-nineteenth century, university students were required to study liberal arts and philosophy for two years prior to entering one of the classical faculties (theology, law, or medicine). In 1848, philosophy was separated from the liberal arts and designated as a faculty parallel with the classical faculties. The liberal arts requirement was tacked onto the university-preparatory general secondary schools (Gymnasien), thus increasing the length of general secondary education from six to eight years. (As is still the case today, students attended four years of primary school prior to entering general secondary schools.) Since this time, general secondary schools rather than universities have been considered the vehicles for conveying a general liberal arts education. When students enter universities after completing general secondary education, they immediately begin intensive study in their major field.

The second phase of university foundings occurred mostly during the nineteenth century in response to the need for more specialized and technical knowledge. The following universities were established: University for Veterinary Medicine in Vienna (Veterinärmedizinische Universität Wien) in 1767, Technical University of Graz (Technische Universität Graz) in 1811, Technical University of Vienna (Technische Universität Wien) in 1815, University for Mining and Metallurgy in Leoben (Montanuniversität Leoben) in 1840, University for Agriculture in Vienna (Universität für Bodenkultur Wien) in 1872, and University for Business Administration in Vienna (Wirtschaftsuniversität Wien) in 1898. Prior to 1975, these universities were known as colleges (*Hochschulen*) and some had slightly different names (see "University Profiles" in this chapter).

The third phase of university foundings has occurred during the current period of school reforms which began shortly after the Austro-Hungarian monarchy collapsed and the First Austrian Republic was established in 1918. The school reforms were temporarily interrupted by an authoritarian administration that assumed power in 1934 and also by German occupation from 1938 through World War II. From 1938 to 1945, German educational laws replaced Austrian laws, and university research was ordered to support the war effort. During this period many of the famous and qualified Austrian scientists and scholars were forced to emigrate. The freedom to research and teach was severely limited, and the number of enrolled university students dropped dramatically. After the war, a reorientation program was formed to remove any remaining Nazi philosophy from the universities. Many of the professors who remained in universities and conducted research during this period were asked to leave, and few of those who emigrated returned. The resulting loss of a generation of scientists and scholars has had a profound effect on the country.

The school reform movement was rekindled after the war. Particularly after Austria regained its sovereignty in 1955, major changes were legislated in the educational system. To pass educational legislation in Parliament, political parties must agree or compromise in order to achieve the required two-thirds majority vote. The political climate was particularly conducive to educational legislation at this time. Two of the most significant laws affecting universities passed within this political climate were the 1966 General University Studies Law (Allgemeines Hochschul-Studiengesetz, AHStG) and the 1975 University Organization Law (Universitäts-Organisationsgesetz, UOG). The AHStG reformed many aspects of university study, while the UOG reformed university organization and instituted a democratic process of university self-governance. The three universities established during this period were the University of Linz (Universität Linz or Johannes-Kepler-Universität Linz) in 1962, University of Salzburg (which had closed in 1810) in 1962, and University for Educational Sciences in Klagenfurt (Universität für Bildungswissenschaften Klagenfurt) in 1970.

Funding and Enrollment

Almost all of the funding for Austrian universities and colleges comes from the federal budget, though approximately 3% of the funds come from such sources as endowments or donations. Austrian nationals pay no tuition. Foreign students pay only a small tuition fee each semester, although this fee may be waived for students from developing countries and from countries where tuition is waived for Austrians. The university-level institutions of higher education (universities, colleges, and the one art academy) and the compulsory schools represent the two most expensive items in the education budget. Money allocated to higher education has increased by 500% since the 1960s and now accounts for approximately one-sixth of the total education budget. The sharpest increase in higher education spending occurred between 1970-80 when expenditures grew from 2.3% to 2.8% of the federal budget. By 1984, the amount spent on higher education equaled roughly 0.9% of the Austrian gross national product.

The rise in expenses is attributed to inflation and to the increased demands placed upon institutions of higher education. Three new universities were founded and educational opportunities were expanded as a result of educational legislation since the 1960s. Although the per-student expenditure on higher education has increased only nominally over the past 20 years, significantly increased numbers of students are now attending institutions of higher education.

Approximately 137,000 Austrian citizens and 14,900 foreign students were enrolled in universities and colleges in 1984-85 compared with 44,600 citizens and 8,600 foreign students in 1970-71. This represents a combined student increase of 286%. Part of the growth is due to a sharp rise in the number of female students. During this period, the percentage of males increased by 219% while the percentage of females increased by 487%. Of all students enrolled in 1982-83, 43% were female, compared with only 25% in 1970-71. Enrollments, which began to increase after World War II, are predicted to level off by 1990.

The number of students who earned the maturity (examination) certificate (*Reifeprüfungszeugnis, Reifezeugnis*) and, thus, qualified for entry into higher education increased from 11,700 students in 1960 to 26,300 students in 1980. Within each age group, the percentage of those having the maturity certificate rose from 10% in 1960 to 21% in 1980.

Slightly more than half of all students who earn the maturity certificate enroll in a university or college. Of those who enroll, approximately three-quarters attended a general secondary school and one-quarter attended a senior vocational school in order to qualify for university entrance. In 1982, 77% of long-form general secondary school graduates, 54% of upper-cycle general secondary school graduates, and 37% of senior vocational school graduates attended a university. In 1970, the corresponding percentages were 69%, 34%, and 25%, respectively.

Legal Basis for University Studies

The legal basis for university organization and study programs differs from that for fine arts colleges. The University Organization Law (UOG) and the

General University Studies Law (AHStG) are described below while the parallel Fine Arts College Organization Law (KOG) and Fine Arts College Studies Law (KHStG) are described in Chapter VII.

Organization and Control

The organization of Austrian universities is regulated by the University Organization Law (Universitäts-Organisationsgesetz, UOG) which was passed in 1975. Prior to this, universities were organized and regulated primarily by higher education laws passed during the nineteenth century (except for the period between 1938 and 1945). Although another university organization law was passed in 1955, this law did not substantially modify the nineteenth century university organization laws in effect at the time. The primary stimulus for university reorganization arose not from the universities themselves but from the political arena and the international student movement in the 1960s.

In addition to reorganizing faculties, departments and other university functions, the UOG clearly defined the boundaries between university self-governance and government control over universities. University autonomy was expanded. The Science and Research Ministry may not interfere with each university's autonomy or self-governance but has general responsibility for ensuring that universities adhere to relevant laws.

The UOG also established a self-governance system that features "co-determination" (Mitbestimmung), a concept that extends authority for determining the direction of university affairs to all members of the academic community. Not only full professors but also students and other middle-level academic and support personnel (including assistant and associate professors)—the so-called "Mittelbau"—have a right and a duty to serve on administrative or governing councils. These three groups are equally represented on some councils and thus cast equal votes, but the ratio of representation on other councils is two full professors to one middle-level representative and one student. By providing for the representation of all university interests, the law attempted to transform universities from traditional elitist institutions to modern democratic ones. Prior to passage of the UOG, only professors belonged to administrative or governing councils.

A nineteenth century (1867) law on the general rights of citizens still provides the legal basis for academic freedom. Scientists and teachers are guaranteed the right, free of state interference, to seek new or reconfirm old knowledge through the scientific method of inquiry, pursue any scientific investigation, publish research findings, postulate any theory or doctrine, and use research findings in teaching.

Some universities are divided into faculties and some are not. Most of the larger universities are divided into faculties and subdivided into institutes (Institute [plural], or Institut [singular]). In faculty-divided universities the highest governing body is the academic senate (Akademische Senat). Smaller universities, however, usually are not divided into faculties but rather into institutes. An institute is the smallest independent organizational unit in which university research and teaching occurs and is equivalent to an academic department in the United States. In these universities the highest governing body is the University Council *(Universitätskollegium)*. In all universities the highest officer is the rector *(Rektor)*.

Regulation of Study Programs

Each study program or major *(Studienrichtung)* is subject to four levels of regulation, of which two have the status of federal law and the other two, decrees *(Verordnungen)*. (See also Bundesministerium für Wissenschaft und Forschung, *Das Österreichische Hochschulsystem.*) These regulations might be visualized as a pyramid where the first or top layer provides the most general regulations and each subsequent layer becomes successively more specific and detailed. The following descriptions of regulations introduce study program characteristics that are defined in later sections of this chapter and in Table 6.1.

The first layer of regulation is the General University Studies Law (Allgemeines Hochschul-Studiengesetz or AHStG) which was passed by Parliament in 1966 and which establishes the basic framework for all study programs. The AHStG generally regulates admission and registration standards, the contents and standardized organization of study programs, the structure and management of examinations, and the award of academic degrees. The AHStG also provides the basis for the remaining three sets of regulations and regulates their interaction.

The second layer of regulation consists of a multitude of special study laws that govern each study program or groups of related ones. These laws regulate the title of each study program, the division of certain majors into study branches *(Studienzweige)*, each major's requisite number of study segments *(Studienabschnitte)*, each major's prescribed minimum study duration *(Mindeststudiendauer)*, the required subjects *(Prüfungsfächer)* for each diploma examination *(Diplomprüfungen* and *Rigorosen)*, the examination process, and the academic degree or title awarded for each major.

The third layer of regulations are decrees known as study ordinances *(Studienordnungen)* which are decided within each university faculty. Study ordinances describe the overall structure of major programs, assign the approximate number of class hours required for each compulsory and elective subject *(Fach)*, and determine specific examination procedures and, in some cases, the types of classes *(Lehrveranstaltungen)*.

The fourth layer of regulations are decrees known as study plans *(Studienpläne)* which are issued by the study commission in each university. See sample study plans in Tables 6.2, 6.3, and 6.4. According to the UOG, members of the study commission are drawn from the following three groups: professors, middle-level academic and support personnel, and students. Study plans determine the individual classes that are necessary to satisfy the subject

Table 6.1 Major Degree Programs, 1985

FACULTY/STUDY GROUPING MAJOR 2nd Segment Specialization	Program Type	Prerequisite Secondary Subjects*	Min. Legal Length in Sems.: Total (Each Segment)	Actual Ave. Length in Semesters	Academic Degree or Title†
AGRICULTURAL STUDIES					
AGRICULTURE§					
Agri. Econ., Anim. Produc., Landscape Arch. & Hort., Plant Produc.	Diploma	—	9(4+5)	13.2	*Dipl.-Ing.*
	Doctoral	—	No legal min.	—	*Dr. nat. techn.*
AGRICULTURE‖	Diploma	Math-1	10(4+6)	16.0	*Dipl.-Ing.*
AGRI. & WATER ENGR.	Diploma	—	10(4+6)	15.3	*Dipl.-Ing.*
FOOD SCI. & BIOTECHNOL.					
FOREST. & WOOD PRODUCTS§					
Forest., Torrent/ Avalanche Control, Wood Products	Diploma	Math-1	9(4+5)	15.0	*Dipl.-Ing.*
CATHOLIC THEOLOGY					
PHILOSOPHY	Diploma	Phil.-1; Lat.-3; Grk.-5	8(4+4)	—	*Mag. phil. fac. theol.*
PHILOSOPHY‖	Doctoral		4	—	*Dr. phil. fac. theol.*
RELIGION EDUCATION	Diploma‡	Lat.-3; Grk.-5	10(4+6)	13.2	*Mag. theol.*
RELIGION EDUCATION# (combined program)	Diploma‡	Lat.-3	8(4+4)	16.8	*Mag. theol.* or *Mag. phil.*
THEOLOGY	Diploma	Lat.-3; Grk.-5	10(4+6)	14.0	*Mag. theol.*
THEOLOGY‖	Doctoral	—	4	—	*Dr. theol.*
EXPERIMENTAL STUDIES PROGRAMS				11.4 (programs combined)	
APPLIED BUS. ADMIN.	Diploma	—	9(4+5)	—	*Mag. rer. soc. oec.*
COMPARATIVE LIT.#	Diploma	Lat.-3	8(4+5)	—	*Mag. phil.*

LAND ECON./ECOLOGY	Diploma	—	10(4+6)	—	*Dipl.-Ing.*
NUMISMATICS#	Diploma	Lat.-3	8(4+4)	—	*Mag. phil.*
OPERATIONS ENGR. (TECH. CHEM.)	Diploma	Math-1	10(5+5)	—	*Dipl.-Ing.*
SCANDINAVIAN STUDIES#	Diploma	Lat.-3	8(4+4)	—	*Mag. phil.*
SOCIOLOGY#	Diploma	—	8(4+4)	—	*Mag. phil.*
HUMAN AND NATURAL SCIENCES				14.2 (programs combined)	
AFRICAN STUDIES#	Diploma	—	8(4+4)	—	*Mag. phil.*
ANCIENT HISTORY#	Diploma	Lat.-1; Grk.-3	8(4+4)	—	*Mag. phil.*
ANCIENT HISTORY & ANTIQUITY#	Diploma	Lat.-1	8(4+4)	—	*Mag. phil.*
ANTHROPOLOGY#	Diploma	—	8(4+4)	—	*Mag. phil.*
ARABIC#	Diploma‡	Lat.-3	8(4+4)	—	*Mag. phil.*
ART EDUCATION#	Diploma‡	—	9(4+5)	—	*Mag. art.*
ART HISTORY	Diploma	Lat.-3	8(4+4)	—	*Mag. phil.*
ASTRONOMY	Diploma	Math-1	8(4+4)	—	*Mag. rer. nat.*
BIOLOGY§ Bct., Genetics, Human Biol., Microbiol., Paleontol., Zoology	Diploma	Biol./Ecol.-1	10(4+6)	—	*Mag. rer. nat.*
BIOL. & EARTH SCI. EDUC.	Diploma‡	Biol./Ecol.-1	9(4+5)	—	*Mag. rer. nat.*
BIOL. & STUDY OF CONSUMER GOODS	Diploma‡	Biol./Ecol.-1	9(4+5)	—	*Mag. phil.*
BULGARIAN#	Diploma	Lat.-3	8(4+4)	—	*Mag. phil.*
BYZANTINE & MODERN GREEK STUDIES§	Diploma	Lat.-3; Grk.-3	8(4+4)	—	*Mag. phil.*
CHEMISTRY§ Biochem., Chem., Food Chem.	Diploma	—	10(5+5)	—	*Mag. rer. nat.*
Chem. Educ.#	Diploma‡	—	9(4+5)	—	*Mag. rer. nat.*
CLASSICAL ARCHEOL.#	Diploma	Lat.-3; Grk.-3	8(4+4)	—	*Mag. phil.*

continued

Program	Diploma	Requirements	Years		Degree
CLASSICAL SEMITIC PHILOL. & ORIENTAL ARCHEOL.#	Diploma	Lat.-3	8(4+4)	—	Mag. phil.
CLASSICS (GREEK)§#					
Class. Grk. Philol.	Diploma	Grk.-1; Lat.-3	8(4+4)	—	Mag. phil.
Class. Grk. Philol. Educ.	Diploma‡	Grk.-1; Lat.-3	9(4+5)	—	Mag. phil.
CLASSICS (LATIN)§#					
Class. Latin Philol.	Diploma	Lat.-3; Grk.-3	8(4+4)	—	Mag. phil.
Class. Lat. Philol. Educ.	Diploma‡	Lat.-3; Grk.-3	9(4+5)	—	Mag. phil.
CZECH§#					
Czech	Diploma	Lat.-3	8(4+4)	—	Mag. phil.
Czech. Educ.	Diploma‡	Lat.-3	9(4+5)	—	Mag. phil.
DESCRIPT. GEOM. EDUC.#	Diploma‡	Math-1; Geom.-1	9(4+5)	—	Mag. rer. nat.
EARTH SCIENCE§ Geol., Geotechnol., Mineral./Crystallogr., Mining/Geol., Paelontol., Petrology	Diploma	Biol./Ecol.-1	10(4+6)	—	Mag. rer. nat.
EDUCATIONAL SCIENCES#	Diploma	Phil.-1	8(4+4)	—	Mag. phil.
EGYPTIAN STUDIES#	Diploma	Lat.-1; Grk.-3	8(4+4)	—	Mag. phil.
ENGLISH & AMER. STUDIES#					
Engl. & Amer. Stud.	Diploma	Lat.-3	8(4+4)	—	Mag. phil.
Engl. & Amer. Stud. Educ.	Diploma‡	Lat.-3	9(4+5)	—	Mag. phil.
ETHNOLOGY (EUROPEAN)#	Diploma	—	8(4+4)	—	Mag. phil.
FINNISH/HUNGARIAN#					
Finnish/Hungarian	Diploma	Lat.-3	8(4+4)	—	Mag. phil.
Hungarian Educ.	Diploma‡	Lat.-3	9(4+5)	—	Mag. phil.
FRENCH§#					
French	Diploma	Lat.-3	8(4+4)	—	Mag. phil.
French Educ.	Diploma‡	Lat.-3	9(4+5)	—	Mag. phil.
GEOGRAPHY§					
Cartogr., Geog., Space Plan. & Research	Diploma	—	9(4+5)	—	Mag. phil.
Geog. & Econ. Educ.#	Diploma‡	—	9(4+5)	—	Mag. phil.

continued

GERMAN PHILOLOGY§#					
German Philology	Diploma	Lat.-3	8(4+4)	—	Mag. phil.
German Philo. Educ.	Diploma‡	Lat.-3	9(4+5)	—	Mag. phil.
HANDICRAFTS EDUC.#	Diploma‡	—	9(4+5)	—	Mag. art.
HISTORY§#					
History	Diploma	Lat.-3	8(4+4)	—	Mag. phil.
Hist. & Soc. Sci. Educ.	Diploma‡	Lat.-3	9(4+5)	—	Mag. phil.
HOME ECONOMICS EDUC.#	Diploma‡	—	9(4+5)	—	Mag. rer. nat.
INDIC STUDIES#	Diploma	—	8(4+4)	—	Mag. phil.
INSTRUM. MUSIC EDUC.#	Diploma‡	—	9(4+5)	—	Mag. art.
ITALIAN§#					
Italian	Diploma	Lat.-3	8(4+4)	—	Mag. phil.
Italian Educ.	Diploma‡	Lat.-3	9(4+5)	—	Mag. phil.
JAPANESE STUDIES#	Diploma	—	8(4+4)	—	Mag. phil.
JEWISH STUDIES#	Diploma	Lat.-3	8(4+4)	—	Mag. phil.
JOURNAL. & MASS COMMUNICA.#	Diploma	—	8(4+4)	—	Mag. phil.
LANGUAGE/CULTURE OF ANCIENT ORIENT#	Diploma	Lat.-3	8(4+4)	—	Mag. phil.
LINGUISTICS§# Appl. Linguis., Gen. Linguis.	Diploma	Lat.-3	8(4+4)	—	Mag. phil.
Indo-Europ. Lang. Study	Diploma	Lat.-3; Grk.-3	8(4+4)	—	Mag. phil.
LOGISTICS	Diploma	Math-1	8(4+4)	—	Mag. phil.
MATHEMATICS§					
Mathematics	Diploma	Math-1	10(4+6)	—	Mag. rer. nat.
Mathematics Educ.#	Diploma‡	Math-1	9(4+5)	—	Mag. rer. nat.
METEOROLOGY/GEOPHYSICS§					
Geophys., Meteorol.	Diploma	Math-1	8(4+4)	—	Mag. rer. nat.
MUSIC EDUCATION#	Diploma‡	—	9(4+5)	—	Mag. art.
MUSICOLOGY#	Diploma	—	8(4+4)	—	Mag. phil.
PHARMACY	Diploma	Biol./Ecol.-1; Lat.-3	9(4+5)	15.3	Mag. pharm.
PHILOSOPHY#	Diploma	Phil.-1; Lat.-3	8(4+4)	—	Mag. phil.

Subject					
PHILOS./EDUC./PSYCH.#	Diploma‡	Phil.-1	9(4+5)	—	Mag. phil.
PHILOS. or NATURAL SCI.‖	Doctoral	—	4	—	Dr. phil. or Dr. rer. nat.
PHYSICS§					
Physics	Diploma	Math-1	10(4+6)	—	Mag. rer. nat.
Physics Educ.#	Diploma‡	Math-1	9(4+5)	—	Mag. rer. nat.
POLISH#	Diploma	Lat.-3	8(4+4)	—	Mag. phil.
POLITICAL SCIENCE#	Diploma	—	8(4+4)	—	Mag. phil.
PORTUGUESE#	Diploma	Lat.-3	8(4+4)	—	Mag. phil.
PSYCHOLOGY	Diploma	Phil.-1	10(4+6)	—	Mag. phil.
ROMANIAN#	Diploma	Lat.-3	8(4+4)	—	Mag. phil.
RUSSIAN§#					
Russian	Diploma	Lat.-3	8(4+4)	—	Mag. phil.
Russian Educ.	Diploma‡	Lat.-3	9(4+5)	—	Mag. phil.
SERBO-CROATIAN§#					
Serbo-Croatian	Diploma	Lat.-3	8(4+4)	—	Mag. phil.
Serbo-Croatian Educ.	Diploma‡	Lat.-3	9(4+5)	—	Mag. phil.
SINOLOGY#	Diploma	—	8(4+4)	—	Mag. phil.
SLOVENE§#					
Slovene	Diploma	Lat.-3	8(4+4)	—	Mag. phil.
Slovene Educ.	Diploma‡	Lat.-3	9(4+5)	—	Mag. phil.
SPANISH§#					
Spanish	Diploma	Lat.-3	8(4+4)	—	Mag. phil.
Spanish Educ.	Diploma‡	Lat.-3	9(4+5)	—	Mag. phil.
SPORTS & PHYS. EDUC.#					
Physical Education	Diploma‡	—	9(4+5)	—	Mag. phil.
Sports Science	Diploma	—	8(4+4)	—	Mag. phil.
TEXTILE DESIGN & PRODUCT.#	Diploma‡	—	9(4+5)	—	Mag. art.
THEATER ARTS#	Diploma	—	8(4+4)	—	Mag. phil.
TIBETAN & BUDDHISM STUD.#	Diploma	—	8(4+4)	—	Mag. phil.
TRANSLATING	Short	—	6	—	Akad. gepr. Übersetzer

TRANSLATING & INTERPRET.§					
Interpreting	Diploma	—	8(4+4)	15.0	*Mag. phil.*
Translating	Diploma	—	8(4+4)	—	*Mag. phil.*
TURKISH STUDIES#	Diploma	Lat.-3	8(4+4)	—	*Mag. phil.*
LAW, SOCIAL SCIENCE, AND BUSINESS					
BUSINESS ADMINISTRATION					
Business Administration	Diploma	—	8(4+4)	12.2	*Mag. rer. soc. oec.*
Public Econ. & Admin.	Diploma	—	8(4+4)	New, 1983	*Mag. rer. soc. oec.*
BUSINESS EDUCATION	Diploma‡	—	9(4+5)	13.4	*Mag. rer. soc. oec.*
COMMERCE	Diploma	—	8(4+4 or 3+5)	11.9	*Mag. rer. soc. oec.*
ECONOMICS	Diploma	—	8(4+4 or 3+5)	13.3	*Mag. rer. soc. oec.*
LAW	Diploma	Lat.-1	8(2+6)	—	*Mag. iur.*
LAW	Doctoral	—	2	—	*Dr. iur.*
MANAGEMENT INFO. SCI.§ Business Info., Econ. & Mgmt. Info.	Diploma	—	8(4+4)	—	*Mag. rer. soc. oec.*
SOCIAL POLICY	Diploma	—	8(4+4 or 3+5)	11.8	*Mag. rer. soc. oec.*
SOC. SCI. & ECONOMICS	Doctoral	—	2	—	*Dr. rer. oec.*
SOCIOLOGY	Diploma	—	8(4+4 or 3+5)	13.0	*Mag. rer. soc. oec.*
STATISTICS	Diploma	—	8(4+4 or 3+5)	—	*Mag. rer. soc. oec.*
MEDICAL STUDIES					
MEDICINE	Doctoral	Biol./Ecol.-1; Lat.-3	12(4+3+5)	15.2	*Dr. med. univ.*
VETERINARY MEDICINE	Diploma	Biol./Ecol.-1; Lat.-3	10(4+4+2)	15.6	*Mag. med. vet.*
Food Science	Extension	—	2	—	No degree awarded
VETERINARY MEDICINE	Doctoral	—	3	—	*Dr. med. vet.*
MINING STUDIES					
MATERIALS ENGR.	Diploma	Math-1; Geom.-3	10(5+5)	15.4	*Dipl.-Ing.*
METALLUR. ENGR.§ Extract. Metall., Founding, Indus. & Energy Mgmt.,					

continued

Program					
Metal Forming, Metals Sci., Nonferrous Metall.	Diploma	Math-1; Geom.-3	10(5+5)	16.2	Dipl.-Ing.
MINING & MINERAL ENGR.	Diploma	Math-1; Geom.-3	10(5+5)	19.7	Dipl.-Ing.
MINE SURVEYING	Diploma	Math-1; Geom.-3	10(5+5)	11.7	Dipl.-Ing.
MINING	Diploma	Math-1; Geom.-3	10(5+5)	14.0	Dipl.-Ing.
MINING & METALLUR. MACHIN.	Diploma	Math-1; Geom.-3	10(5+5)	17.1	Dipl.-Ing.
MINING SCIENCES‖	Doctoral	—	No legal min.	—	Dr. mont.
PETROLEUM ENGINEERING	Diploma	Math-1; Geom.-3	10(5+5)	15.8	Dipl.-Ing.
PLASTICS TECHNOLOGY	Diploma	Math-1; Geom.-3	10(5+5)	17.5	Dipl.-Ing.
PROTESTANT THEOLOGY					
RELIG. EDUC.# (comb. prog.)	Diploma‡	—	9(4+5)	—	Mag. theol.
THEOLOGY	Diploma	Lat.-3; Grk.-5	9(4+5)	16.8	Mag. theol.
THEOLOGY‖	Doctoral‡	—	4	—	Dr. theol.
TECHNICAL STUDIES					
ACTUARIAL MATHEMATICS	Short	Math-1	6	9.2	Akad. gepr. Ver. Math.
ARCHITECTURE	Diploma	Math-1; Geom.-3	10(4+6)	16.9	Dipl.-Ing.
ARCHITECTURE	Diploma	Math-1; Geom.-3	10(4+6)	—	Mag. arch.
ARCHITECTURE	Diploma	Math-1; Geom.-3	8(1 exam)	—	Mag. arch.
CIVIL ENGINEERING§ Bldg. Constr. & Oper., Constr. Engr., Traffic/ Transport, Water Econ. & Hydroengr.	Diploma	Math-1; Geom.-3	10(4+6)	16.8	Dipl.-Ing.
BUS., LAW & ECON.	Contin.	—	4	—	Diplomierter Wirtschaftstechniker
COMPUTER TECHNOLOGY	Short	Math-1	5	6.4	Akad. gepr. Datentechn.
ELECTRICAL ENGINEERING§ Communica. Engr., Indus. Electron. & Control Engr., Elec. Energy Technol.	Diploma	Math-1; Geom.-3	10(4+6)	15.1	Dipl.-Ing.
ENVIRON. PROTECT. TECHNOL.	Contin.	—	4	—	Diplomierter Umwelttechniker

Field	Degree	Secondary school subjects*	Semesters	Duration	Degree title†
INFORMATION SCIENCE	Diploma	Math-1	10(4+6)	11.8	Dipl.-Ing.
MECHANICAL ENGINEERING§ Gen. Mech. Engr., Marine Engr., Oper. Sci., Proces. Engr., Transport & Vehicle Engr.	Diploma	Math-1; Geom.-3	10(4+6)	15.7	Dipl.-Ing.
OPERATIONS ENGR. (CIVIL ENGINEERING)	Diploma	Math-1; Geom.-3	10(4+6)	—	Dipl.-Ing.
OPERATIONS ENGR. (MECH. ENGINEERING)	Diploma	Math-1; Geom.-3	10(4+6)	14.7	Dipl.-Ing.
PROCESSING TECHNOLOGY	Diploma	Math-1; Geom.-3	10(4+6)	15.8	Dipl.-Ing.
SURVEYING	Diploma	Math-1; Geom.-3	10(4+6)	16.5	Dipl.-Ing.
TECHNICAL CHEMISTRY§ Biochem. & Food Chem., Chem. Engr., Inorg. Chem., Organ. Chem.	Diploma	Math-1	10(5+5)	13.2	Dipl.-Ing.
TECHNICAL MATHEMATICS§ Math/Nat. Sci., Econ. & Plan. Math, Inform. & Data Proces.	Diploma	Math-1	10(4+6)	12.3	Dipl.-Ing.
TECHNICAL PHYSICS	Diploma	Math-1	10(4+6)	13.5	Dipl.-Ing.
TECHNICAL SCIENCES‖	Doctoral	—	No legal min.	—	Dr. techn.
URBAN & REGIONAL PLANNING§ Region. Plan., Space Plan.	Diploma	Math-1; Geom.-3	10(4+6)	13.9	Dipl.-Ing.

SOURCE: Adapted and translated from data provided by the Science and Research Ministry.

*Secondary school subjects which are prerequisite for registration for the designated semester (e.g., 1 = first semester, etc.). Biol./Ecol. = Biology and Ecology; Geom. = Descriptive Geometry; Grk. = Greek; Lat. = Latin; Math = Additional Mathematics; Phil. = Introduction to Philosophy.

†The full name of the academic degree (which may be in German or Latin) follows with an English translation:

Akad. gepr. Datentechn. = Akademisch geprüfter Datentechniker/Academically Certified Computer Engineer

Akad. gepr. Übersetzer = Akademisch geprüfter Übersetzer/Academically Certified Translator

Akad. gepr. Ver. Math. = Akademisch geprüfter Versicherungsmathematiker/Academically Certified Actuary

Dipl.-Ing. = Diplom-Ingenieur/Diploma in Engineering

Diplomierter Umwelttechniker/Graduate Environmental Engineer

continued

Diplomierter Wirtschaftstechniker/Graduate Business Technician

Dr. iur. = Doktor der Rechte/Doktor der Rechtswissenschaften/Doctor iuris/Doktor of Law

Dr. med. univ. = Doktor der gesamten Heilkunde/Doctor medicinae universae/Doktor of Medicine

Dr. med. vet. = Doktor der Veterinärmedizin/Doctor medicinae veterinariae/Doktor of Veterinary Medicine

Dr. mont. = Doktor der montanistischen Wissenschaften/Doctor rerum montanarum/Doktor of Mining Sciences

Dr. nat. techn. = Doktor der Bodenkultur/Doctor rerum naturalium technicarum/Doktor of Agriculture

Dr. phil. = Doktor der Philosophie/Doctor philosophiae/Doktor of Philosophy

Dr. phil. fac. theol. = Doktor der Philosophie der Theologischen Fakultät/Doctor philosophiae facultatis theologicae/Doktor of Philosophy from the Theology Faculty

Dr. rer. nat. = Doktor der Naturwissenschaften/Doctor rerum naturalium/Doktor of Natural Sciences

Dr. rer. soc. oec. = Doktor der Sozial– und Wirtschaftswissenschaften/Doctor rerum socialium oeconomicarumque/Doktor of Social and Economic Sciences

Dr. techn. = Doktor der technischen Wissenschaften/Doctor technicae/Doktor of Technical Sciences

Dr. theol. = Doktor der Theologie/Doctor theologiae/Doktor of Theology

Mag. arch. = Magister der Architektur/Magister architecturae/Magister of Architecture

Mag. art. = Magister der Künste/Magister artium/Magister of Arts

Mag. iur. = Magister der Rechtswissenschaften/Magister iuris/Magister of Law

Mag. med. vet. = Diplom-Tierarzt/Magister medicinae veterinariae/Diploma in Veterinary Medicine

Mag. pharm. = Magister der Pharmazie/Magister pharmaciae/Magister of Pharmacy

Mag. phil. = Magister der Philosophie/Magister philosophiae/Magister of Philosophy

Mag. phil. fac. theol. = Magister der Philosophie der Theologischen Fakultät/Magister philosophiae facultatis theologicae/Magister of Philosophy from the Theology Faculty

Mag. rer. nat. = Magister der Naturwissenschaften/Magister rerum naturalium/Magister of Natural Sciences

Mag. rer. soc. oec. = Magister der Sozial– und Wirtschaftswissenschaften/Magister rerum socialium oeconomicarumque/Magister of Social and Economic Sciences

Mag. theol. = Magister der Theologie/Magister theologiae/Magister of Theology

‡Secondary school teacher certification (Lehramt an höheren Schulen).

§The major program has the same first segment curriculum in all specializations; the specialized curriculum exists only in the second segment.

‖Prerequisite for admission to the doctoral program is completion of one of the diploma programs in this faculty or subject grouping.

#This major requires a second major or an approved combination of subjects in order to satisfy requirements for the first academic degree.

Table 6.2. Study Plan for English and American Studies at Karl-Franzens University of Graz

The major in English and American Studies is divided into two study segments (*Studienabschnitte*). Two second-segment study branches (*Studienzweige*) exist; one prepares secondary-school teachers and the other does not. The program that does not train teachers is translated below. Secondary school preparation in Latin is required prior to registration for the third semester. Also, students normally study English for eight years in secondary school.

Students must complete this major as well as a second major in order to satisfy all requirements for the *Magister* of Philosophy degree. If used as a first major, a few more courses are required than if used as a second major. The educational plan described below is that for English and American Studies as a first major. This major may be combined with educational sciences which is described as a second major in Table 6.3. For descriptions of study program characteristics, see "Diploma Study Program."

FIRST STUDY SEGMENT

1. In the first study segment, which lasts a minimum of four semesters, 30 weekly semester hours* in compulsory subjects (*Pflichtfächer*) and 6 weekly semester hours in free subjects (*Freifächer*) are required. Each semester, students must register for a minimum of 15 weekly hours, including subjects required for the second major.

2. The following compulsory subjects are required for the specified number of weekly semester hours: Command of the Language (12), Linguistics (8), Literature (6), Land and Culture (4). Students may register for up to 10 weekly hours of specifically-designated second-segment courses during the first study segment.

3. The following courses (*Lehrveranstaltungen*) are required within each subject (*Fach*):

Subject (*Fach*) Course (*Lehrveranstaltung*)	Type of Class†	Weekly Hours in a Semester*
Command of the Language		
Oral Work I	Ü	2
English Grammar I	PS	2
Oral Work II	Ü	2
English Grammar II	PS	2
Translation (English-German)	Ü	1
Comprehension & Composition	PS	3
Linguistics‡		
English Phonetics	V with Ü	2
Intro. to Linguistics	PS or V	2
Intro. to Old English	PS	2
Linguistics	PS	2
Literature‡		
Intro. to English & American Lit.	PS	2
Literature	PS or V	2
Intro. to Hist. of Engl. & Amer. Lit.	PS or V	2
Land and Culture‡		
Intro. to Land & Culture of England	PS or V	2
Intro. to Land & Culture of America	PS or V	2
Free Subjects	–	6

continued

SECOND STUDY SEGMENT

1. In the second study segment, which lasts a minimum of four semesters, 24 weekly semester hours in compulsory and choice (*Wahlfächer*) subjects and 10 weekly semester hours of free subjects are required. Each semester, students must register for a minimum of 15 weekly hours, including subjects required for the second major.
2. The following compulsory and choice subjects are required for the specified number of weekly semester hours: Command of the Language (4), Linguistics (6), Literature (6), choice subject in English Language and/or Literature (6), Preliminary Examination (*Vorprüfung*) Preparation (2).
3. The following courses are required within each subject:

Subject (*Fach*) Course (*Lehrveranstaltung*)	Type of Class†	Weekly Hours in a Semester*
Command of the Language		
Adv. Oral English	PS	2
Adv. Translation (German-English)	PS	1
Error Analysis	PS	1
Linguistics (as related to the Land and Culture)		
Linguistics	V	2
Review of English Linguistics	V and Ü	2
Linguistics Seminar	S	2
Literature (as related to the Land and Culture)		
Literature	V	2
Literature	PS/V/S	2
Literary Appreciation	V and Ü	2
Choice of English Language	S, P,	
and/or Literature	PS, V	6
Preliminary Exam. Preparation	–	2
Free Subjects	–	10

4. A thesis (*Diplomarbeit*) also is required.

*The weekly hours in a semester (*Semesterwochenstunden, Wochenstunden*) are essentially equivalent to semester hours in the United States.
†P = *Privatissimum* (special research seminar), PS = *Proseminar* (introductory seminar), S = *Seminar* (seminar), Ü = *Übung* (exercise), V = *Vorlesung* (lecture).
‡At least one course within this subject must be taken in English. If the course taken in English is a lecture, then the student also must write a paper in English.

Table 6.3. Study Plan for Educational Sciences at Karl-Franzens University of Graz

The major in Educational Sciences does not prepare graduates for teaching positions in secondary schools. Slightly different second segments exist for those who study Educational Sciences as a second, rather than as a first major. Educational Sciences as a second major (translated below) may be combined with English and American Studies as a first major (see description in Table 6.2) in order to satisfy requirements for the *Magister* of Philosophy degree. For descriptions of each study program characteristic, see "Diploma Study Program."

continued

FIRST STUDY SEGMENT

1. In the first study segment, which lasts a minimum of four semesters, 36 weekly semester hours* of compulsory and choice subjects (*Pflichtfächer* and *Wahlfächer*) and 4 weekly semester hours of free subjects (*Freifächer*) are required. Each semester, students must register for a minimum of 15 weekly hours, including required subjects for the first major.

2. During the first segment, the following subjects are required for the specified number of weekly semester hours: Theory of Education and Training (13), General Methodology (8), Introduction to Comparative Education (2), Educational Psychology (9), and Educational Sociology (4).

3. The following courses (*Lehrveranstaltungen*) are required within each subject (*Fach*):

Subject (*Fach*) Course (*Lehrveranstaltung*)†	Type of Class‡	Weekly Hours in a Semester*
Theory of Education and Training		
Theory of Education (*Bildung*) & Training (*Erziehung*)	V + S	9
History of Problems in Education	V	4
General Methodology		
Methodology	V	2
Statistics	V + Ü	6
Intro. to Comparative Education		
Intro. to Comparative Education	S	2
Educational Psychology		
Developmental Psychology	V	1
Educational Psychology	V + Ü	8
Educational Sociology		
Educational Sociology	V + S	4
Free Subjects	–	4

SECOND STUDY SEGMENT

1. The second segment in Educational Sciences lasts a minimum of four semesters. As a second major, 20 weekly semester hours of compulsory or choice subjects and 4 weekly semester hours of free subjects are required.

2. Within the compulsory and choice subjects, students must choose two of the following subjects, each of which requires 8 weekly semester hours: Experimental Educational System Theories; Theory of Educational Institutions; or one subject chosen from School Education and Teacher Training, Social Education, Health and Special Education, or Adult Education. In addition, one of these subjects is chosen as an area of emphasis and an extra 4 weekly semester hours is required in that subject. The names of classes are the same as those for subjects. An additional 4 weekly semester hours are required in free subjects.

---

*The weekly hours in a semester (*Semesterwochenstunden, Wochenstunden*) are essentially equivalent to semester hours in the United States.

†The name of the class on the class-completion certificate (*Zeugnis, Kolloquienzeugnis*) may differ from that in the study plan. Courses may be subdivided into smaller classes lasting fewer hours. For example, a required course lasting 4 weekly semester hours may be offered as two classes each lasting 2 weekly semester hours.

‡V = *Vorlesung* (lecture), Ü = *Übung* (exercise), P = *Privatissimum* (special research seminar), S = *Seminar* (seminar).

Table 6.4. Short Summary of Selected Study Plans

CIVIL ENGINEERING, TECHNICAL UNIVERSITY OF GRAZ
A total of 91 weekly semester hours is required during the first segment and 155 weekly semester hours are required during the second segment. Of the required 246 weekly semester hours, 10 are free subjects. The first segment, which lasts a minimum of four semesters, covers the background technical and scientific subjects. Required subjects include descriptive geometry, mathematics, mechanics, and physics. The second segment, which lasts a minimum of six semesters, provides the basics of civil engineering. Required subjects include construction business, construction engineering, foundations, hydraulic engineering, statics, and transportation systems. Each subject is subdivided into required classes.

MATHEMATICS, KARL-FRANZENS UNIVERSITY OF GRAZ
A total of 139 weekly semester hours is required for the *Magister* of Natural Sciences degree in mathematics, of which 59 are required in the first segment and 80 in the second segment. In the first segment, which lasts a minimum of four semesters, required subjects are algebra, analysis, geometry, choice subjects, and free subjects. In the second segment, which lasts a minimum of six semesters, required subjects are algebra, analysis, numerical mathematics, topology, a choice subject within the field of mathematics, a choice subject from an area of application, and free subjects.

GEOGRAPHY AND ECONOMICS EDUCATION, UNIVERSITY FOR EDUCATIONAL SCIENCES IN KLAGENFURT
This major provides training for secondary school teachers. A second major also must be completed in order to satisfy requirements for the *Magister* of Philosophy degree. During the first segment which lasts a minimum of four semesters, a total of 51 weekly semester hours (of which 8 are free electives) are required. Required subjects are general human geography, general physical geography, introduction to economics, maps, and regional geography of Austria and central Europe. During the second segment which lasts a minimum of five semesters, 34 weekly semester hours are required in the following subjects: comparative human geography, comparative physical geography, economics, regional geography of Europe and non-European areas, theory and methods of geographers, and subject didactics (for teachers).

requirements in each major (as established by the corresponding study law in layer two) and the study duration of each subject (as defined by the faculty in layer three). In addition, study plans establish prerequisites for enrollment in each class and assign hours to each class (the total of which should equal or exceed that required for each subject).

Prior to passage of the AHStG in 1966, study programs were subject to a series of non-uniform regulations dating from the nineteenth century. From 1966 to 1983, old study programs were replaced by new ones as study programs subject to AHStG requirements were prepared. Students could begin old programs up until they were converted. The program in effect when a student entered was the one which that student had to complete. Primarily the new system will be described here, although reference will be made to both new and old systems. The old system is described in the 1962 World

Education Series volume on Austria (*Austria: A Survey of Austrian Education and Guide to the Academic Placement of Students from Austria in Educational Institutions in the United States of America* by Lily von Klemperer).

Entry Requirements

The requirement for entering a university depends upon whether the student wishes regular student status *(ordentlicher Hörer)*, special student status *(ausserordentlicher Hörer)*, or auditor status *(Gasthörer)*. Approximately 96% of all university students enroll with regular status, 3.5% with special status, and 0.5% as auditors.

Entry with Regular Student Status

Students who wish to earn an academic degree or title must meet admission requirements for regular student status *(ordentlicher Hörer)*. The minimum university entry requirement is the maturity certificate *(Reifeprüfungszeugnis, Reifezeugnis)*. Regardless of age or other personal attributes, all Austrian citizens who have the maturity certificate are guaranteed the right to enter a university with regular status. The quota system *(numerus clausus)* which exists in some other European countries to limit the number of students studying in certain majors does not exist in Austria.

Although the maturity certificate is the minimum requirement for university admission, students also must meet prerequisite subject requirements prior to registration in certain majors. Students who have not completed the subject prerequisites while in secondary school must take additional examinations *(Zusatzprüfungen)* prior to registration for a particular semester. The law requires an additional examination prior to first, third, or fifth semester registration. For example, registration in classical archaeology or Latin majors requires completion of Latin and Greek in secondary school or an additional examination in Latin prior to first-semester university registration and in Greek prior to third-semester registration. (See Table 6.1 for a list of prerequisites in each major.) To prepare for additional examinations, students may study the subject as a special student in a university or through various adult education options. The prerequisite subjects, which not all maturity certificate holders have studied and for which additional examinations exist, are biology/ecology, descriptive geometry, Greek, Latin, additional mathematics, and philosophy. University students receive no university credit for studying these subjects because they are deemed to be secondary-level subjects.

Supplementary examinations *(Ergänzungsprüfungen)* serve as aptitude tests and are required prior to registration for a particular semester in the following majors: art history, music, sports and physical education, and translating and interpreting. Usually the supplementary examination is required prior to one of the two diploma examinations *(Diplomprüfungen)*. In addition, supplementary examinations may be given to foreign or stateless applicants in order to determine the comparability of their academic preparation with that required for the Austrian maturity certificate or to determine German language proficiency.

Students who do not have the maturity certificate may demonstrate their qualification for university study in a particular major by taking an alternate maturity examination which was known as the vocational maturity examination (*Berufsreifeprüfung*) until 1986 and the studies-authorizing examination (*Studienberechtigungsprüfung*) after 1986. These examinations represent maturity examination equivalencies but do not represent completion of all academic studies required for the maturity certificate. Passing either equivalency examination meets the minimum requirement for university entry, although additional examinations (*Zusatzprüfungen*) still are necessary for entering certain majors. Usually less than 1% of each year's entering class qualifies for admission through a maturity examination equivalency, though the law permits a maximum of 3% to qualify in this manner.

Entry with Special Student Status

Students admitted with special student status (*ausserordentlicher Hörer*) may enroll in regular university courses on a space-available basis, in special college or university programs (*Hochschullehrgänge, Universitätslehrgänge*), or in special college or university courses (*Hochschulkurse*), none of which lead to the award of an academic degree. Students with special status are ineligible to take any of the examinations required for an academic degree.

Special-status admission does not require the maturity certificate. Instead, students must be at least 17 years of age and have attained the necessary prerequisite knowledge which is evaluated on an individual basis. Admission to some general programs or courses may be granted to 15-year-olds.

Those who wish to prepare for additional examinations that are prerequisite for regular registration in certain university majors sometimes enroll with special status. Also, foreign students whose secondary-school leaving certificate is judged not equivalent to the Austrian maturity certificate may enter a university with special status and take classes to supplement their secondary-school qualifications. Ultimately, these students may gain admission to a regular program with regular status, but they will receive no "advanced placement" for their special-status study.

Entry with Auditor Status

Auditor status (*Gasthörer*) is a nondegree-seeking status reserved for university graduates who wish to enroll in regular university classes, special college or university programs (*Hochschullehrgänge, Universitätslehrgänge*), or special college or university courses (*Hochschulkurse*), none of which lead to the award of an academic degree. The minimum admission requirement is completion of an academic degree. Students who have completed one degree program and wish to earn another academic degree must seek admission with regular student, not auditor, status.

Regular Study Programs

Regular study programs *(ordentliche Studien)* and special study programs *(ausserordentliche Studien)* exist. Regular study programs culminate in the award of an academic degree or title and enroll the vast majority of students while special study programs (as described in a later section) enroll only a small number of nondegree-seeking students. Students enrolled in regular study programs must enter a university with regular student status *(ordentlicher Hörer)*. See Appendix A for sample university documents.

Although the General University Studies Law (AHStG) was passed in 1966, both old and new systems operated simultaneously for a time as required programmatic changes were made. Conversion to study programs subject to AHStG requirements occurred as the new programs were prepared between 1966 and approximately 1983. The study program in effect when a student entered was the one that the student had to follow. The AHStG provides for the award of a first degree (the *Diplom-Ingenieur* in engineering, *Diplom-Tierarzt* in veterinary medicine, and *Magister* in all other disciplines) and a second degree (the *Doktor*). These same degrees also existed in the pre-AHStG system, but only the *Doktor* was consistently awarded. The first degree was less formally conferred and in certain majors was not required prior to earning the *Doktor*. The names of other first degrees conferred in the old system consisted of the word "diploma" *(Diplom)* and a professional title, e.g., *Diplom-Kaufmann* *(Dkfm.* or *Dipl.-Kfm.)* which is a diploma for business persons or *Diplom-Dolmetscher (Dipl.-Dolm.)* which is a diploma for interpreters. In secondary teacher-training majors, a state examination for teachers *(Lehramtsprüfung)* was required and was reported on a teacher examination certificate *(Lehramts-prüfungszeugnis)*. Teachers also could obtain a *Magister* degree, but it was not uniformly required prior to earning the *Doktor*. Unless specifically designated "pre-AHStG," descriptions in this section apply to the current or "post-AHStG" system.

The AHStG created several standard structures for regular study programs. The most common structure is the diploma program *(Diplomstudium)* which leads to the award of the first academic degree. An enlarged diploma program is the extension program *(Erweiterungsstudium)* which also culminates in the award of the first academic degree. The short program *(Kurzstudium)* leads not to the award of an academic degree but to an academic title (e.g., *Akademisch geprüfter Übersetzer* or Academically Certified Translator). Second degree or title programs, which sometimes are called "postgraduate studies" *(postgraduale Studien)*, are the doctoral program *(Doktoratsstudium)* and the recently-established (1983) continuation program *(Aufbaustudium)*. The doctoral program culminates in the award of the second *(Doktor)* degree and the continuation program in the award of a higher-level academic title (e.g., *Diplomierter*

Umwelttechniker or Graduate Environmental Engineer) than that awarded after a short program. The only study program unchanged by the AHStG was the doctoral program in medicine where the only degree still awarded is the *Doktor.* Other doctoral programs were changed by the AHStG and now require, prior to admission, a completed diploma program and receipt of the first academic degree. Among enrolled university students in 1983-84, 4% were in special study programs (described in a later section) and 96% were in regular study programs (i.e., 80% in diploma programs [including extension programs], 12% in the doctoral program in medicine, 3% in other doctoral programs, and 1% in short programs).

Diploma Study Program *(Diplomstudium)*

Most degree-seeking students are enrolled in diploma study programs which lead to the award of the first academic degree *(Magister, Diplom-Ingenieur, Diplom-Tierarzt).* Diploma programs are divided into study segments, each of which conclude with a diploma examination. Prior to the second diploma examination in the second segment, students must prepare a thesis. Within each segment, coursework is organized into general subjects which are subdivided into specific classes. Diploma programs in some majors require completion of a second major or an approved combination of subjects. A legally-prescribed minimum study duration exists for each major, although most students' actual study duration is considerably longer. Table 6.1 outlines the unique characteristics of each major program.

Various academic credentials document completion of different portions of the diploma program. Each credential is identified along with the description of the educational component that it documents. Students may request from their university a summary of their accomplishments, which is called a Certificate of Study Results *(Nachweis über den Studienerfolg)* or a Departure Certificate *(Abgangsbescheinigung).* These certificates list examinations and classes completed along with the grade received. The university grading scale is described in the section entitled "Grading Scales."

Study Segments

Diploma programs are divided into two study segments *(Studienabschnitte)* in all majors except for veterinary medicine which is divided into three. The first segment of the diploma program serves as an introduction to the academic discipline. The intent is to provide an overview of the relevant scientific literature and to establish a perspective within which to view the discipline in relation to others. The second segment provides for a deeper and more specialized understanding of the discipline. All majors are designed to provide a theoretical and philosophical as well as an historical and sociological framework during the second segment. Technically, a student should complete one study segment with the corresponding diploma examination before starting the next, but study segments often overlap by one or two semesters.

Primarily in the human and natural sciences, some diploma programs require completion of two majors or one major *(Studienrichtung)* plus an approved combination of subjects *(kombinationspflichtige Studienrichtung)*. In each major program, certain components are completed during the first segment and others during the second segment. Diploma programs requiring two majors are identified in Table 6.1.

In some majors, students must choose from among different specializations during the second segment. These second-segment specializations are known as study branches *(Studienzweige)*. A second-segment specialization existing within many disciplines is that for secondary-school teacher training *(Lehramt an höheren Schulen)*. As an example, chemistry majors complete a common first segment but choose one of the following second-segment specializations: biochemistry, chemistry education (for secondary-school teachers), food chemistry, or general chemistry.

Diploma Thesis

During the second segment of diploma programs, students are required to complete a thesis *(Diplomarbeit)* in addition to required coursework. Only in veterinary medicine may students complete a six-month practicum instead of a thesis. The purpose of the thesis is to demonstrate competence in scientifically discussing an academic problem. The thesis theme is chosen by the student but must be approved by a professor and must relate to the student's major field. The thesis is usually 80 to 100 pages in length, although a 150-page thesis is not uncommon. Students work under the guidance of a tenured professor who, after completion of the thesis, judges whether the thesis requirement has been successfully satisfied. Completion of the thesis requirement is reported on a form entitled Assessment of the Diploma Thesis *(Beurteilung der Diplomarbeit)* which also provides the title of the thesis and the grade received.

Subjects and Classes

Coursework within each study segment is organized into several broad, general subjects *(Fächer* [plural] or *Fach* [singular])*, and each subject is subdivided into a number of specific classes *(Lehrveranstaltungen)*. For each major at each university, the required subjects, classes, and number of weekly class hours per semester are published in a study plan *(Studienplan)*. The subjects within each major are established by law, but the faculty in each university department assigns minimum instructional hours to each subject. The study commission in each university department subdivides each subject into individual classes and determines the topics to be covered in each class. See sample study plans in Tables 6.2, 6.3, and 6.4.

Subjects may be compulsory *(Pflichtfächer)*, choice *(Wahlfächer)*, or free subjects *(Freifächer)*. Compulsory subjects are core subjects that are fundamental to each discipline and are required of all students for graduation. Choice subjects supplement the compulsory subjects but are chosen by students within general guidelines. Free subjects are chosen by students from a wide range of subjects that have some meaningful connection with the students' major discipline. The compulsory and choice subjects constitute the subject matter for either a diploma examination *(Diplomprüfung)* or a preliminary examination *(Vorprüfung)* which sometimes preceeds a diploma examination. Elective subject groupings *(Wahlfachgruppe)* exist within the second segment of certain (usually technical) majors. In these majors, students may choose from among different specializations within a subject.

Certain types of class structures have evolved over time, although university professors are free to approach class topics as they wish and determine their own methods of instruction. Sometimes the study plan specifies the type of class structure. In all classes (except for lectures), regular student participation and contribution are required.

The classes for which students register each semester are recorded in a study book *(Studienbuch)* or on a registration certificate *(Inskriptionsschein)* which becomes part of the study book. The study book (or registration certificates) contains the name of the class, each class instructor's name, the number of weekly hours the class met, and the type of class structure. Although the study book indicates the number of semesters and classes for which a student has registered, it never contains an indication of class completion or academic performance and thus cannot be equated with a U.S. transcript. Class completion is reported on individual certificates *(Zeugnis, Kolloquienzeugnis)*. The most common types of class structure are described below and an approximate English translation is provided. These same types of class structures also are found in doctoral, short, and continuation programs.

- Lecture *(Vorlesung)* may be either a general lecture *(allgemeine Vorlesung)* where a general overview of the subject is presented, or a special lecture *(Spezialvorlesung)* where a position relative to an area of research is presented. Lectures may be combined with exercises *(Übungen)*. Attempts have been made to shift away from the lecture format to classes using more of a discussion format. The percentage of class offerings using the lecture model has decreased from 40% to 30% since the 1960s.
- Exercise *(Übung)* is a class in which students work toward the solution of concrete problems that relate to the practical and professional goals of their diploma program.
- Review Class *(Repetitorium)* provides a format for students in diploma programs to review the materials from a lecture in preparation for an examination.
- Introductory Seminar *(Proseminar)* provides an introduction to the basic scientific literature in a subject and provides examples of scientific problem-solving through lectures, discussions, or observations. Introductory seminars usually are preparatory for seminars and may exist at either introductory or upper levels of a study program.
- Seminar *(Seminar)* provides the format for scientific discussions that are preparatory for independent scientific work. Students are required to make an oral or written contribution.

- Special Research Seminar *(Privatissimum)* provides an opportunity for a small group of students to discuss common research techniques and problems while completing their theses.
- Dialogue *(Konversatorium)* is a discussion class where students are encouraged to ask questions of faculty members.
- Study Group *(Arbeitsgemeinschaft)* is (translated literally) a "working community" where scientific team work is introduced and where small groups explore scientific hypotheses and learn research methods and techniques.
- Practicum *(Praktikum)* supplements students' theoretical education by providing opportunities for practical or "hands-on" learning.
- Project Study *(Projekstudium)* provides a format for interdisciplinary study and the application of different research methods and techniques.
- Excursion *(Exkursion)* serves as a practical illustration of a subject. An excursion may be combined with an *Übung* or a *Praktikum*.

Diploma Examinations

Each study segment concludes with a diploma examination *(Diplomprüfung)* and award of a Diploma Examination Certificate *(Diplomprüfungszeugnis)* which indicates in the text whether the certificate corresponds to the first *(erste)* or the second *(zweite)* diploma examination. Diploma examinations are comprehensive examinations that cover the required subjects in each study segment. Sometimes a preliminary examination *(Vorprüfung)* preceeds a diploma examination, and the results of the preliminary examination are reported on a Certificate *(Zeugnis)*. Three types of diploma examinations exist.

- Commission Diploma Examination *(Kommissionelle Diplomprüfung)* consists of a written and an oral portion. After completion of the written examination parts, the student takes an oral examination before the University Examinations Senate *(Prüfungssenat)*. Commission diploma examinations are required in Protestant theology and in the second segment of the philosophy major (from the Catholic theology faculty) but may be chosen for part of the second diploma examination in certain other faculties.
- Subject Examinations *(Fachprüfungen)* are sometimes called partial examinations *(Teilprüfungen)* and are reported on a Partial Examination Certificate *(Teilprüfungszeugnis)* or on a Certificate Covering the First (or Second) Part of the First (or Second) Diploma Examination *(Zeugnis über den ersten [or zweiten] Teil der ersten [or zweiten] Diplomprüfung)*. Subject examinations for each required subject in a study segment together constitute the equivalent of a full diploma examination, and students receive a Diploma Examination Certificate *(Diplomprüfungszeugnis)* after all parts of the examination are complete. See sample documents in Appendix A. Subject examinations are taken after completion of the required classes that constitute that subject. Subject examinations are administered in Catholic theology, law, social sciences and business, and veterinary medicine. For the second diploma examination in Catholic theology (excluding philosophy) or in the social sciences and business, students may choose to

validate one subject through a subject examination and the remaining ones through a commission diploma examination.

- Cumulative Class Examinations *(Lehrveranstaltungsprüfungen)* are used in human and natural sciences majors; the technical, mining, and agricultural majors; and the experimental study programs (excluding business). This diploma examination model is characterized by a cumulative examination system that is sometimes called "exam parts of part exams" *(Prüfungsteile von Teilprüfungen)*. That is to say, the successful completion of all required class examinations in a subject is considered equivalent to a subject examination *(Fachprüfung)*, and two or more subject examinations (or their equivalent in class examinations) constitute a diploma examination. The second diploma examination for these majors contains a commission diploma examination portion that must be taken before the University Examinations Senate. Students may elect to take the two diploma examinations (except for the commission examination portion of the second diploma examination) in the form of subject examinations.

Duration of Study Programs

The duration of study programs is defined in number of semesters. The academic year is divided into two fifteen-week semesters, known as winter *(Wintersemester)* and summer semester *(Sommersemester)*. The winter semester generally lasts from October 1 until January 31 and summer semester from March 1 until June 30.

The AHStG established a minimum study duration *(Mindeststudiendauer)*, which specifies the minimum number of semesters legally required to complete each study program but does not specify a maximum study duration. For diploma study programs, the minimum study duration ranges from four to five years. See Table 6.1 for the minimum study duration in each major as well as the actual average study duration. No minimum study duration existed prior to passage of the AHStG.

The minimum study duration for each study program is established by legislators through the political process, but the content of each program is determined by educators. Educators design a study program which might be completed within the minimum study duration but this is not their primary objective. Many educators place little importance on the legally-specified minimum study duration, and professors often encourage students to take extra time in order to master the subject matter prior to an examination.

Only about 6% of all students in degree programs complete their program within the prescribed minimum study duration. The average student requires an extra five semesters. Within Austrian culture, the practice of exceeding the minimum study duration is completely acceptable and does not reflect negatively upon a student's academic performance. Students must take certain class examinations in order to qualify for the diploma examinations, but they are free to decide when to attend classes and when to take the required examinations. Class registrations are free of charge for Austrian students, who usually register for more classes each semester than U.S. students do. No expectation exists that Austrian students complete each course each semester, and no grade of "incomplete" exists in Austria. Prior to taking an examination, students may register for the same class as many times as they wish, register for additional or related classes, or register for the same class taught by different professors in order to gain different perspectives on the subject matter. As many as half or more of the students who register for a class may decide not to complete the course (i.e., take the final examination) during the current semester.

Another phenomenon that lengthens the study duration in certain departments stems from the "mass" university philosophy. The right to enter any department is guaranteed to any Austrian citizen who has the maturity certificate, but some departments are unable to meet the demand for class spaces each semester. For this reason, students may be unable to gain access to a required course, and thus must extend the duration of their studies. University departments receive the same amount of government funding regardless of the number of students who wish to enroll.

Study reform laws have increased the planned number of weekly class hours per semester (*Wochenstunden, Semesterwochenstunden*). For most majors, registration in at least 20 weekly hours of class per semester was planned, but the actual number ranges from an average of 16 weekly hours in business administration to 24 weekly hours in electrical engineering. Some study plans specify a minimum number of weekly semester hours for which a student must register. See examples of weekly semester hours in sample study plans (Tables 6.2, 6.3, and 6.4).

Alternate Diploma Program Structures

In addition to the already-established diploma study programs, the AHStG established three structures within which students may individually design a diploma program:

- Double Study Program (*Doppelstudium*) provides the opportunity to simultaneously complete two (or more) regular study programs. The study programs need not be thematically related.
- Irregular Study Program (*Studium Irregulare*) offers the chance to individually structure a major program using classes from various regular study programs. The combination of classes must be logical and educationally sound, and the goal of the program must be unique and unavailable through already-established degree programs. The program must be approved by university authorities and the Ministry.
- Experimental Study Programs (*Studienversuche*) are established on a trial basis and later may be approved as regular study programs through federal legislation. When at least 10 students request a particular irregular study program, university authorities may ask the Ministry to establish the program as an experimental study program. Several experimental programs have been established since 1971 and are listed in Table 6.1.

Extension Study Program *(Erweiterungsstudium)*

An extension study program is a formally expanded diploma program. Like a diploma program, the extension program is divided into two segments requiring two diploma examinations and a thesis and concludes with the award of the first academic degree *(Magister, Diplom-Ingenieur,* or *Diplom-Tierarzt)*. To enter an extension program, a student must be enrolled already in a diploma program.

Well-established examples of extension study programs are those for secondary teacher training (known as *Lehramts-Diplomstudium)*. The teacher-education portion of the degree is not itself a degree program but rather a supplement to an academic degree program. The minimum study duration for teacher-education programs is usually nine semesters while the minimum duration of the regular academic program is usually eight semesters. See "University-Trained Teachers," Chapter VIII.

Another extension program is that for food science which may be incorporated into the major for veterinary medicine. In addition to other degree requirements, students who choose this program also must complete an eight-month practicum prior to the last diploma examination.

Doctoral Study Program *(Doktoratsstudium)*

Doctoral study programs enroll around 3% of all university students and led to approximately 6% of the academic degrees awarded in 1984 (excluding the doctoral study program in medicine which is described below). Completion of the requirements in a doctoral study program results in the award of the second academic degree which is the *Doktor*.

To enter a doctoral program, students must complete the diploma program and receive the first academic degree in the same or a closely-related major field within the same faculty. The new doctoral program corresponds to the third and final study segment in the old system; the two study segments that now constitute the diploma program were the first two study segments in the old system. By establishing a formal academic degree as the second-segment conclusion, the AHStG provided for a stronger differentiation between the second and third study segments and, in effect, strengthened the educational quality of the third segment.

Students who proceed to the doctoral program are those who demonstrate a high level of academic success during their diploma studies. University professors usually encourage only a few of their top students to continue studying at the doctoral level. The goal of the doctoral program is to develop a student's competence in independent scientific research to a higher level than that required for the first academic degree. A legal minimum study duration is specified for some disciplines, but not for others. When specified, the minimum length varies by discipline from two to four semesters, but actual study duration is considerably longer. See Table 6.1 for the minimum study duration in each major.

The doctoral program consists of coursework and a dissertation *(Disserta-tion)*, followed by three oral examinations *(Rigorosen)*. The dissertation must go beyond the requirements of the diploma thesis and demonstrate compe-tence to independently research a scientific hypothesis. Students choose the theme of their dissertation from among the compulsory and choice subjects in their doctoral program and also choose a university professor in their major field as their faculty monitor. The dissertation topic need not be thematically related to the diploma thesis. The dissertation is evaluated by two tenured professors while the diploma thesis is evaluated by only one tenured profes-sor. Completion of the dissertation is reported on an Assessment of the Dissertation *(Beurteilung der Dissertation)* form which also lists the dissertation title and the grade awarded.

The three oral examinations constitute the final requirement for the award of the *Doktor* degree. Two of the oral examinations cover the major field (one of which is usually a defense of the dissertation) while the third covers the minor field. All three examinations are taken on the same day and are open to the public. In the old system, the final oral examination covered all subject matter studied by the student since beginning university studies; but in the new system, the final oral examinations cover only subject matter contained in the doctoral program. Completion of these examinations are reported on an Oral Examination Certificate *(Rigorosenzeugnis)*.

Doctoral Study Program in Medicine

The program in medicine is the only one unchanged by the AHStG; and, thus, a *Magister* degree does not exist in medicine. Approximately 18% of the academic degrees awarded in 1984 were the *Doktor* of Medicine *(Doktor der gesamten Heilkunde* or *Doctor medicinae universae)*. The program in medicine trains physicians as well as dentists.

The doctoral program in medicine is divided into three segments, each of which concludes with a set of examinations *(Rigorosen)*. Within each segment, coursework is organized into general subjects *(Fächer)* which are subdivided into classes *(Lehrveranstaltungen)*. (See description of "Subjects and Classes" under "Diploma Study Programs" above.) Compulsory subjects for the first examination are anatomy, histology and embryology, medical biochemistry, medical biology, medical chemistry, medical physics, and medical physiology. Subjects compulsory for the second examination are hygiene, microbiology, pathology and anatomy, functional pathology, pharmacology and toxicology, preventive medicine, and radiology. And subjects compulsory for the third examination are dermatology, ear-nose-throat diseases, forensic medicine, gynecology and obstetrics, internal medicine, law, neurology, ophthalmol-ogy, pediatrics, psychiatry, social medicine, and surgery. In place of a thesis, students may substitute additional specialized coursework. The minimum study duration established by law is six years, but the average actual study duration in 1985 was seven and one-half years.

After completing the program and receiving the degree, additional require-ments exist for those who wish to be dentists, general practitioners, or medical specialists. For dentists, two years of experience in a university dental clinic and passing of a state dental examination *(zahnärztliche Staatsprüfung)* are required prior to entering private practice. For general practitioners, a three-year hospital residency is required. And for medical specialists, additional training totaling approximately six years is required.

Short Study Program *(Kurzstudium)*

Established by the AHStG, short study programs represent complete programs but require a shorter study duration than the parallel diploma programs do. Short programs, which roughly correspond to the first study segment of the diploma program, last a minimum of five or six semesters and conclude with a final examination *(Abschlussprüfung)* (see sample document in Appendix A). In the short program for translators, a student must take, in addition to the final examination, a professional translators' examination *(akademische Übersetzerprüfung)* which tests translating skills from the first or native language to a second language and vice versa.

After successful completion of a short program, an academic title *(Berufsbezeichnung)*—not an academic degree *(Grad)*—is awarded. Currently, three short programs exist and the following academic titles are awarded: Academically Certified Computer Engineer *(Akademisch geprüfter Datentechniker)*, Academically Certified Actuary *(Akademisch geprüfter Versicherungsmathematiker)*, and Academically Certified Translator *(Akademisch geprüfter Übersetzer)*. Regular diploma programs also exist in translating and in interpreting.

Continuation Study Program *(Aufbaustudium)*

Continuation study programs were added to the educational system in 1983. For students who have completed a diploma program and have received the first academic degree, the continuation study program provides an additional qualification in a related area. A continuation program corresponds roughly to the second study segment of a diploma program; the completed diploma program, which must be in a related field, substitutes for the first study segment.

The continuation program lasts a minimum of four semesters and concludes with a final examination *(Abschlussprüfung)* and award of a graduate professional title which is a higher level academic title than that awarded after completion of a short program. Currently, two continuation study programs exist, and both of them require the *Diplom-Ingenieur* degree for admission. After completion of these continuation study programs, the following academic titles are awarded: Graduate Environmental Engineer *(Diplomierter Umwelttechniker)* and Graduate Business Technician *(Diplomierter Wirtschaftstechniker)*.

Special Study Programs

In addition to regular study programs which lead to an academic degree or title, special study programs *(ausserordentliche Studien)* exist to provide adult education and further training for secondary school graduates. Special university or college programs *(Hochschullehrgänge, Universitätslehrgänge)* and courses *(Hochschulkurse)* serve the changing needs of society and the workplace by offering a wide range of educational options. The number of university programs and courses which are available has grown from approximately 10 in 1964-65 to around 30 in 1984-85. Special programs and courses are open to students admitted with regular *(ordentlicher Hörer)*, special *(ausserordentlicher Hörer)*, or auditor *(Gasthörer)* status. The maturity certificate required for entering degree programs is not required for enrollment in special study programs.

Special programs consist of a defined curriculum with a fixed duration, but special courses consist of varying themes and durations. Graduates of special programs that last at least four semesters and correspond to a particular occupation may be awarded an academic title, e.g., *Akademisch geprüfter Fremdenverkehrskaufmann* (Academically Certified Tourist Business Person). Graduates of special courses and programs not meeting these specifications receive a leaving certificate *(Abschlusszeugnis* or *Abschlussbescheinigung)*. See examples of special programs and courses and the academic title or certificate awarded for each in Table 6.5.

Table 6.5. Sample List of Special University Programs and Courses, 1985

PROGRAMS/ COURSES	Admission Requirement*	Length	Final Credential†
BUSINESS PROGRAMS			
Management Training for Tourist Business	Mat. Cert.* or 4 years' exper. in tourist business	4 sems.	Leaving Certificate *(Abschlusszeugnis)* with acad. title: Academically Certified Tourist Business Person *(Akademisch geprüfter Fremdenverkehrs-kaufmann)*
Management Training for Nurses and Medical Technicians	Dipl. in nurs., 3 years' nurs. exper., less than 45 years of age	4 sems.	Leaving Certificate *(Abschlusszeugnis)*
Training in Advertising & Marketing	Mat. Cert.* or min. 3 years' advert. & mktg. exper.	4 sems.	Leaving Certificate *(Abschlusszeugnis)* with acad. title: Academically Certified Advertising Business Person *(Akademisch geprüfter Werbekaufmann)*

continued

Training in Export Business[†]	Mat. Cert.*; some progs. req. univ. grad. or student status	2 sems.	Leaving Certificate *(Abschlusszeugnis)*
Training in Insurance Business	Mat. Cert.* or 5 years' insur. bus. exper., admissions test in bkkpg.	4 sems.	Leaving Certificate *(Abschlusszeugnis)* with acad. title: Academically Certified Insurance Business Person *(Akademisch geprüfter Versicherungskaufmann)*

PROGRAMS AND COURSES FOR CONTINUING PROFESSIONAL EDUCATION

Continuing Education & Didactical Training for English & Math Teachers (2 programs)	Teacher in gen. secondary school or voc. school	4 sems.	Leaving Certificate *(Abschluss-bescheinigung)*
Various Continuing Education Programs for Physicians, Preparatory Programs for State Dental Exams, Programs for Foreign Physicians	*Doktor* degree in medicine	1–4 sems.	Leaving Certificate *(Abschlusszeugnis)*
Training in Media Arts	Gen. admission	4 sems.	Leaving Certificate *(Abschlusszeugnis)* with acad. title: Academically Certified Grad. of Media Arts Program *(Akademisch geprüfter Absolvent des Medienkundlichen Lehrganges)*

PROGRAMS AND COURSES IN GERMAN

German Language Training for Foreigners[†]	Gen. admission	Variable	Leaving Certificate *(Abschlusszeugnis)*

PREPARATORY PROGRAMS FOR MATURITY CERTIFICATE EQUIVALENCY EXAMINATIONS

Preparation for Maturity Certificate Equivalency Exam	Gen. admission	Variable	None

*(Studienberechti-
gungsprüfung)* for
University
Admission with
Regular Status

___

*Maturity Certificate *(Reifeprüfungszeugnis, Reifezeugnis).*
†Prior to 1985, the following title was issued after completion of an export business program lasting 4 semesters: Academically Certified Export Business Person *(Akademisch geprüfter Exportkaufmann).*

Grading Scale

Two different grading scales exist. An individual grade *(Note)* is awarded for a class, thesis, or individual part of a large examination. And a comprehensive grade *(Gesamtnote)*, which is awarded for examinations that consist of several parts, combines several individual grades according to a legally-defined formula.

An Austrian grade with the same characteristics as a U.S. "D" grade does not exist. The U.S. "D" grade is averaged with "B" or "A" grades in order to obtain a satisfactory average grade. A student who receives all "D" grades does not have an overall satisfactory grade, but a student who receives all "sufficient" *(genügend)* grades—the lowest passing individual grade in Austria—does have a satisfactory comprehensive grade. The Austrian comprehensive grade does not represent an "average" grade and, thus, cannot be equated with the U.S. "grade point average." Individual grades are as follows:

Number Grade	Descriptive Grade	Suggested U.S. Equivalent
1	*sehr gut* (very good)	A
2	*gut* (good)	B+/B
3	*befriedigend* (satisfactory)	B−/C+
4	*genügend* (sufficient)	C
5	*nicht genügend* (failing or insufficient)	F

Comprehensive grades are as follows:

Grade	Definition
mit Auszeichnung bestanden (passed with distinction)	At least half of the individual grades are *sehr gut* and all remaining grades are *gut*.
bestanden (pass)	Each individual grade is at least *genügend*, but conditions necessary for the higher comprehensive grade do not exist.
nicht bestanden (not passed)	At least one individual grade of *nicht genügend* exists.

Most failed examinations may be repeated three times, but failed commission diploma examinations may be repeated only twice.

Special Post-*Magister* Schools

The Diplomatic Academy in Vienna and the Institute for Advanced Studies offer post-*Magister* study programs but are legally independent of the regular Austrian university system.

Diplomatic Academy in Vienna (Diplomatische Akademie Wien)

As a politically neutral country, Austria is in a unique position to offer career preparation in international diplomacy and business. Originally established in 1753 as the Academy of Oriental Languages (Akademie der Orientalischen Sprachen), later changed to the Consular Academy (Konsularakademie), the school was closed during the Second World War but reopened in 1964 as the Diplomatic Academy in Vienna. The academy is subject to Austrian laws and regulated by the Foreign Affairs Ministry.

For admission, applicants must be under 30 years of age and have the Austrian *Magister* in geography, history, journalism, law, political science, or social sciences and economics, or have a comparable degree from a foreign university. For U.S.-educated applicants, the bachelor's degree plus a number of graduate courses deemed by the school to be sufficient or the master's degree is required for admission. In addition, applicants must take an admissions examination which sometimes is administered in Austrian embassies or consulates abroad. Applicants who are native German speakers must be proficient also in English and French; and other applicants must be proficient in German, either English or French, and at least one other language.

An intensive four-semester (two year) program is offered in the following six areas: historical and geographical basis for international affairs, international affairs and politics, international business, international law, languages, and public affairs. Faculty members are drawn from among professors at Austrian universities and experts from research institutions, federal ministries, international organizations, and businesses. After completing studies and successfully passing the final diploma examination *(Diplomprüfung)*, graduates receive the Diploma of the Diplomatic Academy *(Diplom der Diplomatischen Akademie)*.

Institute for Advanced Studies (Institut für Höhere Studien)

Established in 1963 in Vienna, the Institute for Advanced Studies (also called the Institute for Advanced Studies and Scientific Research [Institut für Höhere Studien und Wissenschaftliche Forschung] or the "Ford Institute") is a nonprofit, private institution that is funded through contributions from public and private sources and through contract income. Although independent of the regular university system, the institute is a respected institution in Austria. The board of trustees is composed of 14 prominent Austrian business, educational, and political leaders, including the Austrian chancellor, the science and research minister, the mayor and vice-mayor of Vienna, members of Parliament, and professors from Austrian universities. The institute has a council of scientific advisers which consists of 11 professors drawn from Austrian and recognized foreign universities.

The institute trains students who have completed at least the first academic degree *(Magister)*, are proficient in German and English, and have passed the rigorous entrance examination. Two-year programs are available in economics, management science and operations research, mathematical methods and computer science, political science, and sociology. Graduates of the program are prepared for academic or research positions in business, public administration, or international organizations. Graduates receive a diploma *(Diplom)*.

Post-*Doktor* Research Process *(Habilitation)*

Habilitation is a research process that may be undertaken after receipt of the *Doktor* degree. *Habilitation* requires independent research and production of a research monograph *(Habilitationsschrift)*. The monograph must be published and then defended before a jury of peers, half of whom must already have completed the *Habilitation* process themselves. Those who successfully complete the *Habilitation* process become associate professors *(Universitätsdozenten, Dozenten)* and become eligible for university tenure.

Those working on *Habilitation* often hold assistant professorships *(Universitätsassistent)* in universities, although employment at or professional association with a university is not required. The entire research and publication process normally takes several years. The average age at completion of *Habilitation* is 39 years. An average of 200 persons a year completed *Habilitation* between 1981 and 1984.

University Profiles

Technical University of Graz (Technische Universität Graz or Erzherzog-Johann-Universität), Rechbauerstrasse 12, 8010, Graz.

Description: Founded 1811 by Archduke Johann as a natural science institution *(naturwissenschaftliche Lehranstalt)* called the "Joanneum"; elevated to university-level institution and named Technical College in Graz (Technische Hochschule in Graz) in 1872; acquired right to award *Doktor* degree in 1901; reorganized in 1955; changed to current name in 1975. Enrollment (1984-85): 7,026 students. Library: 347,823 bound volumes and 1,837 periodicals. Faculty: 590 faculty members.

Faculties and Majors: (Note: † = Secondary teacher preparation.)

Architecture Faculty—Architecture.

Civil Engineering Faculty—Civil Engineering (Building Construction & Operations, Construction Engineering, Traffic/Transport, Water Economics & Hydroengineering), Operations Engineering (Civil Engineering), Surveying.

Electrical Engineering Faculty—Electrical Engineering.

Mechanical Engineering Faculty—Operations Engineering (Mechanical Engineering), Mechanical Engineering, Processing Technology.

Technical Natural Sciences Faculty—Descriptive Geometry†, Physics†, Technical
   Chemistry (Biochemistry & Food Chemistry, Chemical Engineering, Inorganic
   Chemistry, Organic Chemistry), Technical Mathematics (Mathematics/Natural Sci-
   ences, Information & Data Processing), Technical Physics.
Continuation Study Program: Business/Law/Economics, Environmental Protection
   Technology.
Institutional Partnership Arrangement: Technical University of Budapest, Hungary
   (since 1976).

Technical University of Vienna (Technische Universität Wien), Karlsplatz 13, 1040
Wien.
Description: Founded 1815 as a polytechnical institute *(polytechnisches Institut);* elevated
   in level and title to Technical College of Vienna (Technische Hochschule Wien) in
   1872; acquired right to award *Doktor* degree in 1901; changed name to current one
   and reorganized into current faculty divisions in 1975. Enrollment (1984-85): 12,652
   students. Library: 791,124 bound volumes and 2,466 periodicals. Faculty: 1,214 faculty
   members.
Faculty and Majors: (Note: † = Secondary teacher preparation.)
   Civil Engineering Faculty—Civil Engineering (Building Construction & Operation,
      Construction Engineering, Traffic/Transport, Water Economics & Hydroengineer-
      ing).
   Electrical Engineering Faculty—Electrical Engineering (Communication Engineering,
      Industrial Electronics & Control Engineering, Electrical Energy Technology).
   Land Development and Architecture Faculty—Architecture, Urban & Regional Plan-
      ning.
   Mechanical Engineering Faculty—Mechanical Engineering (General Mechanical Engi-
      neering, Marine Engineering, Operations Science, Processing Engineering, Trans-
      port & Vehicle Engineering).
   Technical Natural Sciences Faculty—Actuarial Mathematics, Chemistry†, Computer
      Technology, Descriptive Geometry†, Information Science, Management Informa-
      tion Sciences, Mathematics†, Physics†, Surveying, Technical Chemistry (Biochem-
      istry & Food Chemistry, Chemical Engineering, Inorganic Chemistry, Organic
      Chemistry), Technical Mathematics (Mathematics/Natural Sciences, Economics &
      Planning Mathematics, Information & Data Processing), Technical Physics.
Continuation Study Programs: Business/Law/Economics, Environmental Protection
   Technology.
Institutional Partnership Arrangements: Technical University of Budapest, Hungary
   (since 1972); University of Tokyo, Japan (1981); University of Trieste, Italy (1979).

University for Agriculture in Vienna (Universität für Bodenkultur Wien), Gregor
Mendel-Strasse 33, 1180 Wien.
Description: Founded 1872 as an Agriculture College (Fachhochschule für das Land-
   wirtschaftliche Studium or Hochschule für Bodenkultur in Wien); changed to current
   name in 1975. Enrollment (1984-85): 4,399 students. Library: 273,277 bound volumes
   and 1,069 periodicals. Faculty: 274 faculty members.
Majors: The university is not faculty-divided. The following majors exist: Agricultural
   & Water Engineering, Agriculture (Agricultural Economics, Animal Production,
   Landscape Architecture & Horticulture, Plant Production), Food Science & Biotech-
   nology, Forestry & Wood Products (Forestry, Torrent/Avalanche Control, Wood
   Products), Land Economy/Ecology, Environmental Protection Technology.
Institutional Partnership Arrangements: University of Minnesota, College of Agricul-
   ture, U.S.A. (since 1981); University of Washington, U.S.A. (1983).

University for Business Administration in Vienna (Wirtschaftsuniversität Wien), Franz-Klein-Gasse 1, 1190 Wien.

Description: Founded 1898 as a private Export Academy (Export-Akademie); elevated to university-level College for World Trade in Vienna (Hochschule für Welthandel in Wien) in 1919; authorized to grant *Doktor* degree in 1930; changed to current name in 1975. Enrollment (1984-85): 13,167 students. Library: 423,727 bound volumes and 2,912 periodicals. Faculty: 253 faculty members.

Majors: The university is not faculty-divided. The following majors exist: Biology & the Study of Consumer Goods, Business Administration, Business Education, Commerce, Economics.

Institutional Partnership Arrangements: Academy of Economics in Katowice, Poland (since 1978); Higher School of St. Gallen for Economics and Social Sciences (Hochschule St. Gallen für Wirtschafts- und Sozialwissenschaft), Switzerland (1969).

University for Educational Sciences in Klagenfurt (Universität für Bildungswissenschaften Klagenfurt), Universitätsstrasse 67, 9020 Klagenfurt.

Description: Founded 1970 as a university-level College for Educational Sciences in Klagenfurt (Hochschule für Bildungswissenschaften Klagenfurt); changed to current name in 1975. Enrollment (1982-83): 2,271 students. Library: 386,413 bound volumes and 2,045 periodicals. Faculty: 134 faculty members.

Majors: (Note: * = Programs with and without secondary teacher preparation available. † = Secondary teacher preparation only.) The university is not faculty-divided. The following majors exist: Applied Business Administration, Comparative Literature, Educational Sciences, English & American Studies, French*, Geography*, German Philology*, History*, Italian*, Linguistics (Applied, General), Mathematics*, Philosophy, Philosophy/Education/Psychology†, Russian*, Serbo-Croatian*, Slovene*.

Institutional Partnership Arrangements: University of Ljubljana, Yugoslavia (since 1982); University of Trieste, Italy (1982); University of Udine, Italy (1982).

University for Mining and Metallurgy in Leoben (Montanuniversität Leoben), Kaiser-Franz-Josef-Strasse 18, 8700 Leoben.

Description: Founded 1840 as a mining school (Montananstalt); elevated to university-level Mining College in Leoben (Montanistiche Hochschule in Leoben) in 1895; changed to current name in 1975. Enrollment (1982-83): 1,512 students. Library: 160,958 bound volumes and 856 periodicals. Faculty: 229 faculty members.

Majors: The university is not faculty-divided. The following majors exist: Earth Science (Mining/Geology), Materials Engineering, Metallurgical Engineering, Mining & Mineral Engineering, Mine Surveying, Mining, Mining & Metallurgical Machinery, Petroleum Engineering, Plastics Technology.

Institutional Partnership Arrangements: Technical University for Heavy Industry in Miskolc, Hungary (since 1982); Technical University of Clausthal (Technische Universität Clausthal), Federal Republic of Germany (1982).

University for Veterinary Medicine in Vienna (Veterinärmedizinische Universität Wien), Linke Bahngasse 11, 1030 Wien.

Description: Founded 1765 through a decree issued by Empress Maria Theresia as the Royal Veterinary Medicine School for Horses (K.k. Pferde- Curen- und Operationsschule); elevated to a university-level institution and renamed the Royal Veterinary Medicine College (K.u.k. Tierärztliche Hochschule) in 1905; acquired right to grant *Doktor* degree in veterinary medicine in 1908; changed to current name in 1975. Enrollment (1984-85): 1,993 students. Library: 107,196 bound volumes and 668 periodicals. Faculty (1985-86): 198 faculty members.

Study Programs: The university is not faculty-divided. Diploma and doctoral study programs exist in veterinary medicine as does an extension study program in food science.

Institutional Partnership Arrangement: University of Veterinary Science in Budapest, Hungary (since 1977).

University of Graz (Universität Graz or Karl-Franzens-Universität Graz), Universitätsplatz 3, 8010 Graz.

Description: Founded 1585; dissolved in 1782; re-established in 1829. Enrollment (1984-85): 20,282 students. Library: 1,947,957 bound volumes and 8,805 periodicals. Faculty: 1,348 faculty members.

Faculties and Majors: (Note: * = Programs with and without secondary teacher preparation available. † = Secondary teacher preparation only.)

Catholic Theology Faculty—Religion Education, Religion Education (combined program), Theology.

Humanities and Natural Sciences Faculty—Ancient History, Art History, Astronomy, Biology (Botany, Zoology), Biology & Earth Science Education†, Biology & the Study of Consumer Goods†, Chemistry*, Classical Archaeology, Classics (Greek)*, Classics (Latin)*, Earth Science (Geo-technology, Geology, Mineralogy/Crystallography, Mining/Geology, Paleontology, Petrology), Economics Education†, Educational Sciences, English & American Studies*, French*, German Philology*, Geography, History, History & Social Science Education†, Interpreting, Italian*, Linguistics (Applied, General, Indo-European Language Study), Mathematics*, Meteorology/Geophysics, Musicology, Pharmacy, Philosophy, Philosophy/Education/Psychology†, Physical Education†, Physics*, Psychology, Russian*, Serbo-Croatian*, Slovene*, Spanish*, Sports Science, Translating (diploma and short study programs).

Law Faculty—Law.

Medicine Faculty—Medicine.

Social Sciences and Economics Faculty—Business Administration, Business Education, Economics.

Institutional Partnership Arrangements: University of Minnesota, U.S.A. (since 1986); University of Zagreb, Yugoslavia (1981).

University of Innsbruck (Universität Innsbruck or Leopold-Franzens Universität Innsbruck), Innrain 52, 6020 Innsbruck.

Description: Founded 1669. Enrollment (1984-85): 17,586 students. Library: 1,882,435 bound volumes and 7,278 periodicals. Faculty: 1,490 faculty members.

Faculties and Majors: (Note: * = Programs with and without secondary teacher preparation available. † = Secondary teacher preparation only.)

Architecture Faculty—Architecture.

Catholic Theology Faculty—Philosophy, Religion Education, Religion Education (combined program), Theology.

Civil Engineering Faculty—Civil Engineering (Building Construction & Operation, Construction Engineering, Traffic/Transport, Water Economics & Hydroengineering), Surveying.

Humanities and Natural Sciences Faculty—Ancient History, Ancient History & Antiquity, Art History, Astronomy, Biology (Botany, Microbiology, Zoology), Biology & Earth Science†, Chemistry*, Classical Archaeology, Classics (Greek)*, Classics (Latin)*, Comparative Literature, Earth Science (Geology, Paleontology, Petrology), Educational Sciences, English & American Studies*, European Ethnology, French*,

Geography*, German Philology*, History*, Interpreting, Italian*, Language & Culture of Ancient Orient, Linguistics (Applied, General, Indo-European Language Study), Mathematics*, Meteorology, Musicology, Pharmacy, Philosophy, Philosophy/Education/Psychologyt, Physics*, Political Science, Portuguese, Russian*, Serbo-Croatian, Spanish*, Sports & Physical Education*, Translating (diploma and short study programs).

Law Faculty—Law.

Medicine Faculty—Medicine.

Social Sciences and Economics Faculty—Business Education, Economics.

Institutional Partnership Arrangements: Albert-Ludwig University of Freiburg/Breisgau, Federal Republic of Germany (since 1979); University of Ljublin (1979); University of New Orleans, U.S.A. (1983); University of Notre Dame, U.S.A. (1982); University of Padua, Italy (1978); University of Sarajevo, Yugoslavia (1980).

University of Linz (Universität Linz or Johannes-Kepler-Universität Linz), Auhof, 4045 Linz.

Description: Founded 1962 as a university-level College for Social and Economic Sciences (Hochschule für Sozial- und Wirtschaftswissenschaften); changed to current name in 1975. Enrollment (1984-85): 7,629 students. Library: 318,230 bound volumes and 2,278 periodicals. Faculty: 348 faculty members.

Faculties and Majors: (Note: t = Secondary teacher preparation.)

Law Faculty—Law.

Social Sciences and Economics Faculty—Business Administration, Business Education, Economics, Management Information Sciences, Social Policy, Sociology, Statistics.

Technical Natural Sciences Faculty—Chemistryt, Computer Technology, Information Science, Mathematicst, Physicst, Technical Mathematics (Mathematics/Natural Sciences, Economics & Planning Mathematics, Information & Data Processing), Technical Physics.

Inter-Faculty Experimental Studies—Operations Engineering (Technical Chemistry).

Institutional Partnership Arrangement: Emory University, U.S.A. (since 1983).

University of Salzburg (Universität Salzburg, sometimes called Paris Lodron-Universität Salzburg), Residenzplatz 1, 5020 Salzburg.

Description: Founded 1623 as a school by Archbishop Paris Lodron; elevated to university-level institution in 1623; closed in 1810; reopened in 1962. Enrollment (1984-85): 8,897 students. Library: 1,204,811 bound volumes and 4,864 periodicals. Faculty: 656 faculty members.

Faculties and Majors: (Note: * = Programs with and without secondary teacher preparation available. t = Secondary teacher preparation only.)

Catholic Theology Faculty—Philosophy, Religion Education, Religion Education (combined program), Theology.

Humanities and Natural Sciences Faculty—Ancient History, Art History, Biology (Botany, Genetics, Zoology), Biology & Earth Sciencest, Bulgarian, Classical Archaeology, Classics (Greek)*, Classics (Latin)*, Earth Science (Geology, Petrology), Educational Sciences, English & American Studies*, French*, Geography*, German Philology*, History*, Italian*, Journalism & Mass Communication, Linguistics (Applied, General, Indo-European Language Study), Mathematics*, Musicology, Philosophy, Philosophy/Education/Psychologyt, Polish, Political Science, Portuguese, Psychology, Romanian, Russian*, Serbo-Croatian, Spanish*, Sports & Physical Education*.

Law Faculty—Law.
Institutional Partnership Arrangements: University of Cracow, Poland (since 1975); University of Perugia, Italy (1983); University of Rheims (Reims), France (1973).

University of Vienna (Universität Wien), Dr. Karl Lueger-Ring 1, 1010 Wien.
Description: Founded 1365 by Rudolph IV of Austria; reorganized in 1377, 1384, and 1850. Enrollment (1984-85): 53,987 students. Library: 4,307,887 bound volumes and 16,343 periodicals. Faculty: 3,764 faculty members.
Faculties and Majors: (Note: * = Programs with and without secondary teacher preparation available. † = Secondary teacher preparation only.)
Basic and Integrated Sciences Faculty—Anthropology, Educational Sciences, Geography (Cartography, Geography*, Space Planning & Research), Journalism & Mass Communication, Philosophy, Philosophy/Education/Psychology†, Political Science, Psychology, Sociology, Sports & Physical Education*, Theater Arts.
Catholic Theology Faculty—Religion Education, Religion Education (combined program), Theology.
Humanities Faculty—African Studies, Ancient History, Ancient History & Antiquity, Arabic, Art History, Byzantine & Modern Greek Studies, Classical Archaeology, Classical Semitic Philology & Oriental Archaeology, Classics (Greek)*, Classics (Latin)*, Comparative Literature (experimental program), Czech*, Egyptian Studies, English & American Studies*, European Ethnology, Finnish-Hungarian*, French*, German Philology*, History*, Indic Studies, Interpreting, Italian*, Japanese Studies, Jewish Studies, Linguistics (Applied, General, Indo-European Language Study), Musicology, Numismatics (experimental program), Polish, Romanian, Russian*, Scandinavian Studies (experimental program), Serbo-Croatian*, Sinology, Slovene*, Spanish*, Tibetan & Buddhism Studies, Translating (diploma and short study programs), Turkish Studies.
Law Faculty—Law.
Medicine Faculty—Medicine.
Protestant Theology Faculty—Religion Education (combined program), Theology.
Social Sciences and Economics Faculty—Business Administration (offered jointly with Technical University of Vienna), Economics, Information Science, Statistics.
Technical and Natural Sciences Faculty—Astronomy, Biology (Botany, Genetics, Human Biology, Microbiology, Paleontology, Zoology), Biology & Earth Science Education†, Biology & the Study of Consumer Goods†, Chemistry (Biochemistry, Chemistry*, Food Chemistry), Earth Science (Geology, Mineralogy/Crystallography, Mining/Geology, Paleontology, Petrology), Home Economics Education†, Logistics, Mathematics*, Meteorology & Geophysics, Pharmacy, Physics*.
Institutional Partnership Arrangements: Humboldt University of Berlin, German Democratic Republic (since 1984); University of Budapest, Hungary (1957); University of Trieste, Italy (1978); University of Warsaw, Poland (1977).

Chapter VII

Fine Arts Education

Introduction

Programs in fine arts colleges *(Kunsthochschulen)* provide Austria's highest-level training in the fine arts and prepare students for professional careers in the fine arts. The fine arts colleges consist of three music colleges *(Musik-hochschulen)*, two art colleges *(Kunsthochschulen)*, and one art academy *(Kunst-akademie)*. All are public institutions that are federally funded and regulated. Since 1970, fine arts colleges are university-level institutions and, thus, are permitted to grant university academic degrees. (See "Introduction to Higher Education" in Chapter VI.) All fine arts majors will culminate in an academic degree after provisions of a 1983 study law are fully implemented; only a few majors led to an academic degree prior to 1983. No private institutions offering training in the fine arts are authorized to grant university-level academic degrees, but private music conservatories *(Konservatorien)* for advanced students and music schools *(Musikschulen)* for beginners also provide training in music.

The fine arts colleges enjoy the same constitutional guarantee of academic freedom that universities have but, in addition, have guaranteed freedom for artistic creativity. The goals of fine arts colleges are to cultivate and advance the arts, impart an integrated academic and artistic education, and provide continuing artistic education to fine arts college graduates.

The number of students enrolled in fine arts colleges has nearly doubled since 1960. In 1983, approximately 3% of all students in higher education were enrolled in a fine arts college. Among entering students in fine arts colleges in 1983, approximately 42% were foreign students.

Brief Historical Overview

Art and music colleges have an historical tradition that is quite different from that of universities. Fine arts colleges arose from a tradition of individual instruction by artistic "masters" and only recently have been established as academic institutions. Individual instruction (private lessons) still exists today and is known as "master instruction" *(Meisterlehre)*.

The Academy of Fine Arts in Vienna (Akademie der bildenden Künste in Wien) was one of the earliest art academies in Europe. Originally founded by Emperor Leopold I in 1696, the school was combined with two other art academies in 1772 by Empress Maria Theresia. Since then, the school's reputation and status have continued to grow. While retaining the same name, the Academy of Fine Arts in Vienna was accorded "college" or "university" *(Hochschule)* status in 1872.

The forerunners of the current music colleges were founded in the early nineteenth century as private music schools or music societies, and the forerunner of the other art college in Vienna was founded in the late nineteenth century to train artists and art teachers for industry. Through the years, the artistic reputations of these schools within Austrian society grew. By the early twentieth century, these music schools had been converted to music conservatories. Conservatories (which still exist in Austria) provide advanced musical training but are not permitted to award academic degrees.

After the annexation of Austria by Germany in 1938, German laws controlled the fine arts colleges until the end of World War II in 1945 when Austrian laws were re-established. After the war, the previously-established tradition of progressive increases in the status of fine arts training within the educational system was restored. In addition, the private Art School of Linz (Kunstschule der Stadt Linz), which later became the sixth fine art college, was founded in 1947. The fine arts schools founded during the nineteenth century were elevated to the postsecondary status of "academy." These schools became known as the Academy for Music and Dramatic Art in Vienna (Akademie für Musik und darstellende Kunst in Wien) in 1947, the Academy for Applied Art in Vienna (Akademie für angewandte Kunst in Wien) in 1948, the Academy for Music and Dramatic Art 'Mozarteum' in Salzburg (Akademie für Musik und darstellende Kunst 'Mozarteum' in Salzburg) in 1953, and the Academy for Music and Dramatic Art in Graz (Akademie für Musik und darstellende Kunst in Graz) in 1963.

In 1970, the Fine Arts College Organization Law (Kunsthochschul-Organisationsgesetz, KOG) again raised the status of fine arts academies to the same university status that the Academy of Fine Arts in Vienna has enjoyed since 1872. Unlike the Academy of Fine Arts in Vienna, the names of the other academies were changed to college (Hochschule). These schools now are known as the College for Music and Dramatic Art in Vienna (Hochschule für Musik und darstellende Kunst in Wien), the College for Applied Art in Vienna (Hochschule für angewandte Kunst in Wien), the College for Music and Dramatic Art 'Mozarteum' in Salzburg (Hochschule für Musik und darstellende Kunst 'Mozarteum' in Salzburg), and the College for Music and Dramatic Art in Graz (Hochschule für Musik und darstellende Kunst in Graz). In 1973, the Art School of Linz was accorded university status and renamed the College for Industrial Arts in Linz (Hochschule für künstlerische und industrielle Gestaltung in Linz).

In 1983, the Fine Arts College Studies Law (Kunsthochschul-Studiengesetz, KHStG) was passed. Although provisions of this law had not been fully implemented by 1985, the law will standardize study programs in each of the six fine arts colleges.

Legal Basis For Fine Arts College Studies

Organization and Control

Except for the Academy of Fine Arts in Vienna, all fine arts colleges are organized according to the Fine Arts College Organization Law (Kunsthochschul-Organisationsgesetz, KOG) of 1970. The Academy of Fine Arts in Vienna is organized according to laws passed in 1872 and 1955. A new law that will assimilate regulations for the art academy with those of other fine arts colleges is now being prepared.

Fine arts colleges are administered in the same way as universities. Although generally regulated by the Science and Research Ministry, fine arts colleges have guaranteed autonomy for self-governance. Except for the Academy of Fine Arts in Vienna, the concept of "co-determination" as applied to universities also extends to fine arts colleges. Professors, middle-level academic and support personnel and students share responsibility for the administration of fine arts colleges. The new law being prepared for the Academy of Fine Arts in Vienna will contain a provision for administrative "co-determination."

Fine arts colleges are subdivided into departments (*Abteilungen*), except for the Academy of Fine Arts in Vienna. Within each department, artistic subjects are taught in classes (known more specifically as classes of artistic education [*Klassen künstlerischer Ausbildung*] in music colleges, master schools [*Meisterschulen*] at the art academy, and master classes [*Meisterklassen*] in the art colleges) which actually are private lessons, i.e., one student and one teacher. Subjects supplementary to artistic subjects are taught in classes (*Lehrkanzeln*) which consist of one teacher and several students. Institutes (*Institute*) exist within departments to fulfill special teaching or research functions.

The highest officer in a fine arts college is the rector (*Rektor*) who is chosen from and also chairs the Comprehensive Council (*Gesamtkollegium*), the highest governing body. As is the case in universities, a Study Commission (*Studienkommission*) exists in each fine arts college and is responsible for dividing required general areas of study known as "subjects" (*Fächer*) into individual classes.

Regulation of Study Programs

Study programs in fine arts colleges (including the Academy of Fine Arts in Vienna) are regulated by the 1983 Fine Arts College Studies Law (Kunsthochschul-Studiengesetz, KHStG) which is parallel to the General University Studies Law (AHStG) for universities. Some study programs have been revised according to KHStG provisions, but many are still in the process of revision. The four layers of regulations that exist for university programs as a result of the AHStG also will exist for fine arts colleges through the KHStG. (See "Regulation of Study Programs" in Chapter VI.)

The primary thrust of the KHStG is to expand and strengthen the academic and theoretical portions of study programs and to better integrate these with the artistic portions of a fine arts education. After implementation of the KHStG, all study programs will conclude with an academic degree. Prior to 1983, only programs in architecture and secondary-school teacher education led to an academic degree because these programs are subject to the AHStG. The KHStG did not alter the "master" instruction (*Meisterlehre*) principle that has traditionally characterized study in fine arts colleges. In "master" instruc-

FINE ARTS EDUCATION

98

tion, which exists only in artistic subjects, a teacher provides instruction to only one student. Study programs existing prior to implementation of the KHStG are not subject to federal regulations, and thus pre-KHStG study programs in the six fine arts colleges are not uniform.

Entry Requirements

The same three types of student status exist in fine arts colleges as in universities. (See "Entry Requirements," Chapter VI.) Degree-seeking students must register with regular student status *(ordentlicher Hörer)*, and nondegree-seeking students register with special student *(ausserordentlicher Hörer)* or auditor *(Gasthörer)* status. Approximately 85% of fine arts college students enroll with regular student status, 12% with special student status, and 3% with auditor status.

Admission with Regular Student Status

For admission with regular student status *(ordentlicher Hörer)* in all majors, a rigorous admissions examination *(Aufnahmsprüfung)* measuring artistic performance and talent is required. In addition to the admissions examination, an academic or an age requirement exists for admission. Admission to the following majors requires completion of the maturity (examination) certificate *(Reifeprüfungszeugnis, Reifezeugnis)* from a general secondary or senior vocational school: architecture and interior architecture, music theater direction, music therapy, performance arts direction, and secondary teacher education. Admission to instrumental music majors requires a minimum age of 15 years and other majors require a minimum age of 17 years. Major programs into which 15-year-olds are admitted usually last a minimum of eight years while those into which 17-year-olds are admitted usually last a minimum of four to seven years.

Admission with Special Student or Auditor Status

Admission with special student *(ausserordentlicher Hörer)* or auditor *(Gasthörer)* status is granted to persons who demonstrate artistic talent and have the necessary prerequisite knowledge for enrollment. Special students and auditors are allowed to register in regular classes on a space-available basis or in special college programs *(Hochschullehrgänge)* or classes *(Hochschulkurse)* offered by fine arts colleges. Those who enroll with special student or auditor status may not complete requirements for an academic degree.

Students younger than the minimum age required for admission with regular status may be admitted as special students into preparatory programs *(Vorbereitungslehrgänge)* until they are old enough for admission to regular study programs. The preparatory program is not a university-level program and does not lead to the maturity certificate or to any other certificate.

At the Academy of Fine Arts in Vienna, students who do not have the maturity certificate enter with special status. After successfully completing one year of study (but before planning the second year), students must transfer to regular status (*ordentlicher Hörer*).

Study Programs

The KHStG changed the organization of study programs. A description of the pre-KHStG system and the post-KHStG system follows. For many study programs (majors) the old system still exists today as revisions legislated by the 1983 KHStG are being prepared.

Pre-KHStG System

Prior to 1983, only study programs in architecture and secondary-school teacher education led to the award of an academic degree. Although located in fine arts colleges, these programs are regulated by the AHStG which is described in Chapter VI. Artistic study programs under the old system lead, not to the award of an academic degree or title, but usually to a diploma or certificate (*Diplom, Diplomzeugnis*). The final diploma previously issued by some fine arts colleges was a maturity certificate (*Reifezeugnis*) which is not equivalent to and should not be confused with the maturity certificate from a general secondary or senior vocational school. Students enrolled under the old system since 1948 may retroactively request the *Magister* degree for a completed artistic study program. Some fine arts colleges issue the *Magister* without requiring further study, but some require additional academic work.

Under the old system artistic study programs are not subject to common federal laws and as a result are not uniform from college to college. Usually students take a diploma examination (*Diplomprüfung*) prior to award of the final diploma or certificate. Program duration is determined by each fine arts college, but continuation in the program each year is contingent upon satisfactory artistic achievements.

The following credentials are issued by some, but not all, fine arts colleges. Often credentials are issued to students only upon request.

- Diploma (*Diplom, Diplomzeugnis, Reifezeugnis*) documents completion of the program. (At the College for Music and Dramatic Art in Vienna, the grading scale used is as follows: "passed with distinction" [*mit Auszeichnung bestanden*] or "passed" [*bestanden*]. A diploma is not issued with a non-passing grade [*nicht bestanden*].)
- Teacher Qualification Certificate (*Lehrbefähigungszeugnis*) provides music teacher certification for music conservatories but not for secondary schools.
- Leaving Certificate (*Abschlusszeugnis*) documents completion of a special program (*Lehrgang*) or course (*Kurs*).
- Yearly Certificate (*Jahreszeugnis*) is issued after each year of study and provides a grade for achievement during that year.

- Summary of Achievement *(Frequenzbestätigung)* is a summary of achievements for students who do not finish requirements for the complete program and is issued only upon request.

Post-KHStG System

The KHStG equalized the curricula and policies governing study programs in all fine arts colleges but did not change the commonly understood differentiation between special study programs *(ausserordentliche Studien)* and regular study programs *(ordentliche Studien)*. Special study programs, like those in universities, exist as programs *(Lehrgänge)* and courses *(Kurse)* in which students admitted with regular, special or auditor status may enroll. Those who complete special study programs receive a leaving certificate *(Abschlusszeugnis)* but no academic degree or title.

Regular study programs, on the other hand, constitute the bulk of study programs in fine arts colleges and, after implementation of KHStG regulations, will lead to an academic degree or title in all majors. Most regular study programs are diploma study programs *(Diplomstudien)*, which lead to the *Magister* of Arts *(Magister der Künste)* degree. The KHStG also created several short study programs *(Kurzstudien)* which culminate in academic titles, e.g., Academically Certified Opera Singer *(Akademisch geprüfter Opernsänger)*. Doctoral study programs *(Doktoratsstudien)* leading to the *Doktor* degree are available in a few majors. Doctoral study in the fine arts is completed at a university but the thesis *(Dissertation)* adviser is a tenured professor from a fine arts college.

The structure and organization of diploma and short study programs are essentially the same as those in universities. (See "Regular Study Programs," Chapter VI.) Diploma study programs usually are divided into two study segments, each of which concludes with a diploma examination *(Diplomprüfung)* and award of a diploma examination certificate *(Diplomprüfungszeugnis)*. Study programs not divided into study segments also conclude with a diploma examination. In addition to coursework, students must complete a thesis during the second segment. Short programs are not divided into segments but conclude with a diploma examination *(Diplomprüfung)* and award of an academic title. Under the KHStG, the minimum study duration is flexible; students may shorten their studies by demonstrating previous knowledge or by developing their artistic talents quickly. In artistic subjects only, an examination is given each semester and the certificate awarded is known as the Assessment of Study Results *(Beurteilung des studien Erfolgs)*. Music students who fail the artistic examination for two consecutive semesters or art students who fail three consecutive semesters must leave the college. In academic subjects for which a certificate *(Zeugnis)* is awarded, students may repeat lectures until they pass the examination. Although not fully implemented yet, regular study programs in fine arts colleges as required by the KHStG are outlined in Table 7.1.

Table 7.1. Major Degree Programs in Fine Arts Colleges per KHStG

DEPARTMENT MAJOR 2nd Segment Specialization	Minimum Entrance Requirement*	Min. Legal Length in Sems. Total (per Seg.)	Academic Degree or Title†
ARTISTIC RESTORATION & PRESERVATION			
ARTISTIC RESTOR. &			
PRESERV.	17 years	10‡	*Mag. art.*
CHURCH MUSIC			
CATHOLIC CHURCH MUSIC			
Choir Conducting &			
Cantor Training	17 years	12 (8 + 4)	*Mag. art.*
Organ	17 years	12 (8 + 4)	*Mag. art.*
PROSTESTANT CHURCH MUSIC			
Choir Conducting &			
Cantor Training	17 years	12 (8 + 4)	*Mag. art.*
Organ	17 years	12 (8 + 4)	*Mag. art.*
COMPOSITION, MUSIC THEORY, CONDUCTING			
COMPOSITION & MUSIC THEORY			
Composition	17 years	12 (4 + 8)	*Mag. art.*
Music Theory	17 years	12 (4 + 8)	*Mag. art.*
MUSIC CONDUCTING			
Choir Conducting	17 years	12 (4 + 8)	*Mag. art.*
Opera Stage Management	17 years	12 (4 + 8)	*Mag. art.*
Orchestra Conducting	17 years	12 (4 + 8)	*Mag. art.*
DESIGN			
CERAMICS	17 years	10 (6 + 4)	*Mag. art.*
FASHION	17 years	10 (6 + 4)	*Mag. art.*
INDUSTRIAL DESIGN	17 years	10 (6 + 4)	*Mag. art.*
METAL	17 years	10 (6 + 4)	*Mag. art.*
PRODUCT DESIGN	17 years	10 (6 + 4)	*Mag. art.*
TEXTILES	17 years	10 (6 + 4)	*Mag. art.*
FILM & TELEVISION			
DIRECTION	17 years	10 (4 + 6)	*Mag. art.*
DRAMATURGY	17 years	10 (4 + 6)	*Mag. art.*
EDITING	17 years	10 (4 + 6)	*Mag. art.*
PHOTOGR. TECHNIQ.			
& CAMERA	17 years	10 (4 + 6)	*Mag. art.*
PRODUCTION	17 years	10 (4 + 6)	*Mag. art.*
INSTRUMENTAL STUDIES			

Majors in each of the following instruments:
Bass Tuba, Bassoon,
Clarinet, Contrabass, Flute,
French Horn, Guitar, Harp,
Harpsichord, Oboe, Organ,
Percussion Instruments,
Piano, Piano Chamber
Music, Piano-Vocal
Accompaniment, Recorder,

continued

Saxophone, Trombone, Trumpet, Viola, Violin, Violoncello	15 years	16 (10 + 6)	*Mag. art.*
INTERIOR ARCHITECTURE			
INTERIOR ARCHITECTURE	Mat. Cert.§	10 (6 + 4)	*Mag. art.*
JAZZ			
JAZZ	15 years	16 (10 + 6)	*Mag. art.*
MUSIC EDUCATION‖			
INSTRUMENTAL (VOCAL) MUSIC EDUCATION	17 years	12 (8 + 4)	*Mag. art.*
MUSIC & MOVEMENT TRAINING	17 years	12 (8 + 4)	*Mag. art.*
PAINTING, GRAPHICS, PLASTICS			
MEDAL ENGRAVING & SMALL SCULPTURE	17 years	8‡	*Mag. art.*
PAINTING & GRAPHICS	17 years	8‡	*Mag. art.*
SCULPTURE	17 years	8‡	*Mag. art.*
PERFORMANCE ARTS			
PERFORMANCE ARTS			
Drama	17 years	8‡	*Mag. art.*
Direction	Mat. Cert.§	8‡	*Mag. art.*
STAGE DESIGN			
STAGE DESIGN	17 years	8‡	*Mag. art.*
VISUAL MEDIA DESIGN			
VISUAL MEDIA DESIGN	17 years	10 (6 + 4)	*Mag. art.*
VOICE & MUSIC THEATER			
VOICE TRAINING			
Choir	17 years	14 (8 + 6)	*Mag. art.*
Dramatic Music Presenta.	17 years	14 (8 + 6)	*Mag. art.*
Lied & Oratorium	17 years	14 (8 + 6)	*Mag. art.*
MUSIC THEATER DIRECTION	Mat. Cert.§	8‡	*Mag. art.*
SHORT STUDY PROGRAMS (*KURZSTUDIUM*)			
CATHOLIC CHURCH MUSIC	17 years	8‡#	*Akad. gepr. Kirchenmusiker*
DRAMATIC MUSIC PRESENTA.	17 years	6‡	*Akad. gepr. Opernsänger*
LIED & ORATORIUM	17 years	6‡	*Akad. gepr. Konzertsänger*
MUSIC THERAPY	Mat. Cert.§	6‡	*Akad. gepr. Musiktherapeut*
PROTESTANT CHURCH MUSIC	17 years	8‡#	*Akad. gepr. Kirchenmusiker*

*In addition to the maturity certificate or a minimum age requirement, all applicants must pass an artistic aptitude test.

†The full name of the academic degree (which may be in German or Latin) or academic title follows with an English translation: *Mag. art.* = *Magister der Künste*/Magister artium/Magister of Arts, *Akad. gepr. Kirchenmusiker* = *Akademisch geprüfter Kirchenmusiker*/Academically Certified Church Musician, *Akad. gepr. Konzertsänger* = *Akademisch geprüfter Konzertsänger*/Academically Certified Concert Singer, *Akad. gepr. Musiktherapeut* = *Akademisch geprüfter Musiktherapeut*/Academically Certified Music Therapist, *Akad gepr. Opernsänger* = *Akademisch geprüfter Opernsänger*/Academically Certified Opera Singer.

‡Not divided into segments.
§Maturity Certificate *(Reifeprüfungszeugnis, Reifezeugnis)*.
‖This major is not intended for secondary school teachers but rather for teachers in music conservatories. Secondary school music teacher training is regulated by the AHStG (which is described in Chapter VI, Table 6.1), although the program is located in a music college.
#This short study program is actually the first study segment of the corresponding diploma program. Those who complete the diploma program also will receive an academic title after completing the first study segment.

Under the new system, examinations given and documentation awarded will be the same as for university programs regulated by the AHStG (see Chapter VI for details). The same five-point individual grading scale used in universities will be used for non-artistic courses. See "Grading Scale," Chapter VI.

For examinations and courses in the core artistic subjects, the following grading scale will be used:

Grade	Suggested U.S. Equivalent
sehr gut (very good)	A
mit Erfolg (with success)	B/C
ohne Erfolg (without success or failing)	F

For diploma examinations which contain more than one part, the following comprehensive grades will be awarded:

Grade	Definition
mit ausgezeichnetem Erfolg (with outstanding success)	Over half of the individual grades are *sehr gut*.
mit Erfolg (with success)	All grades are passing grades.
ohne Erfolg (without success or failing)	Not all individual grades are passing grades.

Fine Arts College Profiles

The following are profiles of fine arts colleges from 1985. Since provisions of the KHStG were not fully implemented by 1985, some of the majors are from the pre-KHStG system.

Academy of Fine Arts in Vienna (Akademie der bildenden Künste in Wien), Schillerplatz 3, 1010 Wien.
Description: Founded 1696 by Kaiser Leopold I as the first art academy in middle Europe and known as the Academy for Painting, Sculpture, Architecture, Perspective and Fortification (Academia für Malerei, Bildhauerei, Architektur, Perspektive, und Fortifikation); combined with two other art academies, The Royal Copperplate Engraver Academy (Kaiserlich-königliche Kupferstecher-Akademie) and the Engraver Academy (Graveurakademie), in 1772 by Empress Maria Theresia and renamed the Royal United Academy of Fine Arts (Kaiserlich-königlich vereinigten Akademie der bildenden Künste); elevated to university-level institution (with current name) in 1872; reorganized in 1955. Enrollment (1984-85): 460 students. Full- and Part-time Academic Staff (1984-85): 144 staff members.

Majors (1985): The school is not divided into departments. Majors exist in Architecture, Art Education, Graphics, Handicrafts Education, Medal Engraving & Small Sculpture, Painting, Preservation & Technology, Sculpture, Stage Design, and Textile Design & Production.

College for Applied Art in Vienna (Hochschule für angewandte Kunst in Wien), Oskar-Kokoschka-Platz 2, 1010 Wien.

Description: Founded 1867 as an industrial arts school (Kunstgewerbeschule des Kaiserlich-königlichen österreichischen Museums für Kunst und Industrie); elevated to status of art academy (Akademie für angewandte Kunst in Wien) in 1948; elevated to university-level institution and changed to current name in 1970. Enrollment (1984-85): 816 students. Library: 125,000 volumes. Full- and Part-time Academic Staff (1984-85): 176 staff members.

Departments and Majors (1985):

Department of Architecture—Architecture, Interior Architecture.

Department of Art Education—Art Education, Handicrafts Education, Textile Design & Production.

Department of Fine Art—Artistic Restoration & Preservation, Decorative Designs & Textiles, Painting.

Department of Plastic Formation and Design—Fashion Design, Industrial Design, Product Formation & Ceramics, Product Formation & Medal, Sculpture.

Department of Visual Communication—Artistic Lettering & Book Design; Commercial Art, Illustrations & Photography, Graphics & Print Graphics; Stage & Film Design.

College for Industrial Arts in Linz (Hochschule für künstlerische und industrielle Gestaltung in Linz), Hauptplatz 8, 4020 Linz.

Description: Founded 1947 as the Art School of Linz (Kunstschule der Stadt Linz); elevated to university-level institution with current name in 1973. Enrollment (1984-85): 383 students. Full- and Part-time Academic Staff (1984-85): 112 staff members.

Departments and Majors (1985):

Department of Applied Graphics and Artistic Handwork—Visual Media Design with emphases in Artistic Lettering & Book Design, Commercial Graphic Arts.

Department of Environmental Design—Industrial Design, Interior Architecture.

Department of General Art and Art Education—Art Education, Industrial Arts, Metal, Painting & Graphics, Sculpture, Textile Design & Production, Textiles.

College for Music and Dramatic Art in Graz (Hochschule für Musik und darstellende Kunst in Graz), Leonhardstrasse 15, 8010 Graz.

Description: Founded 1803 as a provincial school of music; became a music conservatory in 1815; elevated to a music academy (Akademie für Musik und darstellende Kunst in Graz) in 1963; elevated to university-level institution with current name in 1970. Enrollment (1984-85): 1,020 students. Library: 30,000 volumes. Full- and Part-time Academic Staff (1984-85): 232 staff members.

Departments and Majors (1985):

Department of Church Music—Catholic Church Music, Protestant Church Music.

Department of Composition, Music Theory, and Conducting—Composition, Conducting, Sound Engineering.

Department of Jazz—Contrabass, Guitar, Jazz Theory/Composition/Arrangement, Percussion Instruments, Piano, Saxophone, Trombone, Trumpet.

Department of Keyboard Instruments—Harpsichord, Organ, Piano, Piano Chamber Music & Vocal Accompaniment.

Department of Music Education—Instrumental Music Education, Instrumental & Vocal Education, Music Education.

Department of String Instruments—Contrabass, Guitar, Harp, Viola, Violin, Violoncello.

Department of Voice, Choir Conducting, and Performance Arts—Choir Conducting, Directing, Drama, Stage Design, Voice (Choir), Voice (Lied & Oratorium), Voice (Opera).

Department of Wind and Percussion Instruments—Bass Tuba, Bassoon, Clarinet, Flute, French Horn, Oboe, Percussion Instruments, Recorder, Saxophone, Trombone, Trumpet.

College for Music and Dramatic Art in Vienna (Hochschule für Musik und darstellende Kunst in Wien), Lothringerstrasse 18, 1030 Wien.

Description: Founded 1817 as a private vocational school *(Fachschule)* which shortly therafter became a music conservatory (Konservatorium der Musikfreunde); became a public art institution (Kaiserlich-königliche Akademie für Musik und darstellende Kunst) in 1909; elevated to legal status as art academy (Akademie für Musik und darstellende Kunst in Wien) in 1947; became university-level institution with current name in 1970. Enrollment (1984-85): 2,131 students. Library: 81,700 volumes. Full- and Part-time Academic Staff (1984-85): 437 staff members.

Departments and Majors (1985):

Department of Drama and Direction ("Max-Reinhardt Seminar")—Directing, Drama.

Department of Church Music—Catholic Church Music, Protestant Church Music.

Department of Composition, Music Theory and Conducting—Choir Conducting, Composition, Conducting, Opera Rehearsal (piano accompaniment).

Department of Film and Television—Directing, Dramaturgy, Editing, Photography Techniques/Camera, Production.

Department of Keyboard Instruments—Harpsichord, Organ, Piano, Piano Chamber Music, Piano Vocal Accompaniment.

Department of Music Education—Diploma programs for training secondary school teachers in Instrumental Music Education, and Music Education; and doctoral programs in Instrumental & Vocal Music Education, Rhythmical Music Education.

Department of Solo and Dramatic Music Performance—Dramatic Music Performance, Lied & Oratorium, Opera Direction, Voice Training.

Department of String Instruments—Contrabass, Guitar, Harp, Viola, Violin, Violoncello.

Department of Wind and Percussion Instruments—Bass Tuba, Bassoon, Clarinet, Flute, French Horn, Oboe, Percussion Instruments, Recorder, Trombone, Trumpet.

College for Music and Dramatic Art 'Mozarteum' in Salzburg (Hochschule für Musik und darstellende Kunst 'Mozarteum' in Salzburg), Mirabellplatz 1, 5020 Salzburg.

Description: Founded 1841; transferred to the private Mozarteum foundation in 1881; became a private music conservatory in 1914 and a state institution in 1922; elevated to a music academy (Akademie für Musik und darstellende Kunst 'Mozarteum' in Salzburg) in 1953; elevated to university-level institution with current name in 1970. Enrollment (1984-85): 1,228 students. Library: 43,000 volumes. Full- and Part-time Academic Staff (1984-85): 272 staff members.

Departments and Majors (1985):

Department of Art Education (for teachers in secondary schools)—Art Education, Handicrafts Education, Textile Design & Production.

Department of Church Music—Catholic Church Music, Protestant Church Music.

Department of Composition, Music Theory, and Conducting—Composition, Music
Conducting.
Department of Keyboard Instruments—Harpsichord, Organ, Piano, Piano Chamber
Music, Piano Vocal Accompaniment.
Department of Music Education in Innsbruck—Music Education.
Department of Music Education—Instrumental Music Education, Instrumental &
Vocal Education, Music Education.
Department of Performance Arts—Directing, Drama, Stage Design.
Department of Solo and Dramatic Music Performance—Dramatic Music Performance,
Lied & Oratorium.
Department of String Instruments—Contrabass, Guitar, Harp, Viola, Violin, Violon-
cello.
Department of Wind and Percussion Instruments—Bass Tuba, Bassoon, Clarinet &
Saxophone, Flute, French Horn, Oboe, Percussion Instruments, Recorder, Trom-
bone, Trumpet.
Orff Institute—Music & Movement Training.

Institutional Partnership Arrangements: College of Music in Munich (Hochschule für
Musik in München), Federal Republic of Germany (since 1984); National Conservatory
of Music "Benedetto Marcello" Venedig (Conservatorio Nazionale di Musica "Benedetto Marcello" Venedig), Italy (1982).

Other Institutions Offering Training in the Fine Arts

Music Conservatories

Music conservatories *(Konservatorien)* are private institutions that are managed
by cities, provinces, or private individuals. No state music conservatory exists.
Students usually enter a music conservatory after 15 years of age, although
part-time enrollment at a younger age is possible. Teachers in conservatories
usually are trained in music colleges.

The goal of music conservatories is to create professional musicians but,
unlike the three university-level music colleges, music conservatories are not
permitted to grant academic degrees. Thus, credentials issued by music conservatories attest only to musical and not to academic accomplishments. The
final credential may be a certificate of attendance *(Schulbesuchsbestätigung)* or
a maturity certificate *(Reifezeugnis)* which is not equivalent to and should not
be confused with the maturity certificate issued after completion of a general
secondary or senior vocational school.

Music Schools

Music schools *(Musikschulen)* exist for beginning music students. Usually younger
children enroll part-time in music schools while they are regularly enrolled in
a primary or secondary school. All music schools are private. An annual
certification *(Jahresausweis)* may be issued. Similar schools for beginning artists
are dance schools *(Tanzschulen)* and ballet schools *(Balletschulen)*.

Chapter VIII

Teacher Education

Introduction

Teacher training occurs in the following types of institutions: universities, nonuniversity postsecondary institutions, and secondary-level intermediate and senior vocational schools. Descriptions of teacher education in this chapter are organized according to the school type or subject for which the teacher is being trained. The unique pedagogical features of university programs for training teachers are described in this chapter, but general descriptions of university programs are provided in Chapters VI, "University Education," and VII, "Fine Arts Education."

Teacher training at universities is regulated by the Science and Research Ministry. Except for the training of Roman Catholic religion teachers and agriculture and forestry teachers, all other teacher training is regulated by the Education, Arts and Sports Ministry. Teacher training in the Roman Catholic religion is regulated by the Church according to treaties between the Austrian government and the Vatican and funded by the Church and state. Agriculture and forestry teacher training is financed and administered by the Agriculture and Forestry Ministry while educational matters are handled by the Education, Arts and Sports Ministry.

Preschool Teachers

Recent legislation elevated preschool teacher training from the intermediate to the senior vocational school level. Until August 1985, preschool teacher training institutions were equivalent to four-year intermediate vocational schools (*Bildungsanstalten für Kindergärtnerinnen*) and since then have been parallel to five-year senior vocational schools (*Bildungsanstalten für Kindergartenpädagogik*). The new generic school name no longer implies (in the German language) that preschool teacher training is intended only for girls. For admission to either the old or new program, students must have completed eight years of school and have passed an aptitude test. The old program, which requires 12 years of total study, does not qualify graduates for entry into postsecondary education; but the new program, which requires 13 years, does meet postsecondary education entry requirements.

Students who entered the program in the fall of 1984 or before will have until 1988 to complete the old program. Those who complete the old program receive a qualification examination certificate for preschool teachers (*Befähigungsprüfungszeugnis für Kindergärtnerinnen*). Starting in 1985, new students follow the new program leading to the maturity and qualification examination certificate (*Reife- und Befähigungsprüfungszeugnis*) for the preschool teacher. This certificate will be issued in 1990.

The new five-year curriculum along with instructional hours is presented in Table 8.1. The old four-year curriculum required fewer science and education courses and no foreign language. In place of these, courses in domestic sciences were required. The student who wishes to be an educational assistant in a day-care center (*Erzieher an Horten*) also may complete the program for preschool teachers.

A program (*Lehrgang*) exists within some preschool teacher training schools for training preschool teachers who wish to specialize in preschool-level special education. The one and one-half year program may be extended to two years for employed adults. Those who complete the program and pass the final examination receive a qualification examination certificate in preschool special education (*Befähigungsprüfungszeugnis für Sonderkindergartenpädagogik*).

Table 8.1. Course List for Senior Vocational School Training for Preschool Teachers

Compulsory Subjects	Hrs./Wk. by Semester				
	1	2	3	4	5
Art	2	2	2	2	0/2
Biology & Ecology	2	2	1	2	–
Chemistry	–	2	2	–	–
Didactics	1	2	3	3	3
Geography & Economics	2	3	1	1	–
German (Language & Children's Lit.)	4	3	3	3	3
Handicrafts	5	2	2	2	2/0
Health	–	–	–	–	1
History & Social Studies	2	2	2	–	2
Instrumental Music					
Flute	–	1	1	–	1/0
Guitar	2	1	1	–	0/1
Law	–	–	–	1	1
Mathematics	3	3	2	2	–
Modern Foreign Language	3	3	2	2	2
Music	2	2	1	2	2
Pedagogy	–	2	3	3	3
Physical Education	3	2	2	2	3
Physics	–	2	2	2	–
Practical Experience	1	2	5	5	5
Religion	2	2	2	2	2
Rhythmical Music	–	1	1	–	–
Special Education	–	–	–	1	1
Supplementary Instruction	3	–	–	1	2
Total	37	39	38	36	33

Electives also are available.

Educational Assistants

Educational assistants (*Erzieher*) may work in day-care centers (for children of compulsory school age during school vacations), private homes, youth hostels, and dormitories attached to boarding schools. Institutes for training educational assistants (*Institut für Heimerziehung* and *Bildungsanstalt für Erzieher*) were raised from four-year intermediate to five-year senior vocational schools for students beginning their studies in 1985. The intermediate vocational school program leading to the qualification examination certificate for educational assistants (*Befähigungsprüfungszeugnis für Erzieher*) will be awarded until 1988, and the new senior vocational school program leading to the maturity and qualification examination certificate for educational assistants (*Reife- und Befähigungsprüfungszeugnis für Erzieher*) will be awarded starting in 1990. Admission to both the old and new programs requires completion of eight years of education as well as an aptitude test (*Eignungsprüfung*). The new certificate (requiring 13 total years of education) will entitle graduates to enter a postsecondary institution but the old certificate (requiring 12 years of education) does not.

The required course of study for the new five-year program is essentially equivalent to that of the new five-year program for training preschool teachers described above. The former four-year program for educational assistants required fewer science courses than the new five-year program does.

Training for educational assistants also is available in a vocational institute (*Kolleg*) for those who have graduated from a general secondary school. Since the maturity certificate (*Reifeprüfungszeugnis, Reifezeugnis*) is required for admission to a vocational institute, the academic courses required for entering postsecondary education are completed by students prior to entry. Thus, the two-year *Kolleg* curriculum consists only of the vocational courses in the regular senior vocational school curriculum. Upon completing the program and passing the final examination, students receive a second maturity and qualification examination certificate for educational assistants (*Reife- und Befähigungsprüfungszeugnis für Erzieher*).

A two-year program (*Lehrgang*) also exists in some schools to train educational assistants in special education. For admission to this program the educational assistant qualification certificate is required. Those who finish the program receive a leaving certificate (*Abschlusszeugnis*).

Compulsory School Teachers

Fourteen pedagogical academies (*pädagogische Akademien*) train teachers for compulsory schools, i.e., primary schools, lower secondary schools, prevocational programs, and special education schools for handicapped children. Pedagogical academies are considered tertiary-level institutions because the entry requirement is the maturity certificate (*Reifeprüfungszeugnis, Reifezeugnis*) and because equivalent training does not exist at the secondary level. The

1962 School Organization Act elevated all compulsory school teacher training from the upper secondary vocational level to the tertiary level, thereby creating a nonuniversity stream of higher education. The first pedagogical academies opened in 1968, and by 1984, pedagogical academies enrolled 5% of all students in higher education. (Universities and fine arts colleges enrolled 92% of all students in higher education while the other nonuniversity postsecondary institutions each enrolled 1% or fewer.)

Although subject to federal laws, which are regulated by the Education, Arts and Sports Ministry, pedagogical academies are financed by either the Church or state and administered by the federal government, the Roman Catholic Church, or private foundations. Because public and private pedagogical academies are subject to the same federal laws, the curriculum and the final teacher qualification credentials are equivalent.

Pedagogical academies have divisions for primary, lower secondary, prevocational program, and special education teacher training. Each division is paired with corresponding "practice" schools (*Übungsschulen*) that enroll children from the community. An important part of teacher education is the practical training (including observations, practica, and student teaching) that occurs in the "practice" schools. Classes in pedagogical academies are structured similarly to those in universities. Lectures (*Vorlesungen*), seminars (*Seminare*), and exercises (*Übungen*) exist in both and are described in Chapter VI.

Common compulsory subjects for prospective teachers in all schools are human sciences (i.e., biology, educational psychology, educational sciences, educational sociology, hygiene, religion, and school law); teaching methods and practical teaching experience; and other education courses such as audiovisual technology, child development, extracurricular education, and political science. Students preparing for primary school teaching are required to take additional education courses specifically related to the primary school. Those preparing for lower secondary schools and prevocational programs are required to complete two major concentrations of which one must be English, German, or mathematics and the other one chosen from among the remaining subjects taught in these schools. To prepare for teaching in prevocational programs, students take extra coursework in vocational preparation (see Table 8.2 for course list and instructional hours). Those preparing for special education are required to take additional elementary and special education courses that emphasize teaching skills for at least two different types of handicaps.

For students beginning their primary school teacher training prior to August 1985, the program duration was four semesters (two years). Those who started in 1985 enrolled in a new six-semester program. Teacher training programs for lower secondary schools, prevocational programs and special education have always been six-semester programs.

For reporting success in individual classes, two systems exist. In some academies, students receive a certificate (*Zeugnis* or *Prüfungsnachweis*) for each examination they pass (a system similar to that used in universities). The number of certificates obtained varies by program and by school. In other academies, students have a study book (*Studienbuch*) within which is written

Table 8.2. Course List for Lower Secondary School and Prevocational Teacher Training Program, 1985

Compulsory Subjects	Semester Hrs./Wk.*		Semester Hrs./Wk.*
		Human Sciences	
Biological Fndns. of		Emphasis from Human Sciences	6
Education; Hygiene	2	Gen. Special Education	3
Educational Psychology	6	Instructional Sciences	6
Educational Sciences	6	Religion Education	6
Educational Sociology	6	School Law	2
		Majors	
First Major (must be		Second Major (can be any	
English, German or	28-30	other subject taught in the	28-30
Math)	} 38	relevant school type)	} 38
Didactics Related to		Didactics Related to	
First Major	8-10	Second Major	8-10
Alternative Studies	4	**Practical School Training**	
Practicum	–	Instructional Analyses	
Student Teaching	–	Instructional Discussions	
		Instructional Visits	} 28
		Teaching Exercises	
		Teaching Methods	
		Supplementary Studies	
Computer Science	1	Physical Education	1
Educational Research	(6)	Political Education	2
First Aid	1	Practical Writing	
Intro. to Adult Educ.	1	Techniq. & Graphics	1
Instructional Technol.	1	Study Techniques	1
Language Education	1	Theater Arts	1
Media Didactics	1	Traffic Safety	1
		Total	164
			(170)

Elective subjects are also available.

SOURCE: Information provided by the Ministry for Education, Arts and Sports.
*Semester weekly hours are equivalent to the number of weekly classes in one semester and are scheduled by individual schools over the entire six-semester program. For example, 6 semester weekly hours might mean one class/week for six semesters or two classes/week for three semesters, etc. Each semester lasts 16–17 weeks, and each class lasts 45 minutes.

the name of the class, the number of lessons per week, the grade, and the professor's name and signature. The professor's signature indicates that the student attended the required number of lessons and otherwise met the minimum requirements for the class, although sometimes no grade is given. Students who fail to get five professors' signatures may not continue their studies the following year.

Teacher training culminates with a teacher qualification examination (*Lehramtsprüfung*). This examination is monitored by an Examinations Commission

within the Education, Arts and Sports Ministry. Those who successfully pass
the examination receive a teacher qualification certificate for lower secondary
schools (*Zeugnis über die Lehramtsprüfung für Hauptschulen*), for primary schools
(*Zeugnis über die Lehramtsprüfung für Volksschulen*), for lower secondary schools
and prevocational programs (*Zeugnis über die Lehramtsprüfung für Hauptschulen
und Polytechnische Lehrgänge*), or for special education schools (*Zeugnis über die
Lehramtsprüfung für Sonderschulen*). See sample document in Appendix A.

Although lower secondary school and prevocational program teachers have
specialized training in two major subjects, they are considered "general"
teachers and may teach subjects for which they have no specialized training.
Although efforts are made to place teachers according to their specialized
training, teachers become lifetime employees of the state and their employment may not be terminated if demand for their specialization declines.

Vocational Teachers

A 1976 amendment to the School Organization Act elevated teacher training
for vocational subjects from the secondary to the tertiary level. The four
tertiary-level vocational pedagogical academies (*berufspädagogische Akademien*)
were formerly secondary-level vocational teacher-training institutions (*berufspädagogische Lehranstalten*). Vocational pedagogical academies train teachers of
vocational subjects in vocational schools for apprentices (*Berufsschulen, berufsbildende Pflichtschulen*) and in intermediate and senior vocational schools (*berufsbildende mittlere und höhere Schulen*) as well as teachers of stenography,
dictaphone operation, and word processing in all schools.

Vocational teachers are required for the approximately 230 vocations that
currently exist. Training occurs within the following ten basic teacher-training
curricula: vocational schools for apprentices (four semesters:); vocational schools
for apprentices (two); domestic science subjects (four); domestic science subjects (six); industrial vocations with a specialization in women's clothing (four);
industrial vocations with a specialization in men's clothing (four); industrial
vocations with specializations in artistic stitchery (four); industrial vocations
outside the clothing industry (two); industrial vocations outside the clothing
industry (four); stenography, dictaphone operation, and word processing
subjects (four).

In all curricula, the following courses are required: didactics and student
teaching; human sciences (e.g., biology, business sociology, educational science, educational psychology, educational sociology, health education, hygiene,
instructional science, religion, and school law); and the study and practice of
one or more vocational skills.

The Education, Arts and Sports Ministry has outlined specific admission
requirements along with the length and kind of previous vocational experience
required for entry into each curriculum. Usually, one to six years of relevant
vocational experience is required. The maturity certificate (*Reifeprüfungszeugnis, Reifezeugnis*) is required for admission to the curriculum in domestic

science and to that in stenography, dictaphone operation, and word processing. In the latter curriculum, proof of practical skills in typing and shorthand also is required. In other curricula a master craftsman's examination (*Meisterprüfung*) may substitute for the maturity certificate. The approximate proportion of students in recent years who have the maturity certificate upon entry is as follows: two-thirds in the vocational school for apprentices curricula, none in the clothing construction curricula, and half in all remaining curricula.

Passing a teacher qualification examination (*Lehramtsprüfung*) at the conclusion of studies is necessary to obtain the vocational teacher qualification examination certificate (*Lehramtsprüfungszeugnis* or *Zeugnis über die Lehramtsprüfung*) which entitles graduates to teach within their specialization in relevant vocational schools.

Teacher Training in Special Subjects

Agriculture and Forestry Teachers

The Federal Seminar for Agricultural Education (Bundesseminar für das landwirtschaftliche Bildungswesen) in Vienna is the only agriculture and forestry teacher-training institution in the country, although the law does not prohibit the formation of others. While the Agriculture and Forestry Ministry handles funding and staffing for the school, pedagogical concerns are handled by the Education, Arts and Sports Ministry. This institution provides teacher education, continuing education, and courses for agricultural extension agents. Two different teacher education programs are offered.

One is a two-semester teacher education program (which may soon be raised to a four-semester program) that requires the maturity certificate (*Reifeprüfungszeugnis, Reifezeugnis*) from a senior vocational school in agriculture or forestry for admission. The curriculum includes agricultural organization and research, agriculture education, art, curriculum development, didactic presentations, extracurricular activities, history of education, industrial arts, music, physical education, practical teaching experiences, psychology, religion, sociology, speech, supplementary instruction and administration, teaching methods, and youth development. In addition, students may choose to study English and additional physical education. After successful completion of the program and a two-year practicum, students receive a teacher qualification examination certificate (*Befähigungsprüfungszeugnis*). Those who do not yet have the practical experience receive a leaving examination certificate (*Abschlussprüfungszeugnis*). Sometimes the leaving certificate is a combination of these two certificates (*Abschluss- und Befähigungsprüfungszeugnis*).

The other teacher education program is a four-week program which requires either the *Magister* degree from the University for Agriculture in Vienna or the maturity certificate from a senior vocational school in agriculture or forestry with at least four years of relevant experience in the field. The program includes curriculum development, methods of instruction with practical teaching experiences, psychology, teaching methods, and youth work. After successfully completing the program, students receive the teacher qualification examination certificate (*Befähigungsprüfungszeugnis*).

Students in continuing agriculture and forestry education, including the courses for agriculture extension agents, receive no academic credentials, only confirmations of attendance (*Besuchsbestätigungszeugnis, Kursbestätigung*).

Handicraft Teachers

Since legislation has been passed to eliminate teacher training schools that are below the senior vocational school level, schools for training handicraft teachers (*Bildungsanstalten für Arbeitslehrerinnen*), which are equivalent to intermediate vocational schools, are being phased out of the educational system. The last class, which entered in 1984, will graduate in 1988. Graduates of these schools have a qualification examination certificate for handicraft teachers (*Befähigungsprüfungszeugnis für Arbeitslehrerinnen*) and are qualified to teach housekeeping and handicraft subjects in compulsory schools. The total program requires 12 years of education. Compulsory subjects are art, education, geography and economics, German, handicrafts, history and social studies, mathematics, music, physical education, religion, student teaching, and theoretical and practical vocational training. Some elective subjects also are available. After 1988, all handicraft teachers will be trained in pedagogical academies where a major in handicrafts already exists.

Physical Education and Sports Teachers

Most physical education and sports teachers are trained in universities and pedagogical academies, but the federal institutions for physical education (Bundesanstalten für Leibeserziehung) in Vienna and Innsbruck are secondary-level institutions for training physical education and sports teachers. Teachers trained in secondary schools usually work in health clubs or spas but in some cases also teach in schools. Those admitted must be at least 16 years of age and have completed at least eight years of education. In addition, a test measuring physical and mental aptitude is required.

The school in Vienna has a four-semester (two year) program for training physical education and sports teachers. The first year of the program consists of general theoretical and practical foundation courses. The second year consists of further general instruction as well as specialized instruction in all of the sports recognized by the Austrian Federal Sports Organization. Students may add a course entitled "Physical Education in the Schools" which qualifies them to teach in vocational schools for apprentices or compulsory schools (excluding elementary and special education schools). After successfully completing the program, students not prepared for teaching in a school receive a leaving examination certificate (*Abschlussprüfungszeugnis*) and those prepared for teaching in a school receive a leaving and (teacher) qualification examination certificate (*Abschluss- und Befähigungsprüfungszeugnis*). In addition, students receive the vocational title of State Certified Sports Teacher (*Staatlich geprüfter Sportlehrer*).

The school in Innsbruck has a program lasting two winter semesters (or one year) for skiing instructors only. Graduates of this program receive a leaving certificate (*Abschlusszeugnis*) and the vocational title of State Certified Skiing Instructor (*Staatlich geprüfter Schilehrer*).

Roman Catholic Religion Teachers

Teachers of the Roman Catholic religion are trained in four religion pedagogical academies (*religionspädagogische Akademien*) and three branch centers (*Expositur*) which are operated by the Church. The state does not control the educational level or training of religion teachers. Roman Catholic religion instruction is regulated by treaties between the Holy See and the Austrian government. Since priests are trained in the Catholic theology faculties of the Universities of Vienna, Graz, Salzburg, and Innsbruck, those trained in religion pedagogical academies usually are not priests.

Three programs of differing lengths all conclude with the same teacher qualification examination certificate (*Lehramtsprüfungszeugnis*, or *Zeugnis über die Lehramtsprüfung*) necessary for teaching Roman Catholic religion in schools. The most common program is fulltime for four semesters, but one school offers the same four-semester program over eight semesters for employed persons. Three schools offer a twelve-week private program that requires additional independent study of scriptures. Members of the Roman Catholic Church who have the maturity certificate and the aptitude required for teaching may be admitted to these programs. The required course of study covers primarily theology but also includes courses in the human sciences (education, psychology, sociology), teaching methods, student teaching, and elective subjects, mostly in music.

Protestant Religion Teachers

The Protestant Women's School for Church and Social Service (Evangelische Frauenschule für kirchlichen und sozialen Dienst) in Vienna and the Protestant Mission School (Evangelische Missionsschule) in Salzburg train Protestant religion teachers. For admission, both schools require completion of compulsory education or vocational education and the attainment of age 18 (17 for the Salzburg school). Although the maturity certificate (*Reifeprüfungszeugnis, Reifezeugnis*) is preferred for general admission, it is a requirement for leading positions in the church or for head-teacher positions.

The program in each school lasts three years. The curriculum consists primarily of religious doctrine but also contains courses in health, music, pedagogy, psychology, and social work. Those who successfully complete the program receive a diploma examination certificate (*Diplomprüfungszeugnis*) which is below the maturity certificate level. Graduates of the program usually spend approximately two years in a religious practicum or religious service before teaching in the schools.

University Trained Teachers

The law requires university training for teachers of academic subjects in the following types of schools: general secondary schools, most vocational schools, nonuniversity postsecondary institutions, and universities. In some vocational schools, academic subjects are taught by teachers trained in nonuniversity postsecondary institutions. In nonuniversity postsecondary institutions, lecturers are university trained but instructors in the practical phases of the program (e.g., student teacher supervisors) are trained in nonuniversity postsecondary institutions. In secondary and nonuniversity postsecondary institutions, the *Magister* degree is the minimum requirement for teachers, although lecturers in nonuniversity postsecondary institutions often have the *Doktor* degree. For a tenured university professorship, the *Doktor* plus the post-*Doktor* research and publication process known as *Habilitation* is required. For complete descriptions of university education and *Habilitation*, see Chapters VI and VII.

A special university major program for secondary school teacher training (*Lehramt an höheren Schulen*) exists for each academic subject taught in general secondary and vocational schools. Prospective teachers usually study two major subjects. Characteristics of each major program are described in Table 6.1, Chapter VI. The minimum study duration for subjects with a teaching qualification is usually nine semesters while the same ,subject without the teaching qualification is usually eight semesters (although students rarely complete a degree in the legally-prescribed minimum study duration). As are most other university degree programs, teaching programs are divided into two study segments (*Studienabschnitte*), each of which concludes with a diploma examination (*Diplomprüfung*) and award of a diploma examination certificate (*Diplomprüfungszeugnis*).

Recently pedagogical training has been added to new study regulations in teaching majors. Practical pedagogical training occurs during the second segment and requires approximately 10 weekly lessons for one semester and a school practicum consisting of a four-week orientation and an eight-week practical phase.

Graduates of teacher-training programs under the new system receive only the *Magister* degree. Under the old system, graduates receive a graduation document (*Sponsionsurkunde*) listing the degree conferred as well as an examination certificate (*Prüfungszeugnis*) issued by the Federal Examination Commission for Teachers in Secondary Schools (Bundesstaatliche Prüfungskommission für das Lehramt an höheren Schulen). Essentially these two documents certify the same thing, i.e., the individual is certified to teach in general secondary schools or senior vocational schools.

After receipt of the *Magister* degree in a teaching major, a teacher must complete one year as a "trial" teacher (*Probelehrer*) under the supervision of an experienced teacher in a regular school. After completion of the "trial" year (*Probejahr*), a certificate (*Zeugnis*) is issued.

To become eligible for a tenured university professorship, those who have the *Doktor* degree must complete a post-*Doktor* research and publication process known as *Habilitation*. Although not a requirement, those working on *Habilitation* often hold assistant professorships in universities (*Universitätsassistent*). (See "Post-*Doktor* Research Process [*Habilitation*]"in Chapter VI.)

In-Service Teacher Training

While pedagogical academies train pre-service teachers, ten pedagogical institutes (*Pädagogische Institute*) train in-service teachers. Pedagogical academies report directly to the Education, Arts and Sports Ministry at the federal level, while pedagogical institutes report indirectly to the same ministry through the provincial school councils. One vocational pedagogical institute (*Berufspädagogisches Institut*) also exists and is a private institution devoted solely to further training of teachers from developing countries.

Pedagogical institutes may be divided into the following departments:
- Department for compulsory school teachers,
- Department for teachers in vocational schools for apprentices,
- Department for teachers in general secondary schools, (which includes preschool teachers and educational assistants),
- Department for teachers in intermediate and senior vocational schools and social work academies.

Although a department exists for general secondary school teachers who were originally trained in universities, pedagogical institutes are considered to be part of the nonuniversity postsecondary educational system. Most of the programs in pedagogical institutes serve to supplement teachers' professional skills. The programs last a minimum of one semester. For completion of these programs, teachers receive a certificate of attendance (*Besuchsbestätigung*).

Compulsory school teachers or teachers of vocational subjects may complete the requirements for certification in another related field, take the required examination, and receive the teacher qualification examination certificate (*Lehramtsprüfungszeugnis* or *Zeugnis über die Lehramtsprüfung*). Courses not already completed but required for the second teacher qualification certificate constitute the required course of study.

Chapter IX
Paramedical Education

Introduction

The training of paramedical personnel is considered professional rather than academic training and occurs outside the regular academic educational system. According to federal laws, curricula and examinations used in schools for training paramedical personnel are regulated by the Health and Environmental Protection Ministry while the schools themselves are administered and financed by provincial or local authorities.

Although legally organized as programs (*Lehrgänge*), the paramedical-training programs are usually referred to as schools, e.g., medical technology schools (*medizinisch-technische Schulen*) and nursing schools (*Krankenpflegeschulen*). These schools are located in 36 public and private hospitals (*Krankenanstalten*), which are approved for educational programs by the Health and Environmental Protection Ministry. Junior medical technician, medical assistant, and nursing programs operate parallel to secondary education. Senior medical technician programs in dietetics, eye care technology, medical laboratory technology, occupational therapy, physical therapy, radiology technology, and speech therapy and audiology normally require the maturity (examination) certificate (*Reifeprüfungszeugnis, Reifezeugnis*) for admission and are considered part of the nonuniversity postsecondary educational system. Paramedical programs conclude with an examination and award of a professional title (*Berufsbezeichnung*), not an academic degree (*Grad*). The professional title confers the necessary qualification for employment in the field; no further licensing requirements exist. Applicants for all paramedical training programs must be Austrian citizens under 35 years of age with no criminal record and suited physically and mentally for health-care work.

Dentists, pharmacists, physicians, and veterinarians are trained in universities and receive professional academic degrees upon completion. See "Regular Study Programs" in Chapter VI.

Training of Nurses

Nurses are trained in secondary-level nursing schools attached to approved teaching hospitals. Programs exist in general nursing (*Krankenpflege*), pediatric nursing (*Kinderkrankenpflege*) including neonatal nursing (*Säuglingspflege*), psychiatric nursing (*psychiatrische Krankenpflege*), and nurse midwifery (*Hebammenberuf*).

General and Pediatric Nurses

Schools that provide general and pediatric (including neonatal) nurses' training are called *allgemeine Krankenpflegeschulen* and *Kinderkrankenpflegeschulen*, respectively. Admission to the four-year general and pediatric (including neonatal) nursing programs requires completion of the minimum nine-year compulsory education requirement, though some schools prefer to admit students who have the maturity certificate (which is normally required for entering postsecondary education). Applicants over 16 years of age who have completed 10 years of education may be admitted to the second year of the nursing program, since the first year of the four-year program consists primarily of general education. Before 1973, the nursing program lasted three years but students were required to complete 10 years of education prior to admission. In all cases, the total program requires a minimum of 13 years of study.

The programs in general and pediatric (including neonatal) nursing are identical for the first three years but vary according to specialization in the fourth and final year. The first year of the program deepens the student's general educational background and provides preparation for entry into the theoretical and practical training that constitutes the second through fourth years. The courses required in the general nursing program are listed in Table 9.1. Instruction is provided primarily by physicians but also may be provided by professionals in related fields (i.e., chemists or lawyers) who have at least three years of professional experience.

At the conclusion of each year, students take an examination. At the end of the fourth year, students take a comprehensive board examination (*kommissionelle Prüfung* or *Diplomprüfung*) which is supervised by the school's Examinations Commission. After passing the board examination, students receive a diploma (*Diplom*) and a professional title which entitles them to practice the nursing profession. The titles awarded are Certified General Nurse (*Diplomierte Krankenschwester* or *Diplomierte[r] Krankenpfleger[in]*) or Certified Pediatric and Neonatal Nurse (*Diplomierte Kinderkranken- und Säuglingsschwester* or *Diplomierter Kinderkranken- und Säuglingspfleger*). Those who complete only part of the program may request a certificate (*Zeugnis*) but this does not entitle them to practice nursing.

Psychiatric Nurses

Psychiatric nursing schools, which are attached to approved hospitals, are known as *Ausbildungsstätte für die psychiatrische Krankenpflege*. Training in psychiatric nursing lasts three years. Students must be at least 18 years of age and have completed the nine-year compulsory education requirement prior to admission. The total program requires a minimum of 12 years of study. Theoretical instruction during each year of the program consists of 825, 555, and 470 hours per year, respectively. In addition, a total of 2,600 hours of practical training is required.

Students take an examination after completing the first and second years of the program and a board examination after completing the third year. Those who pass the examination receive the diploma (*Diplom*) and professional title of Certified Psychiatric Nurse (*Diplomierte psychiatrische Krankenschwester* or *Diplomierter psychiatrischer Krankenpfleger*) which is required for professional

Table 9.1. Course List for General Nursing

Subject	Min. Hours	Subject	Min. Hours
Second Year (11th year of education, minimum)			
Anatomy	40	Intro. in Psychology	30
Developmental Psychology	30	Intro. in Soc. Hygiene	15
English for Medical Personnel	70	Laboratory Techniques	20
First Aid	20	Nutrition, Disease & Dietetics	40
Fundamentals of Hosp. Proced.	15	Pathology	40
Fundamentals of Phys. Therapy	20	Physical Education	80
Fundamentals of Sanitation Law	15	Physiology	60
Fundamentals of Soc. Insur. &		Practicums Required (in at	
Worker's Rights	15	least 3 of the following	
Fndns. of Welfare Work	20	areas): blood bank,	600
Gen. Nursing Hygiene	60	dietetics, health-care	
Gen. Nursing Techniques	180	admin., lab, pharmacy,	
History & Ethics	20	preventative medicine,	
Intro. in Pedagogy	20	school health	
Third and Fourth Years			
Ear, Nose & Throat Diseases and		Psychology	80
Intro. to Audiology	15	Skin Diseases	40
Eye Diseases	30	Sociology & Hygiene	20
Geriatrics	20	Surgery	110
Infectious Diseases	40	X-Ray Technology	20
Internal Medicine	120	Required Practicums	
Intro. to Rehabilitation	20	Gynecology & Obstetrics	
Neurology	40	with Newborn Care	440
Obstetrics & Gynecology	60	Internal Medicine	600
Occupational Therapy	30	Pediatrics	400
Pedagogy	20	Public Health	160
Pediatrics	60	Surgery	600
Pharmacology & Toxicology	30	Addl. Specialization Choice	–
Physical Education	160	Electives (English, Fine Arts,	
Psychiatry	40	Physical Education)	–

employment. Those who do not complete the program may request a certificate (*Zeugnis*) but are not entitled to work as nurses.

Nurse Midwives

Nurse midwives are trained in federal midwife training institutions (*Bundeshebammenlehranstalten*) that are attached to hospitals. To enter the two-year program in nurse midwifery, students must be at least 17 years of age and have completed at least nine years of compulsory education. The total program consists of a minimum of 11 years of study. Those who already have a nursing diploma but who also wish a midwife diploma complete a one-year program.

Midwife training is both theoretical and practical. The regular program consists of a minimum of 509 hours of theoretical instruction. Practical experience is required in obstetrical and neonatal care. Students must assist with a minimum of 30 births. After passing the final diploma examination (*Diplomprüfung*), students receive the diploma (*Diplom*) and professional title of Midwife (*Hebamme*). The diploma is often referred to as the midwife diploma (*Hebammendiplom*).

Courses for Medical Assistants

Short courses (as opposed to programs) exist in hospitals to train various types of medical assistants. Those admitted must be at least 17 years of age. A final course examination is required prior to award of the final course certificate (*Kursabschlusszeugnis* or *Zeugnis*) and a vocational title. The programs, their duration, and the vocational titles awarded are as follows.

Programs	Hours	Vocational Title
Ambulance attendants	135	*Sanitätsgehilf(e)(in)*
General practitioner's assistant	135	*Ordinationsgehilf(e)(in)*
Hospital station assistants	185	*Stationsgehilf(e)(in)*
Hydro- and balneotherapists	70	*Heilbadegehilf(e)(in)*
Laboratory assistants	135	*Laborgehilf(e)(in)*
Mortuary assistants	135	*Prosektursgehilf(e)(in)*
Occupational therapy assistants	135	*Beschäftigungs- und Arbeitstherapiegehilf(e)(in)*
Operating room assistants	135	*Operationsgehilf(e)(in)*
Public health assistants	130	*Desinfektionsgehilf(e)(in)*
Thermo-, hydro-, and balneotherapists	210	*Heilbademeister(in) und Heilmasseur(in)*

Training of Junior-Level Medical Technician Specialists

The program to train junior-level medical technician specialists (*medizinisch-technische Fachkraft*) exists at the upper secondary level while the training program for senior-level medical technician assistants (*medizinisch-technische[r] Assistent[in]*) occurs at the nonuniversity postsecondary level (see "Postsecondary Training of Senior-Level Medical Technicians" below). Though the salary scale for medical technician specialists is lower than that for medical technician assistants, they often work side by side. Those who enter the fulltime, 30-month hospital training program for junior-level medical technician specialists must be at least 17 years of age and have completed the nine-year compulsory education requirement.

The study program is divided into three segments consisting of theoretical and practical instruction and is then followed by three months of practical training. The first segment, lasting 11 months, provides the basic background subjects as well as introductory laboratory procedures. The second segment, lasting 10 months, provides training in the use of x-rays for different diagnostic and therapeutic goals; and the third segment, lasting six months, provides further training in therapeutic management. The total program consists of 610 hours of theoretical instruction in the medical sciences and 2,800 hours of practical instruction.

At the conclusion of the program, students take a final diploma examination (*Diplomprüfung*). Those who pass the examination receive a diploma (*Diplom*) and the title of Certified Medical Technician Specialist (*Diplomierte medizinisch-technische Fachkraft*). Those who successfully complete only part of the program may request a certificate (*Zeugnis*) but may not work as a medical technician specialist.

Postsecondary Training of Senior-Level Medical Technicians

Dieticians, eye care technicians, (senior level) medical technician assistants, occupational therapists, physical therapists, radiology technicians, and speech therapists and audiologists are trained in medical technology schools (*medizinisch-technische Schulen*) which are attached to approved teaching hospitals. Medical technology schools are part of the nonuniversity postsecondary stream of higher education which was established in the early 1960s. Prior to 1961, all medical technicians were trained in upper secondary vocational schools.

Dietetics

Entry into dietetics (*Diätdienst*) requires the maturity certificate (*Reifeprüfungszeugnis, Reifezeugnis*), a diploma (*Diplom*) from a nursing program, or a leaving certificate (*Abschlusszeugnis*) from a three-year intermediate vocational school in domestic sciences (*Fachschule für wirtschaftliche Frauenberufe*). Skills in cooking as well as skills in typing and shorthand also are required for admission. After passing a final diploma examination (*Diplomprüfung*), graduates receive a diploma (*Diplom*) and the title of Certified Dietician (*Diplomierte[r] Diätassistent[in]*). Dieticians may practice independently and sometimes work in the tourist industry, though dieticians also work under the supervision of physicians in hospitals or other institutions (i.e., sanitariums) or in medical research. Those who fail to complete the entire program may request a certificate (*Zeugnis*) but may not work as professional dieticians.

The two-year program consists of 1,600 hours of practical training and 900 hours of theoretical instruction in calories and calorie calculation (60); economics and business for dieticians (95); first aid and bandaging techniques (10); fundamentals of chemistry, physics, and food chemistry (60); general and special dietetics (130); hospital administration (10); kitchen and food hygiene (15); laboratory methods (10); law (30); medical English (25); normal and pathological anatomy as related to the digestive organs (70); nutrition (90); nutrition for newborns and small children (5); physiology and pathology of the digestive organs and digestion (60); planning diets for special needs (200); and psychology, rhetoric, and negotiating techniques (30).

Eye Care Technology

Admission to eye care technology (*orthoptischer Dienst*) requires the maturity certificate or a diploma from a nursing program. After completing the program and passing the final diploma examination, graduates receive a diploma and the title of Certified Eye Care Technician (*Diplomierte[r] Orthoptist[in]*). Graduates must work under the supervision of a physician. Those who complete only part of the program may request a certificate (*Zeugnis*) but may not enter professional practice.

The program lasts two years and six months and consists of 1,900 hours of practical training and 900 hours of theoretical instruction in anatomy and physiology with special emphasis on the eyes (140 hours); child and educational psychology (60); drugs and anaesthesia (20); equipment (20); first aid and bandaging techniques (20); general pathology with special emphasis on the eyes (60); hospital administration (10); hygiene (20); law (30); ophthalmology examination methods (60); phototechniques (60); physics, especially optics and lenses (70); theoretical fundamentals of treatment (230); and treating cross-eyed or squint conditions (100).

Medical Laboratory Technology

Entry into medical laboratory technology (*medizinisch-technischer Laboratoriumsdienst*) requires the maturity certificate, a diploma from a nursing program, or a diploma from a junior-level medical technician specialist program. Knowledge of typing and shorthand also is required. After completion of the program, graduates receive a diploma and the title of Certified Medical Technician Assistant (*Diplomierte[r] medizinisch-technische Assistent[in]*). Medical technicians must work under the supervision of physicians in hospitals, in private practice, or in other institutions (e.g., sanitariums) or may engage in medical research along with physicians. Those who complete only part of the program may request a certificate (*Zeugnis*) but may not enter professional practice.

The program, which lasts two years and three months, consists of theoretical instruction lasting 1,160 hours and practical training lasting 1,680 hours. The hours of theoretical instruction are distributed as follows: Anatomy (60 hours); cytology (40); first aid and bandaging techniques (20); general and inorganic chemistry including chemical analysis techniques (120); general laboratory techniques (50); general pathology (60); hematology (100); histology and histopathology (100); hospital administration (10); hygiene and environmental protection (40); immunohematology (30); law (30); medical documentation and accounting techniques (60); medical laboratory automation (20); medical technology (40); microbiology (60); organic and physiological chemistry including chemical analysis techniques as well as work with radioactive isotopes in the medical laboratory (180); photography and microphotography (40); physiology (60); radiology and radiation protection (10); and serology (30). Practical instruction consists of clinical chemistry and microscopic examination methods; examination methods in chemistry, hematology, histology and cytology, immunohematology, microbiology, and serology; and techniques of photography and microphotography.

Occupational Therapy

The occupational therapy program is accredited by the World Federation of Occupational Therapy. Required for entry into occupational therapy (*beschäf-*

tigungs- und arbeitstherapeutischer Dienst) is the maturity certificate or a diploma from a nursing program. After passing the final diploma examination, graduates receive a diploma and the title of Certified Occupational Therapist (*Diplomierte[r] Beschäftigungs- und Arbeitstherapeut[in]*). Graduates work under the supervision of physicians in hospitals or other related institutions, in medical research, or in private practice along with physicians. Those who do not complete the entire program may request a certificate (*Zeugnis*) but may not work as an occupational therapist. See sample document in Appendix A.

The three-year program requires a minimum of 1,800 hours of practical instruction as well as 2,400 hours of theoretical instruction in anatomy (120 hours); fundamentals of rehabilitation and cooperative working within the rehabilitation team (80); general pathology (50); geriatrics (30); hospital administration (10); hygiene (20); instruction in manual skills and activities (900); internal medicine (60); law (30); mechanical (or movement) therapy (40); movement training (30); neurology (60); occupations and physiology (30); orthopedics (60); pediatrics (60); physical medicine (40); physiology (120); psychiatry (80); psychology and occupational psychology (50); surgery including first aid and bandaging techniques (80); and the theory of occupational therapy in relation to the medical sciences (450).

Physical Therapy

Required for entry into physical therapy (*physikotherapeutischer Dienst*) is the maturity certificate or a diploma from a nursing program as well as skills in typing and shorthand. After passing the final diploma examination, graduates receive a diploma and the title of Certified Assistant for Physical Medicine (*Diplomierte[r] Assistent[in] für physikalische Medizin*). Physical therapists may practice independently but also may work under the supervision of physicians in hospitals and other related institutions or in medical research. Those who complete only part of the program may request a certificate (*Zeugnis*) but may not enter professional practice.

The program lasts two years and six months and consists of 1,760 hours of theoretical instruction and 1,250 hours of practical training. The hours of theoretical instruction are distributed as follows: anatomy and physiology with special consideration of movement functions (240 hours); general pathology (50); gynecology (15); hospital administration (10); hygiene (20); internal medicine (60); law (30); mechanical (or movement) therapy (440); methods for conductiong group physical training (160); neurology and psychiatry (60); orthopedics (60); pediatrics (15); physical training (200); psychology (20); rehabilitation (40); surgery and emergency surgery including first aid and bandaging techniques (80); and thermo-, electro-, and phototherapy as well as hydro- and balneo-therapy (260). Practical training is provided in geriatrics, gynecology, internal medicine, neurology, orthopedics, pediatrics, psychiatry, rehabilitation, and surgery.

Radiology Technology

Those who enter radiology technology (*radiologisch-technischer Dienst*) must have the maturity certificate, a diploma from a nursing program, or a diploma from a junior-level medical technician program. Knowledge of typing and shorthand also is required. After completing the program, graduates receive a diploma and the title of Certified Radiology Technician Assistant (*Diplomierte[r] radiologisch-technische Assistent[in]* or *Diplomierte[r] Röntgenassistent[in]*). Graduates must work under the supervision of physicians. Although those who do not complete the program may request a certificate (*Zeugnis*), they may not enter professional practice.

In addition to 1,920 hours (minimum) of practical instruction, the two-year program consists of 830 hours of theoretical instruction in anatomy and physiology as related to radiology (110 hours); documentation, statistics and medical accounting (25); first aid as related to radiology (25); general photography (30); general physics and physical basis of radiology (50); hospital administration (10); law (30); nuclear medicine (60); occupational and social hygiene (20); pathology as related to radiology (60); physical radiation protection (30); radiobiology and radiation protection (30); radiochemistry (40); radiographic equipment (30); radiology and physics, including radiological exposure in diagnosis and treatment (60); radiological photography (30); radiological techniques and equipment (40); radiotherapy (50); special procedures in radiology (30); and x-ray positioning (70).

Speech Therapy and Audiology

Those who enter speech therapy and audiology (*logopädisch-phoniatrisch-audiometrischer Dienst*) must have a maturity certificate, a diploma from a nursing program, or the qualification examination certificate for preschool teachers (*Befähigungsprüfungszeugnis für Kindergärtnerinnen*) which after 1990 will be the maturity and qualification certificate (*Reife- und Befähigungsprüfungszeugnis*) for preschool teachers. (See "Preschool Teachers" in Chapter VIII.) After passing the final diploma examination, graduates receive a diploma and the title of Certified Speech Therapist and Audiologist (*Diplomierte[r] Logopäd[e][in]*). Graduates of the speech therapy and audiology program may practice independently or may work under the supervision of physicians in hospitals or in medical research.

The two-year program requires a minimum of 1,400 hours of practical instruction and 1,000 hours of theoretical instruction consisting of anatomy and physiology with special emphasis on the speech and hearing organs (140 hours); audiology (60); biolinguistics (50); children's communication disorders (60); first aid and bandaging techniques (20); general hygiene (20); general pathology with special emphasis on the throat, nose, and ears as well as teeth and oral-facial anomalies (100); hearing aids (40); law (30); neurology as related to the speech and hearing organs (60); psychology (50); treatment of communication disorders (200); voice and language assessment (110); and voice training (60).

Chapter X
International Education

Introduction

Austria has a large international community. Vienna serves as headquarters to approximately 50 international business and diplomatic organizations, including the United Nations. The international community also consists of many foreign students who pay only a nominal tuition at Austrian colleges and universities. In 1984-85, Austrian universities and fine arts colleges enrolled approximately 14,900 foreign students, a figure which represents approximately 10% of the total enrollment. Approximately 65% of the foreign students come from Europe, 24% from Asia, 4% from North America, 3% from Africa, 2% from South America, and less than .002% from Australia and Oceania. (Note: The origin of the remaining foreign students was unspecified.)

Approximately 51% of the foreign students in Austrian universities and colleges come from one of the seven bordering countries (45% come from only two of the neighboring countries, Italy and the Federal Republic of Germany) and approximately 3% come from the United States. Many more U.S. students study in Austria through programs sponsored by U.S. universities, colleges or private organizations, though the exact number is unknown. Sponsors of foreign educational programs in Austria have no legal obligation to notify the Austrian government or the appropriate foreign embassy that a foreign educational program exists. Foreign college and university programs are not officially recognized by the Austrian government.

Austrian College or University Enrollment for Foreign Students

Foreign students are admitted to Austrian universities and fine arts colleges on a space-available basis and entry into certain high-demand majors may be either limited or prohibited. Foreign students seeking admission to Austrian universities or fine arts colleges should direct their application to the office of the university director or rector (*Universitätsdirektion, Rektorat*) at the appropriate university. Required for admission is demonstrated proficiency in German, good health, a character reference, a transcript with passing grades from previous schools attended, and previous education that is deemed equivalent to the Austrian maturity certificate. Non-native German speakers should inquire about German language proficiency during the application process but should be prepared to take the University Language Examination (*Hochschulsprachprüfung*) prior to enrollment.

As a Council of Europe member, Austria honors the European agreement on the equivalence of diplomas leading to university admission. As part of this agreement, entry into Austrian colleges and universities is granted to students who have academic secondary-school diplomas from the following countries: Belgium, Cyprus, Denmark, France, Federal Republic of Germany, Great Britain and Northern Ireland, Greece, Iceland, Ireland, Israel, Italy, Luxembourg, Malta, Netherlands, New Zealand, Norway, Spain, Sweden, Turkey, and Yugoslavia. Austria has bilateral agreements with the following countries whereby the Austrian maturity certificate and the university-preparatory leaving certificate from that country are considered equivalent: Bulgaria, Finland, Liechtenstein, Luxembourg, Portugal (ratification pending), Rumania, and Yugoslavia. The U.S. high school diploma usually is not recognized as equivalent to the Austrian maturity certificate (see Chapter III, "Other Academic Secondary Schools;" Chapter VI, "Entry Requirements;" and Chapter VII, "Entry Requirements"). Similarly, the U.S. bachelor's degree usually is not considered equivalent to the first Austrian academic degree, the *Magister*, or *Diplom-Ingenieur*.

Foreign students may seek admission to regular degree programs in Austrian universities and fine arts colleges (see Chapter VI, "Regular Study Programs;" and Chapter VII, "Study Programs") or to special nondegree programs (see Chapter VI, "Special Study Programs"). Special study programs exist at some universities for students who wish to study German as a second language (see Chapter VI, Table 7.2, and also in this chapter, "German Language Courses"). Special study programs also exist for those who wish to prepare for the maturity certificate equivalency examinations in order to enter a university with regular degree-seeking status.

Staff members in offices of the Austrian Foreign Student Service (Österreichischer Auslandsstudentendienst, ÖAD) provide assistance to foreign students who wish to study in an Austrian university. Addresses of these offices are as follows:

*Hauptgebäude der Universität Wien, Stiege IX, A-1010 Wien, Dr. Karl Lueger-Ring 1.

*Universität Graz, A-8010 Graz, Schubertstrasse 2-4.

*Universität Innsbruck, A-6020 Innsbruck, Innrain 52.

*Universität Salzburg, A-5020 Salzburg, Mozartplatz 1, Stiege 4, IV. Stock.

*Montanuniversität, A-8700 Leoben, Franz-Josef-Strasse 18.

*Universität Linz, A-4040 Linz, Schloss Auhof.

*Universität für Bildungswissenschaften, A-9020 Klagenfurt, Universitätsstrasse 67.

German Language Courses

The Austrian Foreign Student Service (see addresses above) provides information and a printed brochure on German language courses available in Austria. In addition, the Science and Research Ministry, in its publication *Universitäten/Hochschulen: Studium und Beruf* (1985), lists the following German language programs. Regardless of previous language instruction, non-native

German speakers may be required to take the University Language Examination (*Hochschulsprachprüfung*) prior to entrance into Austrian university or fine arts college degree programs.

*Austrian-American Society (Österreichisch-Amerikanische Gesellschaft, A-1010 Wien, Stallburggasse 2)—in cooperation with the Goethe-Institut.

*Austrian Committee for International Study Exchange (Österreichisches Komitee für Internationalen Studienaustausch, ÖKISTA, A-1090 Wien, Türkenstrasse 4).

*Austrian Hammer-Purgstall Society (Österreichisches Orient-Gesellschaft Hammer-Purgstall, A-1010 Wien, Dominikanerbastei 6/6).

*The Berlitz School of Languages (A-1010 Wien, Graben 13).

*Birkbrunn Student House of the Austrian Cultural Society (Studentenhaus Birkbrunn der Österreichischen Kulturgemeinschaft, A-1190 Wien, Linneplatz 3).

*"German in Graz," an international university course at the University of Graz ("Deutsch in Graz," Internationale Universitätskurs, Karl-Franzens-Universität Graz, A-8043 Graz, Postfach 27).

*International Cultural Institute (Internationales Kulturinstitut, A-1010 Wien, Opernring 7).

*International Summer Course for German Language and German Studies (Internationale Ferienkurse für deutsche Sprache und Germanistik [IFK], A-5020 Salzburg, Franz-Josef-Strasse 19).

*International Summer Course of the Tirolean Provincial Tourist Bureau (Internationale Ferienkurse Tiroler Landereisebüro, A-6290 Mayrhofen, Hauptstrasse 409).

*Lerch Language School (Sprachschule Lerch, A-6020 Innsbruck, Kapuzinergasse 10).

*University for Educational Sciences (Universität für Bildungswissenschaften Klagenfurt, A-9020 Klagenfurt, Universitätsstrasse 67).

*University of Innsbruck (Universität Innsbruck, A-6020 Innsbruck, Innrain 52).

*Vienna International University Courses, University of Vienna (Wiener Internationale Hochschulkurse, Universität Wien, A-1010 Wien, Dr. Karl Lueger-Ring 1).

*Vienna Language Institute (Sprachinstitut Vienna, A-1010 Wien, Universitätsstrasse 6).

U.S. Programs in Austria

Many of the U.S. programs located in Austria exist for students who are not fluent enough in German for enrollment in Austrian institutions, although students fluent in German sometimes enroll in U.S. rather than Austrian programs in order to facilitate credit transfer to a U.S. degree program. In addition, U.S. students may lack the secondary-school course prerequisites for entering certain Austrian degree programs (e.g., secondary school Latin or its equivalent is required for enrollment in European language majors).

A comprehensive listing of U.S. programs in Austria is provided by the Institute of International Education (IIE), 809 United Nations Plaza, New York, NY 10017, in its publications *Academic Year Abroad* and *Vacation Study Abroad*. Another listing, entitled *American University and College Programs in Austria*, is available from the Office of the Cultural Attaché of the U.S. Embassy in Vienna, A1082 Wien, Schmidgasse 14.

U.S. university and college programs may operate independently or may be affiliated in various ways with Austrian universities or other organizations. Some study-abroad sponsors arrange for U.S. students' enrollment in special study programs at Austrian universities (see Chapter VI, "Special Study Programs"). In this case, the Austrian university may issue a Certificate of Study Results (*Nachweis über den Studienerfolg*) which serves as a transcript of classes completed and provides a grade. (See sample documents in Appendix A.)

Chapter XI
Placement Recommendations

The Role of the National Council on the Evaluation of Foreign Educational Credentials

The placement recommendations that follow have been approved by the National Council on the Evaluation of Foreign Educational Credentials. In order that these recommendations may be of maximum use to admissions officers, the following information on the development of the terminology used in stating the recommendations, along with instructions for their use, is offered by the Council and the World Education Series Committee.

The recommendations deal with all levels of formal education in roughly chronological order up through the highest degree conferred. Recommendations, as developed through discussion and consensus in the Council, are not directives. Rather, they are general guidelines to help admissions officers determine the admissibility and appropriate level of placement of students from the country under study.

The recommendations should be applied flexibly rather than literally. Before applying the recommendations, admissions officers should read the supporting pages in the text and take into account their own institutional policies and practices. For example, a recommendation may be stated as follows: ". . . may be considered for up to 30 semester hours of transfer credit. . ." The implication is that the U.S. institution may consider giving less than or as much as one year of transfer credit, the decision to be based on various factors—the currentness of the applicant's transfer study, applicability of the study to the U.S. curriculum, quality of grades, and the receiving institution's own policies regarding transfer credit. Similarly, the recommendation ". . . may be considered for freshman admission" indicates possible eligibility only; it is not a recommendation that the candidate be admitted. Although consideration for admission at the same level may be recommended for holders of two different kinds of diplomas, use of identical phrasing in the recommendations does not mean that the two diplomas are identical in nature, quality, or in the quantity of education they represent.

In most cases, the Council will not have attempted to make judgments about the quality of individual schools or types of educational programs within the system under study. Quality clues are provided by the author and must be inferred from a careful reading of the text.

Certain phrases used repeatedly in the recommendations have acquired, within Council usage, specific meanings. For example, "through a course-by-course analysis" means that in dealing with transfer credit, each course taken at the foreign institution is to be judged on an individual basis for its transferability to the receiving institution. Another phrase "where technical training is considered appropriate preparation" suggests that the curriculum followed by the candidate is specialized, and this wording is often a hint that within the foreign system the candidate's educational placement options are limited to certain curriculums. However, while the Council is aware of the educational policies of the country under study, the Council's policies are not necessarily set in conformity with that country's policies. Rather, the recommendations reflect U.S. philosophy and structure of education.

In voting on individual recommendations, Council decisions are made by simple majority. Although consistency among volumes is sought, some differences in philosophy and practice may occur from volume to volume.

Placement Recommendations

Credential	Entrance Requirement	Length of Study	Gives Access in Country to	Placement Recommendations
A. Compulsory Education Credentials				
Primary School *(Volksschule)*				
1. *Jahres- und Abschlusszeugnis* (Yearly and Leaving Certificate) from lower cycle primary school (pp. 11–12)	Age 6	4 years	Lower secondary education	May be placed in grade 5.
2. *Abgangszeugnis or Abschlusszeugnis* (Leaving Certificate) or *Jahres- und Abschlusszeugnis* from upper cycle primary school (p. 12)	Age 6	8 years	Ninth year of education	May be placed in grade 9.
Lower Secondary School *(Hauptschule, Gesamtschule)*				
3. *Jahreszeugnis* (Yearly Certificate) (pp. 12–14)	Received at end of each year of study in a lower secondary school		—	May be placed in secondary school on a year-for-year basis.
4. *Jahres- und Abschlusszeugnis* (pp. 12–14)	4 years of education	4 years	Ninth year of education	May be placed in grade 9.
Prevocational Program *(Polytechnischer Lehrgang)*				
5. *Jahres- und Abschlusszeugnis* (p. 15)	8 years of education	1 year	Apprenticeship or employment	May be placed in grade 10.
B. General Secondary Education Credentials				
6. *Jahreszeugnis* (Yearly Certificate) (p. 17)	Received at end of each year of study in a general secondary school		—	May be placed in secondary school on year-for-year basis.
7a. *Zeugnis über die Ablegung einer Vorprüfung zur Reifeprüfung* (Certificate for Passing a Preliminary Exam for the Maturity Exam) (pp. 23–26)	—		—	Represents partial completion of external maturity certificate.
b. *Externistenprüfungszeugnis or Externistenprüfungszeugnis über den Lehrstoff einzelner Unterrichtsgegenstände* (External Exam Certificate for each subject) (p. 23–26)	—		—	Represents partial completion of external maturity certificate.

continued

Credential	Prior education	Duration	Leads to	Placement recommendation
c. *Externistenreifeprüfungszeugnis* (External Maturity Exam Certificate) (pp. 23–27)	9 years of education minimum	Equivalent to 3 years of school enrollment and/or independent study	Postsecondary education	May be considered for freshman admission.
8. *Reifeprüfungszeugnis/Reifezeugnis* (Maturity Exam Certificate or Maturity Certificate) from a general secondary school (pp. 16–27)	4 to 8 years of education	5 to 9 years (total education lasting 12 or 13 years)	Postsecondary education	May be considered for freshman admission.

C. Vocational Education Credentials

Vocational Schools for Apprentices (Berufsschulen, Berufsbildende Pflichtschulen)

Credential	Prior education	Duration	Leads to	Placement recommendation
9. *Jahreszeugnis* (Yearly Certificate) (pp. 29–30)	—	Received at end of each year of apprenticeship and academic study	—	May be placed in secondary school at an appropriate level.
10. *Abschlusszeugnis* (Leaving Certificate) or *Jahres- und Abschlusszeugnis* (Yearly and Leaving Certificate) plus a Final Apprenticeship Exam Certificate (*Lehrabschlussprüfungszeugnis, Lehrbrief, Gehilfenprüfungszeugnis, Gehilfenbrief, Lehrlingsprüfungszeugnis*). (Student should have both an academic and an apprenticeship credential.) (pp. 29–30)	9 years of education	2–4 years of apprenticeship and academic study	Employment	After two-year programs, may be considered for placement in grade 12; after three- to four-year programs, may be considered for freshman admission where vocational training is considered appropriate preparation.

Intermediate and Senior Vocational Schools

Credential	Prior education	Duration	Leads to	Placement recommendation
11. *Jahreszeugnis* (pp. 30–40)	—	Received at end of each year of fulltime study	—	May be placed in secondary school on year-for-year basis.
12. *Abschlusszeugnis* or *Jahres- und Abschlusszeugnis* from an intermediate vocational school (pp. 30–40)	8 years of education	1–4 years	Employment	May be placed in secondary school on year-for-year basis; after four-year programs, may be considered for freshman admission where vocational training is considered appropriate preparation.
13. *Abschlussprüfungszeugnis* (Leaving Exam Certificate) from *Fachschule*	8 years of education	3–5 years	Employment	After three-year programs, may be considered for placement in grade

Credential	Education requirement	Length	Purpose	Placement recommendation
(intermediate industrial/trade/artisan and agriculture/forestry school) and *Modeschule* (Fashion School) (pp. 30–36)	8 years of education	5 years	Employment or post-secondary education	12; after four- or five-year programs, may be considered for freshman admission to programs where vocational training is considered appropriate preparation.
14. *Reifeprüfungszeugnis* or *Reifezeugnis* (Maturity Exam Certificate) from *höhere Lehranstalt, höhere technische Lehranstalt, höhere gewerbliche Lehranstalt,* and *Handelsakademie* (senior vocational schools) (pp. 30–40, 46–47)	12–13 years of education and first Maturity (Exam) Certificate	1½ or 2 years	Employment or post-secondary education	May be considered for freshman admission.
15. *Reifeprüfungszeugnis* (a [second] Maturity Exam Certificate from a *Kolleg* (vocational institute) (p. 41–44, 46–47)			Employment or post-secondary education	May be considered for freshman admission.
16. *Reifeprüfungszeugnis* or *Reifezeugnis* (Maturity [Exam] Certificate) from *höhere Lehranstalt für Reproduktions- und Drucktechnik* (higher institution for reproduction and printing technology) (p. 45–47)	8–12 years of education	5–3 years (total education of 13–15 years)	Employment or post-secondary education	May be considered for freshman admission.
17. *Ingenieurkunde* (Certification of "Engineer" Title) pp. 36, 44)	Maturity (Exam) Certificate	3 years of work experience	Employment	An employment qualification; admission and placement should be based upon other credentials.
18. *Abschlusszeugnis* from *Meisterschulen, Bauhandwerkerschulen, Werkmeisterschulen, Meisterklassen,* or *Schulen* (master craftsman schools or classes) (p. 45–46)	10–12 years of education	Variable	Employment	A vocational qualification; admission and placement should be based upon other credentials.
19. *Abschlusszeugnis, Lehrgangszeugnis* (Program Certificate), or *Kurszeugnis* (Course Certificate) from courses, programs, and special programs (p. 45)	Variable	Variable	Employment	A vocational qualification; admission and placement should be based upon other credentials.
20. Diploma for the European Secretary/ *Diplom der Europasekretärin/Diplôme*	Maturity (Exam) Certificate	2 years	Employment	May be considered for undergraduate admission with possible transfer

continued

Credential	Entry Requirement	Length	Gives Access To	Placement Recommendation
de Secrétaire Européene from Euro-päische Sekretärinnenakademie (European Secretary Academy) (p. 48)				credit based on a careful review of the syllabus. *continued*

D. Social Work Education

Note: A *Jahreszeugnis* (Yearly Certificate) usually is issued after each year of study and sometimes the last yearly certificate is combined with the leaving certificate (*Jahres- und Abschlusszeugnis*).

	Credential	Entry Requirement	Length	Gives Access To	Placement Recommendation
21.	*Abschlusszeugnis* (Leaving Certificate) from *Schule für Sozialdienste, Fachschule für Sozialberufe* (intermediate vocational school in social work) (p. 50)	8 years of education	2–3 years	Employment	May be placed in secondary school on a year-for-year basis.
22.	*Abschlusszeugnis* from *Kinderpflegerinnenschule* (Child-Care School) or *Fachschule für Sozialberufe-Behindertenarbeit* (social work school for those who work with physically handicapped persons) (p. 51)	9 years of education	3 years	Employment	May be considered for freshman admission where vocational training is considered appropriate preparation.
23.	*Abschlusszeugnis* from *Familienhelferinnenschule* (family helper school) (p. 51)	Minimum 9 years of education and age 17	2 years	Employment	Represents specialized training; should be considered for admission and placement in combination with other credentials.
24.	*Abschlusszeugnis* from *Fachschule für Altendienste* (geriatric social worker school) (p. 51)	9 years of education and age 19 (minimum)	1 year	Employment	Represents specialized training; should be considered for admission and placement in combination with other credentials.
25.	*Jahreszeugnis* (Yearly Certificate) from preparatory program of *Akademie für Sozialarbeit* (Social Work Academy) (Note: Not awarded to those who already have the Maturity [Exam] Certificate) pp. 51–52)	9–13 years of education	1 year	Admission to regular program at social work academy	Represents one year of secondary level education; should be considered for admission and placement in combination with other credentials.
26.	*Diplom* (Diploma) from *Akademie für Sozialarbeit* (Social Work Academy) (pp. 51–52)	Maturity (Exam) Certificate or Yearly Certificate from the preparatory program	2 years	Employment	May be considered for undergraduate admission with 0–60 semester hours of transfer credit determined through a course-by-course analysis.

	Credential	Requirements	Minimum length		Placement recommendation
27.	*Abschlusszeugnis* from *Schule für Ehe- und Familienberater, Lehranstalt für Familientherapie* or *Lehranstalt für Ehe- und Familienberater* (Marriage and Family Counseling School) (p. 52)	Maturity (Exam) Certificate	3½ years part-time	Employment	May be considered for undergraduate admission with 0–30 semester hours of transfer credit determined through a course-by-course analysis.
28.	*Abschlusszeugnis* from *Diakonenschule* (School for Protestant Deacons) (p. 52)	10–12 + years of education and age 19	2 years	Employment	May be considered for freshman admission where vocational training is considered appropriate preparation.
29.	*Abschlusszeugnis* from Lehranstalt für pastorale Berufe (School for Pastoral Professions) (p. 53)	Maturity (Exam) Certificate + 1 year practical experience	4 years including 1 year of practical training	Employment	May be considered for undergraduate admission with 0–90 semester hours of transfer credit determined through a course-by-course analysis.

E. University Credentials

Note: 1) The *Berufsreifeprüfung* (vocational maturity exam) or *Studienberechtigungsprüfung* (studies-authorizing exam) are alternatives to the maturity certificate and meet the entry requirements for university study. 2) An *Ergänzungsprüfung* (supplementary exam) or *Zusatzprüfung* (additional exam) are required in addition to the *Reifeprüfungszeugnis* or *Reifezeugnis* (maturity certificate) for admission to certain university majors. 3) Undergraduate transfer credit, determined through a course-by-course analysis of class completion certificates (*Zeugnis, Kolioquienzeugnis*), may be considered for students who have not completed a full academic program.

	Credential	Requirements	Minimum length		Placement recommendation
30.	*Diplomprüfungszeugnis* (Diploma Exam Certificate) after first (*erste*) study segment (pp. 75–81)	Maturity (Exam) Certificate	Minimum length varies by major from 1 to 2½ years	Further university studies	May be considered for undergraduate admission with transfer credit determined through a course-by-course analysis.
31.	*Diplom-Dolmetscher* in interpreting, *Diplom-Ingenieur* in engineering and technical fields, *Diplom-Kaufmann* in business, *Diplom-Tierarzt* in veterinary medicine, *Lehramtsprüfungszeugnis* (Teacher Exam Certificate), and *Magister* in other fields (pre-AHStG system) (pp. 72–73, 75)	Maturity (Exam) Certificate	Variable	Further university studies	May be considered for graduate admission.
32.	*Diplom-Ingenieur* in engineering and technical fields or *Magister* in all other fields except for veterinary medicine (post-AHStG system) (pp. 75–81)	First *Diplomprüfungszeugnis* (Diploma Exam Certificate)	Minimum length varies by major from 2–3 years	Admission to doctoral program	May be considered for graduate admission.

continued

33. *Diplom-Tierarzt* in veterinary medicine (post-AHStG system) (pp. 75–81)	Maturity (Exam) Certificate	5 years minimum	—	A first professional degree in the field; may be considered for graduate admission.
34. *Doktor* (pre-AHStG system) (pp. 72–73, 75, 82)	Maturity (Exam) Certificate or first academic degree	Variable	*Habilitation* (Post-*Doktor* Research Process)	May be considered comparable to an earned doctorate in the United States.
35. *Doktor* (post-AHStG system) (pp. 75–76, 82–83)	*Magister, Diplom-Ingenieur,* or *Diplom-Tierarzt*	1–2 years legal minimum in some fields; no legal minimum in other fields	*Habilitation* (Post-*Doktor* Research Process)	May be considered comparable to an earned doctorate in the United States.
36. *Doktor* in Medicine (pp. 83–84)	Maturity (Exam) Certificate	6 years minimum	Entrance into a hospital residency or additional medical training	A first professional degree in medicine; may be considered for graduate admission.
37. *Habilitation* (Post-*Doktor* Research Process) (p. 89)	*Doktor* degree	Variable	Eligibility for university tenure	Represents recognition of published scholarly research.
38. *Akademisch geprüfter Datentechniker* (Academically Certified Computer Engineer), *Akademisch geprüfter Versicherungsmathematiker* (Academically Certified Actuary), *Akademisch geprüfter Übersetzer* (Academically Certified Translator) (pp. 75–76, 84)	Maturity (Exam) Certificate	2½ to 3 years minimum	Employment	May be considered for undergraduate admission with transfer credit determined through a course-by-course analysis.
39. *Diplomierter Umwelttechniker* (Graduate Environmental Engineer) or *Diplomierter Wirtschaftstechniker* (Graduate Business Technician) (p. 84)	*Diplom-Ingenieur* degree	2 years minimum	Employment	May be considered for graduate admission with transfer credit determined through a course-by-course analysis.
40. *Abschlusszeugnis* (Leaving Certificate) from special university programs with award of an academic title, e.g., *Akademisch geprüfter Fremdenverkehrskaufmann* (Academically Certified Tourist Business Person), *Akademisch geprüfter Werbekaufmann* (Academically Certified Advertising Busi-	Maturity (Exam) Certificate or variable years of experience	2 years	Employment	Undergraduate admission should be based on other academic credentials; may be considered for undergraduate transfer credit determined through a course-by-course analysis.

ness Person), *Akademisch geprüfter Versicherungskaufmann* (Academically Certified Insurance Business Person), *Akademisch geprüfter Absolvent des Medienkundlichen Lehrganges* (Academically Certified Graduate of Media Arts Program) (pp. 85–87)

Credential	Entrance Requirement	Length of Program	Gives Access to	Placement Recommendation
41. *Abschlusszeugnis* or *Abschlussbescheinigung* (Leaving Certificate) from special university programs or courses (pp. 85–87)	Maturity (Exam) Certificate usually; some programs require an academic degree	Variable	—	Undergraduate admission should be based on other academic credentials; may be considered for undergraduate transfer credit determined through a course-by-course analysis.
42. *Diplom* (Diploma) from the Diplomatic Academy in Vienna or the Institute for Advanced Studies (pp. 88–89)	*Magister* degree	2 years	—	May be considered comparable to a U.S. master's degree.

F. Fine Arts Credentials

Note: Those who have completed fine arts college coursework but who do not yet have the next higher credential/degree/title/diploma may be considered for undergraduate transfer credit determined through a course-by-course analysis.

Credential	Entrance Requirement	Length of Program	Gives Access to	Placement Recommendation
43. *Diplom, Diplomzeugnis, Reifezeugnis** (Diploma); *Lehrbefähigungszeugnis* (Teacher Qualification Certificate); *Abschlusszeugnis* (Leaving Certificate); *Jahreszeugnis* (Yearly Certificate) (pre-KHStG system) (pp. 97–100)	Age 15–17 or Maturity (Exam) Certificate	Variable	Professional fine arts qualification	May be considered for admission and placement as are students from U.S. fine arts schools.

*This *Reifezeugnis* (Maturity Certificate) is not equivalent to and should not be confused with the maturity certificate from a general secondary or senior vocational school.

Credential	Entrance Requirement	Length of Program	Gives Access to	Placement Recommendation
44. *Magister der Künste/Magister artium* (post-KHStG system) (pp. 97–98, 100–103)	Age 15–17 or Maturity (Exam) Certificate	4–8 years	Admission to doctoral studies	May be considered for graduate admission.
45. *Akademisch geprüfter Opernsänger* (Academically Certified Opera Singer), *Akademisch geprüfter Konzertsänger* (Academically Certified Concert Singer), or *Akademisch geprüfter*	Age 17	3 years	Employment	May be considered for admission and placement as are students from U.S. music schools.

continued

Credential	Admission Requirement	Length	Purpose	Placement Recommendation
Musiktherapeut (Academically Certified Music Therapist) (pp. 97–98, 100–103)				
46. Akademisch geprüfter Kirchenmusiker (Academically Certified Church Musician) (pp. 97–98, 100–103)	Age 17	4 years	Employment	May be considered for admission and placement as are students from U.S. music schools.
47. Schulbesuchsbestätigung (Certificate of Attendance) or Reifezeugnis (Maturity Certificate) from a music conservatory (p. 106)	Variable	Variable	Not an academic qualification	Primarily a music qualification; admission and placement should be based on other credentials.

G. Teacher Education Credentials

Note: Partial completion of any program for which undergraduate credit is recommended may be considered for transfer credit through a course-by-course analysis.

Credential	Admission Requirement	Length	Purpose	Placement Recommendation
48. Befähigungsprüfungszeugnis für Kindergartnerinnen (Qualification Exam Certificate for Preschool Teachers) and Befähigungsprüfungszeugnis für Erzieher (Qualification Exam Certificate for Educational Assistants) (awarded prior to spring 1988) (pp. 107–108)	8 years of education + aptitude test	4 years	Employment	May be considered for freshman admission where vocational training is considered appropriate preparation.
49. Reife- und Befähigungsprüfungszeugnis (für Erzieher) (Maturity and Qualification Exam Certificate) for preschool teachers or for educational assistants (awarded beginning in 1990) (p. 109)	8 years of education + aptitude test	5 years	Employment or post-secondary education	May be considered for freshman admission.
50. Befähigungsprüfungszeugnis für Sonderkindergartenpädagogik (Qualification Exam Certificate in Preschool Special Education) or Abschlusszeugnis (Leaving Certificate) in special education for educational assistants (pp. 108–109)	Qualification Exam Certificate for Preschool Teachers or Educational Assistants	1½ to 2 years	Employment	May be considered for freshman admission.
51. Reife- und Befähigungsprüfungszeugnis für Erzieher ([second] Maturity and Qualification Exam Certificate for Educational Assistants) from a Kolleg (vocational institute) (p. 109)	(first) Maturity (Exam) Certificate	2 years	Employment	May be considered for freshman admission.

52. *Zeugnis über die Lehramtsprüfung für Volksschulen* (Teacher Qualification Certificate for Primary Schools) (prior to 1986) (pp. 109–112)	Maturity (Exam) Certificate	2 years	Employment	May be considered for undergraduate admission with 0–60 semester hours of transfer credit determined through a course-by-course analysis.
53. *Zeugnis über die Lehramtsprüfung für Hauptschulen* (Teacher Qualification Certificate for Lower Secondary Schools), *Zeugnis über die Lehramtsprüfung für Hauptschulen und Polytechnische Lehrgänge* (Teacher Qualification Certificate for Lower Secondary Schools and Prevocational Programs), and *Zeugnis über die Lehramtsprüfung für Sonderschulen* (Teacher Qualification Certificate for Special Education Schools) (pp. 109–112)	Maturity (Exam) Certificate	3 years	Employment	May be considered for undergraduate admission with 0–90 semester hours of transfer credit determined through a course-by-course analysis.
54. *Lehramtsprüfungszeugnis* or *Zeugnis über die Lehramtsprüfung* (Qualification Exam Certificate) for vocational teachers (pp. 112–113)	Usually the Maturity (Exam) Certificate; sometimes a *Meisterprüfung* (Master Craftsman Exam)	1–3 years	Employment	May be considered for undergraduate admission with transfer credit determined through a course-by-course analysis.
55. *Befähigungsprüfungszeugnis* (Qualification Exam Certificate) for agriculture and forestry teachers, *Abschlussprüfungszeugnis* (Leaving Exam Certificate) or *Abschluss- und Befähigungsprüfungszeugnis* (Leaving and Qualification Exam Certificate) from Bundesseminar für das landwirtschaftliche Bildungswesen (Federal Seminar for Agricultural Education) (pp. 113–114)	Maturity (Exam) Certificate	1 year	Employment	May be considered for undergraduate admission with 0–30 semester hours of transfer credit determined through a course-by-course analysis.
56. *Befähigungsprüfungszeugnis* (Qualification Exam Certificate) for agriculture	*Magister* degree or Maturity (Exam) Certif-	4 weeks	Employment	Admission should be based on other educational credentials.

continued

and forestry teachers from Bundesseminar für das landwirtschaftliche Bildungswesen (pp. 113–114) | icate + work experience

Note: Handicraft teachers also are trained in pedagogical academies; see placement recommendation for compulsory school teachers.

Credential	Entry requirement	Duration		Recommendation
57. Befähigungsprüfungszeugnis für Arbeitslehrerinnen (Qualification Exam Certificate for Handicraft Teachers) (prior to 1988) (p. 114)	8 years of education	4 years	Employment	May be considered for freshman admission to programs where vocational training is considered appropriate preparation.

Note: Physical education teachers also are trained in pedagogical academies and universities; see placement recommendations 30, 31, 32, 34, 35 or 53.

Credential	Entry requirement	Duration		Recommendation
58. Abschlussprüfungszeugnis ([Non-Teacher Qualifying] Leaving Exam Certificate) or Abschluss- und Befähigungsprüfungszeugnis for physical education teachers and Staatlich geprüfter Sportlehrer (State Certified Sports Teacher) vocational title (pp. 114–115)	Minimum 8 years of education and age 16	2 years	Employment	Represents specialized training; admission and placement should be based on other credentials.
59. Abschlusszeugnis for skiing instructors and Staatlich geprüfter Schilehrer (State Certified Skiing Instructor) vocational title (pp. 114–115)	Minimum 8 years of education and age 16	1 year	Employment	Represents specialized training; admission and placement should be based on other credentials.
60. Lehramtsprüfungszeugnis or Zeugnis über die Lehramtsprüfung for Roman Catholic religion teachers (p. 115)	Maturity (Exam) Certificate	2 years, 4 years part-time, or 12 weeks + independent study	Employment	May be considered for undergraduate admission with 0–60 semester hours of transfer credit determined through a course-by-course analysis.
61. Diplomprüfungszeugnis (Diploma Exam Certificate) for Protestant religion teachers (pp. 115–116)	Minimum 9 years of education and minimum age of 17–18	3 years	Employment	May be considered for freshman admission where the specialized program is considered appropriate preparation.
62. Besuchsbestätigung (Certificate of Attendance) at a Pädagogisches Institut (pedagogical institute) for in-service teachers (p. 117)	A teacher qualification certificate	Variable	—	An in-service teacher training credential; consider for admission and placement on the basis of other credentials.

H. Paramedical Education

Note: A *Zeugnis* (certificate) represents partial completion of the secondary level nursing and junior- or senior-level medical technician programs and is not a professional qualification.

63. *Diplom* (Diploma) with title of *Diplomierte Krankenschwester or Diplomierte(r) Krankenpfleger(in)* (Certified General Nurse) or *Diplomierte Kinderkranken- und Säuglingsschwester or Diplomierter Kinderkranken- und Säuglingspfleger* (Certified Pediatric and Neonatal Nurse) (pp. 118–119)	Variable	Employment	May be considered for freshman admission where specialized training is considered appropriate preparation.
64. *Diplom* (Diploma) with title of *Diplomierte psychiatrische Krankenschwester or Diplomierter psychiatrischer Krankenpfleger* (Certified Psychiatric Nurse) (pp. 119–120)	Minimum 9 years of education and age 18	Employment	May be considered for freshman admission where specialized training is considered appropriate preparation.
65. *Diplom* (Diploma) with title of *Hebamme* (Midwife) (pp. 120–121)	Minimum of 9 years of education and age 17	Employment	Represents specialized secondary training; should be considered for admission and placement in combination with other credentials.
66. *Kursabschlusszeugnis or Zeugnis* (Final Course Certificate) and vocational title representing completion of short course for medical assistants (p. 121)	Minimum age 17	Employment	Primarily a vocational qualification; admission and placement should be based on other credentials.
67. *Diplom* (Diploma) with title of *Diplomierte medizinisch-technische Fachkraft* (Certified Medical Technician Specialist) (pp. 121–122)	Minimum 9 years of education and age 17	Employment	May be considered for freshman admission where specialized training is considered appropriate preparation.
68. *Diplom* (Diploma) with title of *Diplomierte(r) Diatassistent(in)* (Certified Dietician) (p. 121); *Diplomierte(r) radiologisch-technische Assistent(in) or Diplomierte(r) Röntgenassistent(in)*	Maturity (Exam) Certificate, diploma from a nursing program, or leaving certificate from certain 11–13	2 years	Employment

continued

(Certified Radiology Technician Assistant) (p. 125); or *Diplomierte(r) Logopäd(e)(in)* (Certified Speech Therapist and Audiologist) (p. 125)	year vocational programs			
69. *Diplom* (Diploma) with title of *Diplomierte(r) medizinisch-technische Assistent(in)* (Certified Medical Technician Assistant) (p. 123)	Maturity (Exam) Certificate; diploma from a nursing or junior-level medical technician specialist program	2 years and 3 months	Employment	May be considered for undergraduate admission with transfer credit determined through a course-by-course analysis.
70. *Diplom* (Diploma) with title of *Diplomierte(r) Orthoptist(in)* (Certified Eye Care Technician); or *Diplomierte(r) Assistent(in) für physikalische Medizin* (Certified Assistant for Physical Medicine) (pp. 122–124)	Maturity (Exam) Certificate or diploma from a nursing program	2 years and 6 months	Employment	May be considered for undergraduate admission with transfer credit determined through a course-by-course analysis.
71. *Diplom* (Diploma) with title of *Diplomierte(r) Beschäftigungs- und Arbeitstherapeut(in)* (Certified Occupational Therapist) (pp. 123–124)	Maturity (Exam) Certificate or diploma from a nursing program	3 years	Employment	May be considered for undergraduate admission with transfer credit determined through a course-by-course analysis.

Appendix A

Sample Documents

BUNDESGYMNASIUM WIEN XIII
FICHTNERGASSE 15, 1130 WIEN
(Bezeichnung und Standort der Schule)

Schülerstammblatt-Nr.: _____

Zahl des Prüfungsprotokolls: _____

Schuljahr 19_____
(school year)

Reifeprüfungszeugnis

SAMPLE DOCUMENT

(student's name)
Familien- und Vorname

, geboren am _____ (date of birth)

hat sich an dieser Schule vor der zuständigen Prüfungskommission gemäß den Vorschriften der Verordnung des Bundesministers für Unterricht und Kunst vom 20. Dezember 1974 über die Reifeprüfung in den allgemeinbildenden höheren Schulen, BGBl. Nr. 105/1975, in der geltenden Fassung der

Reifeprüfung

unterzogen und diese

_____ mit gutem Erfolg _____

bestanden.

Gesamtbeurteilung: mit ausgezeichnetem Erfolg bestanden, mit gutem Erfolg bestanden, bestanden, nicht bestanden

1. The first page of the Maturity (Examination) Certificate (*Reifeprüfungszeug-nis* or *Reifezeugnis*) contains the school name and address at the top, school year, student's name, date of birth, and the comprehensive grade (*Gesamtbeurteilung*). Preceding the word *bestanden* (passed), which is printed on the form, the words *mit ausgezeichnetem Erfolg* (with high distinction), *mit gutem Erfolg* (with distinction), or *nicht* (not) may be written; a blank line indicates the student passed. The sample Maturity Certificate above is from a language-oriented *(Gymnasium)* type of general secondary school (*allgemeinbildende höhere Schule*, AHS). Although not shown, the first page of a Maturity Certificate from a senior vocational school or vocational institute *(Kolleg)* has many of the same features as that from a general secondary school, except the school name at the top is a senior vocational school and the type of vocational program is noted (e.g., *höhere Lehranstalt für wirtschaftliche Frauenberufe* [higher institute for domestic sciences] or *Kolleg)*. Although the Maturity Certificate for a *Kolleg* program is actually the "second" Maturity Certificate, this is not noted on the certificate.

Die Leistungen in den Prüfungsgebieten der Reifeprüfung bzw. bei der/den Zusatzprüfung(en) gemäß § 41 Abs. 1 des Schulunterrichtsgesetzes wurden wie folgt beurteilt:

Prüfungsgebiete	Beurteilung
Religion (röm. kath.)	Sehr gut
Deutsch	Gut
Englisch	Gut
Latein	Befriedigend
Geographie	Sehr gut
Mathematik	Gut

Zusatzprüfung(en)	Beurteilung

Er / Sie hat damit die Berechtigung für Abgänger eines *neusprachlichen*

Gymnasiums

zum Besuch einer Universität gemäß der Hochschulberechtigungsverordnung erworben.

Wien , am *11. Juni* 198

Für die Prüfungskommission:

Vorsitzender

Schulleiter   Klassenvorstand

Beurteilungsstufen: Sehr gut, Gut, Befriedigend, Genügend, Nicht genügend

2. The second page of the Maturity (Examination) Certificate provides a list of the examination subjects *(Prüfungsgebiete)* and individual grades *(Beurteilung)*. If students take additional examinations *(Zusatzprüfungen)*, the results are reported here. Though usually not included on the second page of the Maturity Certificate from a senior vocational school, the Maturity Certificate from a general secondary school may indicate the type of general secondary school curriculum completed. In the document above, the modern language branch *(neusprachliches Gymnasium)* which requires the study of Latin was completed. Thus, the student qualifies for entry into university majors for which Latin is a prerequisite.

Stundentafel der Höheren Lehranstalt für wirtschaftliche Frauenberufe

(Gesamtstundenzahl und Stundenausmaß der einzelnen Unterrichtsgegenstände)

PFLICHTGEGENSTAND	Wochenstunden im Jahrgang				
	I	II	III	IV	V
Religion	2	2	2	2	2
Deutsch	3	3	3	3	3
Englisch	3	3	3	3	2
Französisch	3	3	3	3	3
Geschichte und Sozialkunde	2	2		2	2
Geographie und Wirtschaftskunde	2	2			
Staatsbürgerkunde und Rechtskunde	—	—		2	2
Volkswirtschaftslehre	—	—		—	2
Musikerziehung	1	1	1	1	1
Bildnerische Erziehung	2	2		—	—
Lebenskunde	1			—	—
Psychologie und Erziehungslehre	—			2	3
Naturgeschichte	2	2	2	2	2
Physik und Chemie	2	2	2	2	—
Wirtschaftliches Rechnen	3	2	2	1	—
Kaufmännische Betriebskunde und Schriftverkehr	—		2	1	2
Buchhaltung, Bilanz- und Steuerlehre	—	—	2	3	4
Stenotypie — Kurzschrift	2	1	1	—	—
Stenotypie — Maschinschreiben	1	2	1	—	—
Küchenpraxis und Küchenführung	—	—	10	10	—
Ernährungslehre, Lebensmittel- und Diätkunde	—	—	1	1	2
Hausnaltspflege	2	2	—	—	—
Hauswirtschaftliche Betriebspraxis und Organisationsübungen	—	—	2	2	—
Organisationslehre der Beherbergungs- und Verpflegungsbetriebe	—	—	—	—	2
Werkstätte für Textilverarbeitung	8	8	—	—	—
Leibesübungen	3	3	3	3	3
Gesamtwochenstundenzahl	42	40	43	43	35

Ferialpraktikum, 12 Wochen zwischen dem III. und IV. Jahrgang in Beherbergungs- und Verpflegungsbetrieben sowie sonstigen Fremdenverkehrseinrichtungen (lt. Verordnung des BMfU v. 20. 4. 1966, BGBI. Nr. 56/1966)

FREIGEGENSTAND					
Mathematik	—	2	2	2	2
Einführung in die Philosophie	—	—	—	—	2
Englische Konversation und literaturkundliche Übungen	—	—	—	—	2
Bildnerische Erziehung	—	—	2	—	2
Leibesübungen	2	2	2	2	2
UNVERBINDLICHE ÜBUNGEN					
Arbeitsgemeinschaft	2	2	2	2	2

3. The third page of the Maturity Certificate from senior vocational schools and vocational institutes (Kolleg) contains a course list with instructional hours (Stundentafel). The sample above is a course list from a five-year senior vocational school for domestic sciences (höhere Lehranstalt für wirtschaftliche Frauenberufe). The Maturity Certificate from a general secondary school does not contain a course list.

4. Registration Certificate *(Inskriptionsschein)* records the university classes for which a student registered each semester but does not contain an indication of class completion or academic performance.

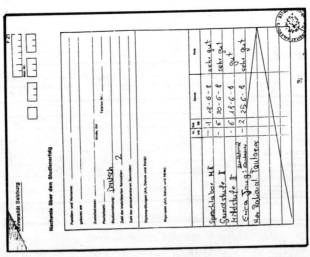

5. Certificate of Study Results *(Nachweis über den Studienerfolg)* provides a summary of accomplishments. The certificate lists the examinations *(Diplomprüfungen, Rigorosen)* taken, courses completed, number of weekly semester hours *(W. Std.* or *Wochenstunden)*, date, and grade.

Teilprüfungszeugnis (form, Universität in Graz): geboren am __; in __; hat am __ 2. Oktober 19__ die Teilprüfung aus __Englisch__; der __I.__ Diplomprüfung · des __geististswirtsch.__ Studienrichtung mit __sehr gut__ Erfolg abgelegt. Graz, am 22. Oktober 19__. Der Präses der Prüfungskommission. Für die Richtigkeit der Ausfertigung: Der Universitätsdirektor. (UNIVERSITÄT GRAZ seal)

6. Partial Examination Certificate *(Teilprüfungszeugnis)* reports partial completion of a diploma examination. The text of the sample document indicates partial completion of the first (I.) diploma examination *(Diplomprüfung)*, but the same certificate may be used to indicate partial completion of the second (II.) diploma examination.

Technische Universität Graz — *Zeugnis über den ersten Teil der zweiten Diplomprüfung* — Prüfungsprotokoll Nr.; Mat. Nr.; Name __; geboren am __; hat am __ 8.02.198__ den ersten Teil der zweiten Diplomprüfung der Studienrichtung __Verfahrenstechnik, Wahlfachgruppe Chemieanlagenbau__ bestehend aus den folgenden Prüfungsfächern:

Prüfungsfach	Note		Datum
Theoretische Maschinenlehre	gut	(2)	8.02.198
Maschinenbau	gut	(2)	8.02.198
Verfahrenstechnik	sehr gut	(1)	8.02.198
Apparate- und Anlagenbau	gut	(2)	8.02.198
Chemieanlagenbau	sehr gut	(1)	8.02.198

7. Certificate Covering the First Part of the Second Diploma Examination *(Zeugnis über den ersten Teil der zweiten Diplomprüfung)* reports partial completion of the second *(zweite)* diploma examination. The same certificate may be used for the first *(erste)* diploma examination. The certificate lists the major *(Studienrichtung)*, the examination subjects *(Prüfungsfach)*, grade received in each subject, and date.

8a. The first page of the Diploma Examination Certificate *(Diplomprüfungs-zeugnis)* reports completion of either the first *(erste)* or second *(zweite)* diploma examination and provides a comprehensive grade *(Gesamtnote)*. In the sample document, the text indicates the second diploma examination was completed.

8b. The second page of the Diploma Examination Certificate reports the examination subjects *(Prüfungsgegenstand)*, grade received in each subject, and date.

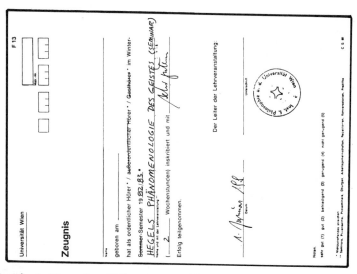

9. Certificate (*Zeugnis* or *Kolloquienzeugnis*) reports class completion and provides the class name, grade received, and number of weekly semester hours (*Wochenstunden*). The irrelevant types of student status are crossed out. In the example above, the student had regular student status (*ordentlicher Hörer*).

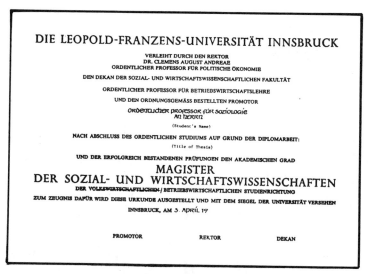

10. *Magister* of Social and Economic Sciences (*Magister der Sozial- und Wirtschaftswissenschaften*) degree.

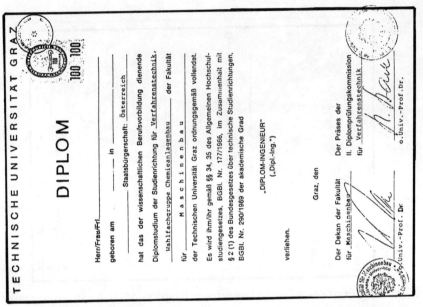

11. *Diplom-Ingenieur* degree.

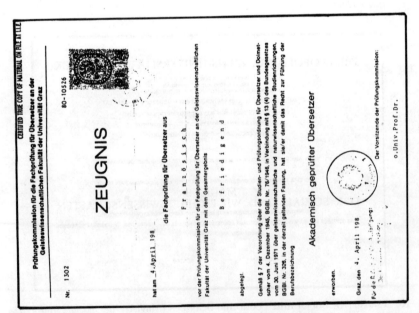

12. Academically Certified Translator (*Akademisch geprüfter Übersetzer*) title.

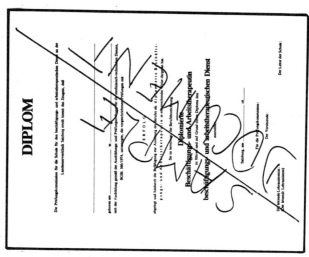

13. Diploma *(Diplom)* with title of Certified Occupational Therapist *(Diplomierte Beschäftigungs- und Arbeitstherapeutin).*

14. Teacher Qualification Certificate for Lower Secondary Schools *(Zeugnis über die Lehramtsprüfung für Hauptschulen),* first page only.

Appendix B

Selected Secondary-Level Vocational Schools

The following secondary-level vocational schools are listed by legal category. The names of the schools selected for this list are similar to the names of other schools within the same legal category. The departments within each of the sample schools illustrate the way in which different types and levels of vocational training are organized. The actual number of schools within each legal category in 1985 was as follows: 124 industrial, trade and artisan schools (consisting of 85 industrial-technical schools, 20 fashion and clothing industry schools, and 19 tourist industry schools); 134 business schools; 132 domestic science schools; 135 agriculture and forestry schools; 16 secondary-level social work schools; 34 secondary-level teacher-training schools; and 61 hospital nursing schools (including 14 that also offer postsecondary medical-technician training).

The departments that exist within each school are abbreviated as follows: CP = continuation program (Aufbaulehrgang); IVS = intermediate vocational school (berufsbildende mittlere Schule); MC = master class (Meisterklasse); MS = master or craftsman school (Meisterschule, Bauhandwerkerschule, Werkmeisterschule); P = program (Lehrgang); SP = special program (Speziallehrgang); SVS = senior vocational school (berufsbildende höhere Schule); WA = working adults (Berufstätige); VI = vocational institute (Kolleg).

A list of vocational specializations in German along with an English translation is included in Table 4.1, Chapter IV.

INDUSTRIAL, TRADE AND ARTISAN SCHOOLS (Chapter IV)

TECHNICAL-INDUSTRIAL SCHOOLS

Bundesfachschule, 3822 Karlstein, Raabser Strasse 23. IVS: Micromech. & Microelectron., Micromech., Watchmaking. MC: Watchmaking.

Höhere technische Bundes- Lehr- und Versuchsanstalt, 3100 St. Pölten, Waldstrasse 3. IVS (Fachschulen für): Elec. Engr. & Produc. Technol., Mech. Engr. Technol., Telecommunica. & Elec. Engr. Technol. SVS: Elec. Engr. Technol., Mech. Engr. & Indus. Technol., Mech. Engr. Technol., Telecommunica. & Elec. Engr. Technol. SVS for WA: Elec. Engr. Technol., Mech. Engr. Technol. SP for WA: Automation Technol.

Höhere technische Bundeslehranstalt, 8018 Graz, Ortweinplatz 1. IVS: Appl. Arts with various specializations. MS: Carpentry, Ceramics, Fashion, Masonry, Metal Formations, Painting, Textile Handwork (Weaving), Wood & Stone Carving. SVS: Appl. Arts (with various specializations), Above-Ground Bldg. Constr. Technol., Below-Ground Constr. Technol. VI: Below-Ground Bldg. Constr. Technol.

Kolleg für elektrische Nachrichtentechnik und Elektronik des Wirtschaftsförderungsinstituts, 8700 Leoben, Peter-Tunner-Strasse 15. VI: Telecommunica. & Elec. Engr. Technol.

Landesfachschule für Textilgewerbe, 3812 Gross-Siegharts, Schlossplatz 2. IVS (Fachschule für): Men's & Women's Clothing Indus., Textile Indus. (Weaving).

Lehranstalt für Chemotechniker des Förderungsvereines Chemotechnik, 8010 Graz, Elisabethstrasse 11. P: Advd. Training Prog. for Chem. Technologists. SVS: Chem. Indus. Technol.

Private Glasfachschule, 6233 Kramsach, Mariatal. IVS: Glass Blowing.

Technisch-gewerbliche Abendschule für Berufstätige der Kammer für Arbeiter und Angestellte, 5020 Salzburg, St. Julien-Strasse 2. MS for WA: Elec. Engr. Technol., Mech. Engr. Technol.

Technologisches Gewerbemuseum, Höhere technische Bundes- Lehr- und Versuchsanstalt, 1200 Wien, Wexstrasse 19-23. CP for WA: Mech. Engr. & Indus. Technol., Telecommunica. & Elec. Engr. Technol. MS for WA: Mech Engr. & Indus. Technol. SP: Electron. Data Proces. & Appl. Microelectron. SVS: Electron. & Biomed. Technol., Elec. Engr. Technol., Mech. & Automotive Engr. Technol., Mech. Engr. & Indus. Technol., Mech. Engr. & Weld. Technol., Mech. Engr. Technol., Plastics & Synthetics Technol., Silicate Technol. & Inorganic Mats., Telecommunica. & Elec. Engr. Technol. SVS for WA: Mech. Engr. & Indus. Technol., Telecommunica. & Elec. Engr. Technol. VI: Plastics & Synthetics Technol., Telecommunica. & Elec. Engr. Technol. VI for WA: Mech. Engr. & Indus. Technol.

Werkmeisterschule für Berufstätige des Wirtschaftsförderungsinstituts, 9020 Klagenfurt, Bahnhofstrasse 40-42. MS for WA: Elec. Engr. Technol., Indus. Electron., Mech. Engr. Technol.

FASHION AND CLOTHING INDUSTRY SCHOOLS

Fachschule der Schwestern vom Heiligen Kreuz, 8600 Bruck an der Mur, Leobner Strasse 61. IVS: Fashion & Clothing Technol.

Höhere Bundeslehranstalt für wirtschaftliche Frauenberufe, 9020 Klagenfurt, Fromillerstrasse 15. IVS: Fashion & Clothing Technol. MC: Women's Clothing Construction.

Höhere gewerbliche Bundeslehranstalt, 4020 Linz, Prinz-Eugen-Strasse 11. IVS: Fashion & Clothing Technol. MC: Women's Clothing Construction. SVS: Fashion & Clothing Technol.

TOURIST INDUSTRY SCHOOLS

Fremdenverkehrsschulen der Wiener Handelskammer, 1190 Wien, Peter-Jordan-Strasse 78-80. IVS: Hotel Management. SVS, VI: Tourist Business.

Höhere Bundeslehranstalt für wirtschaftliche Frauenberufe, 7400 Oberwart, Badgasse 7. IVS: Tourist Business.

Höhere gewerbliche Landeslehranstalt, 9500 Villach, Europaplatz 1. IVS: Hotel Management. SVS: Tourist Business.

Höhere Lehranstalt für Fremdenverkehrsberufe Villa Blanka, 6020 Innsbruck, Weiherburggasse 8. IVS: Hotel Management. SVS: Tourist Business.

Salzburger Unterrichtsanstalten für Fremdenverkehrsberufe, 5071 Siezenheim, Schloss Klessheim. IVS, SVS, VI: Tourist Business. P: Hotel Management & Tourist Business for Adult Students.

BUSINESS SCHOOLS (Chapter IV)

Bundeshandelsakademie und Bundeshandelsschule, 7000 Eisenstadt, Bad-Kissingen-Platz 3. IVS, SVS, VI: Business.

Bundeshandelsschule, 2070 Retz, Rupert-Rockenbauer-Platz 2. IVS, SVS: Business.

Büroschule des Wirtschaftsförderungsinstituts, 4020 Linz, Wiener Strasse 150. IVS: Office Training.

Büro- und Verwaltungsschule der Diözese Gurk, 9313 St. Georgen am Längsee. IVS: Office & Administration.

Schule für Datenverarbeitungskaufleute, 2100 Korneuburg, Wiener Strasse 42. IVS: Data Processing.

DOMESTIC SCIENCE SCHOOLS (Chapter IV)

Fachschule für wirtschaftliche Frauenberufe der Schwestern vom Göttlichen Erlöser, 7453 Steinberg an der Rabnitz, Untere Hauptstrasse 17. IVS: Domestic Science/Housekeeping.

Höhere Bundeslehranstalt für wirtschaftliche Frauenberufe, 4820 Bad Ischl, Kalten-bachstrasse 23. IVS: Domestic Science/Housekeeping. SVS: Domestic Science.

SOCIAL WORK SCHOOLS (Chapter V)

Fachschule für Sozialberufe der Caritas der Diözese Graz-Seckau, 8010 Graz, Wieland-gasse 31. IVS: Family Helper School, Geriatric Social Work School, Social Work.

Kinderpflegerinnenschule der Stadt Wien, 1180 Wien, Bastiengasse 36-38. IVS: Child Care School.

Schule für Sozialdienste der Caritas der Diözese, 3100 St. Pölten, Dr.-Ofner-Gasse 6-10. IVS: Social Work.

AGRICULTURE AND FORESTRY SCHOOLS (Chapter IV)

Forstliche Bundesfachschule, 3340 Waidhofen an der Ybbs, Schlossweg 2. IVS: Forestry.

Höhere Bundeslehranstalt für Forstwirtschaft, 2540 Bad Vöslau-Gainfarn, Hauptstrasse 14. SVS: Forestry.

Höhere Bundeslehranstalt für landwirtschaftliche Frauenberufe Elmberg, 4045 Linz, Elmbergweg 65. SVS: Rural Domestic Sciences.

Höhere Bundes- Lehr- und Versuchsanstalt für Wein- und Obstbau, 3400 Klosterneu-burg, Wiener Strasse 74. SVS: Fruit Growing & Wine Making.

Höhere landwirtschaftliche Bundeslehranstalt Francisco-Josephinum, 3250 Wieselburg, Schloss Weinzierl. SVS: Gen. Agri., Agri. Technol.

Landwirtschaftliche Fachschule, 7000 Eisenstadt, Neusiedler Str. 6. IVS: Wine Produc.

Ländliche Haushaltungsschule St. Martin, 8230 Hartberg, Edelseegasse 18. IVS: Rural Domestic Sciences.

SECONDARY-LEVEL TEACHER-TRAINING SCHOOLS (Chapter VIII)

Bildungsanstalten der Schulschwestern, 3300 Amstetten, Rathausstrasse 16. IVS, SVS: Kindergarten Teacher Training.

Bundes-Bildungsanstalt für Kindergartenpädagogik, 5500 Bischofshofen, Südtiroler Strasse 75. IVS, SVS: Kindergarten Teacher Training.

Bundesinstitut für Heimerziehung, 2500 Baden, Braitnerstrasse 26. IVS, SVS, VI: Edu-cational Asst. Training. P: Program to train Educational Assts. in Special Education.

Schule der Kreuzschwestern, 4020 Linz, Stockhofstrasse 10. IVS, SVS: Kindergarten Teacher Training.

NURSES' TRAINING (Chapter IX)

(Note: The following is a partial list of hospitals providing secondary-level nurses' training only. A complete list of hospitals providing postsecondary training for medical technicians is included in Appendix C. Many hospitals offering postsecondary training also provide secondary-level nurses' training.)

Allgemeines Öffentliches Krankenhaus, 5700 Zell am See. P: General Nursing.

Kinderklinik Glanzing der Stadt, 1190 Wien, Glanzinggasse 35-39. P: Pediatric Nursing.

Krankenpflegeschule des Bundeslandes Burgenland, 7400 Oberwart, Ambrosigasse 15. P: General Nursing.

Landesfrauenklinik, 4020 Linz, Ledererergasse 47. P: Midwife Training.

Psychiatrisches Krankenhaus Baumgartner Höhe der Stadt, 1145 Wien, Baumgartner Höhe 1. P: Psychiatric Nursing.

Appendix C
Nonuniversity Postsecondary Institutions

The following is a list of nonuniversity postsecondary institutions in existence in 1985 and the program(s) offered in each. Descriptions of schools in each section are provided in the referenced chapter. Institutions in the parallel university sector of higher education are listed and described in Chapters VI and VII.

Variations commonly exist in the names of Austrian institutions. For example, one source might list a school as Pädagogische Akademie der Diözese and another source might list the same school as Pädagogische Akademie der Diözese Linz.

DIPLOMATIC ACADEMY IN VIENNA (CHAPTER VI)
Diplomatische Akademie Wien, 1040 Wien, Favoritenstrasse 15.

EUROPEAN SECRETARY ACADEMY (CHAPTER IV)
Europäische Sekretärinnen-Akademie, 1010 Wien, Getreidemarkt 14.

INSTITUTE FOR ADVANCED STUDIES (CHAPTER VI)
Institut für Höhere Studien, 1060 Wien, Stumpergasse 56.

MEDICAL TECHNOLOGY SCHOOLS (CHAPTER IX)
Allgemeines Krankenhaus der Stadt, 1090 Wien, Alser Strasse 4. *Programs:* Dietetics, Eye Care Technol., Med. Lab Technol., Occupa. Therapy, Physical Therapy, Radiol. Technol., Speech Therapy & Audiol.

Allgemeines öffentliches Krankenhaus der Elisabethinen, 4010 Linz, Fadingerstrasse 1. *Program:* Dietetics.

Allgemeines öffentliches Krankenhaus der Stadt, 4020 Linz, Krankenhausstrasse 9. *Programs:* Med. Lab Technol., Radiol. Technol., Speech Therapy & Audiol.

Allgemeines öffentliches Krankenhaus der Stadtgemeinde, 3100 St. Pölten, Kremser Landstrasse 36. *Programs:* Dietetics, Med. Lab Technol., Physical Therapy.

Allgemeines öffentliches Krankenhaus der Stadtgemeinde, 2700 Wiener Neustadt, Corvinusring 20. *Program:* Radiol. Technol.

Allgemeines öffentliches Krankenhaus des Gemeindeverbandes, 2130 Mistelbach, Liechtensteinstrasse 65. *Program:* Med. Lab Technol.

Allgemeines öffentliches Krankenhaus, 9020 Klagenfurt, St. Veiter-Strasse 47. *Programs:* Dietetics, Med. Lab Technol., Physical Therapy, Radiol. Technol.

Allgemeines öffentliches Landeskrankenhaus, 8036 Graz, Auenbruggerplatz 24. *Programs:* Med. Lab Technol., Physical Therapy, Radiol. Technol., Speech Therapy & Audiol.

Allgemeines öffentliches Landeskrankenhaus, 6020 Innsbruck, Anichstrasse 35. *Programs:* Dietetics, Med. Lab Technol., Physical Therapy, Radiol. Technol., Speech Therapy & Audiol.

Allgemeines öffentliches Landeskrankenhaus, 4400 Steyr, Sierninger Strasse 170. *Program:* Med. Lab Technol.

Allgemeines öffentliches niederösterreichisches Landeskrankenhaus, 2340 Mödling, Weyprechtgasse 12. *Programs:* Dietetics, Physical Therapy.

Hanuschkrankenhaus der Wiener Gebietskrankenkasse, 1140 Wien, Heinrich-Collin-Strasse 30. *Program:* Physical Therapy.

Krankenhaus Lainz der Stadt, 1130 Wien, Wolkersbergenstrasse 1. *Program:* Radiol. Technol.

Landeskrankenanstalten, 5020 Salzburg, Müllner Hauptstrasse 48. *Programs:* Eye Care Technol., Med. Lab Technol., Physical Therapy, Radiol. Technol.

Landes-Nervenklinik, 5020 Salzburg, Ignaz-Harrer-Strasse 79. *Program:* Occupa. Therapy.

Rehabilitationszentrum, 6323 Bad Häring. *Program:* Occupa. Therapy.
Wilhelminenspital der Stadt, 1161 Wien, Montleartstrasse 37. *Program:* Physical Therapy.

SOCIAL WORK SCHOOLS (CHAPTER V)
Akademie für Berufstätige für Sozialarbeit der Caritas der Erzdiözese, 5020 Salzburg, Schumacherstrasse 20. *Program:* Social Work.
Akademie für Sozialarbeit der Caritas der Diözese, 6020 Innsbruck, Maximilianstrasse 41. *Program:* Social Work.
Akademie für Sozialarbeit der Caritas der Erzdiözese, 1090 Wien, Seegasse 30. *Program:* Social Work.
Akademie für Sozialarbeit der Stadt Wien, 1210 Wien, Freytaggasse 32. *Program:* Social Work.
Akademie für Sozialarbeit des Landes Oberösterreich, 4020 Linz, Mitterberger Weg 4. *Program:* Social Work.
Akademie für Sozialarbeit des Landes, 8010 Graz, Paulustorgasse 4. *Program:* Social Work.
Akademie für Sozialarbeit des Trägervereins Vorarlberg, 6900 Bregenz, Kirchstrasse 36. *Program:* Social Work.
Bundesakademie für Sozialarbeit, 3100 St. Pölten, Schulring 18. *Program:* Social Work.
Bundesakademie für Sozialarbeit, 1050 Wien, Rainergasse 38. *Program:* Social Work.
Lehranstalt für Ehe- und Familienberater des Zentrums für Ehe- und Familienfragen, 6020 Innsbruck, Museumstrasse 27. *Program:* Marriage & Family Counseling.
Lehranstalt für Familientherapie für Berufstätige der Diözese Graz-Seckau, 8010 Graz, Carnerigasse 34. *Program:* Marriage & Family Counseling.
Lehranstalt für Familientherapie für Berufstätige der Erzdiözese, 1030 Wien, Ungargasse 3. *Program:* Marriage & Family Counseling.
Lehranstalt für pastorale Berufe, 1130 Wien, Wolfrathplatz 2. *Program:* Social Work & Theol.
Schule für Ehe- und Familienberater, 5020 Salzburg, Franz-Josefs-Strasse 21. *Program:* Marriage & Family Counseling.

TEACHER TRAINING INSTITUTIONS (CHAPTER VIII)
Aussenstelle des Pädagogischen Instituts des Bundes, 2020 Hollabrunn, Dechant-Pfeifer-Strasse 3. *Program:* In-Service Teacher Trng.
Aussenstelle des Pädagogischen Instituts des Bundes, 4020 Linz, Kaplanhofstrasse 40. *Program:* In-Service Teacher Trng.
Aussenstelle des Pädagogischen Instituts des Bundes, 5020 Salzburg, Kaigasse 28-30. *Program:* In-Service Teacher Trng.
Berufspädagogische Akademie des Bundes, 8010 Graz, Theodor-Körner-Strasse 38. *Program:* Voc. Teacher Trng.
Berufspädagogische Akademie des Bundes, 6020 Innsbruck, Pastorstrasse 7. *Program:* Voc. Teacher Trng.
Berufspädagogische Akademie des Bundes, 4020 Linz, Kaplanhofstrasse 40. *Program:* Voc. Teacher Trng.
Berufspädagogische Akademie des Bundes, 1120 Wien, Zeleborgasse 21. *Program:* Voc. Teacher Trng.
Berufspädagogisches Institut zur Aus- und Fortbildung von Lehrern und Facharbeitern für das Ausland der Österreichischen Jungarbeiterbewegung aus Entwicklungsländern, 2340 Mödling, Guntramsdorfer Strasse 10a. *Program:* In-Service Teacher (from devel. countries) Trng.
Bundesseminar für das landwirtschaftliche Bildungswesen, 1130 Wien, Angermayergasse 1. *Program:* Agri. Teacher Trng.
Expositur der Religionspädagogischen Akademie der Erzdiözese Wien, 9020 Klagenfurt, Rudolfsbahngürtel 2. *Program:* Roman Catholic Religion Teacher Trng.
Expositur der Religionspädagogischen Akademie der Erzdiözese Wien, 5020 Salzburg, Kapitelplatz 2. *Program:* Roman Catholic Religion Teacher Trng.

Expositur des Pädagogischen Instituts des Landes, 6020 Innsbruck, Lohbachufer 6a. *Program:* In-Service Teacher Trng.

Pädagogische Akademie der Diözese, 4020 Linz, Salesianumweg 3. *Program:* Compulsory School Teacher Trng.

Pädagogische Akademie der Diözese Graz/Seckau, 8026 Graz-Eggenberg, Georgigasse 85-87. *Program:* Compulsory School Teacher Trng.

Pädagogische Akademie der Diözese Innsbruck, 6511 Zams, Klostergasse 8. *Program:* Compulsory School Teacher Trng.

Pädagogische Akademie der Diözese St. Pölten, 3500 Krems, Dr.-Gschmeidler-Strasse 22-30. *Program:* Compulsory School Teacher Trng.

Pädagogische Akademie der Erzdiözese, 1210 Wien, Mayerweckstrasse 1. *Program:* Compulsory School Teacher Trng.

Pädagogische Akademie des Bundes, 2500 Baden, Mühlgasse 67. *Program:* Compulsory School Teacher Trng.

Pädagogische Akademie des Bundes, 8010 Graz, Hasnerplatz 12. *Program:* Compulsory School Teacher Trng.

Pädagogische Akademie des Bundes, 9022 Klagenfurt, Hubertusstrasse 1. *Program:* Compulsory School Teacher Trng.

Pädagogische Akademie des Bundes, 6010 Innsbruck, Pastorstrasse 7. *Program:* Compulsory School Teacher Trng.

Pädagogische Akademie des Bundes, 5020 Salzburg, Akademiestrasse 23. *Program:* Compulsory School Teacher Trng.

Pädagogische Akademie des Bundes Oberösterreich, 4020 Linz, Kaplanhofstrasse 40. *Program:* Compulsory School Teacher Trng.

Pädagogische Akademie des Bundes in Vorarlberg, 6807 Feldkirch, Liechtensteiner Strasse 33-37. *Program:* Compulsory School Teacher Trng.

Pädagogische Akademie des Bundes in Wien, 1100 Wien, Ettenreichgasse 45a. *Program:* Compulsory School Teacher Trng.

Pädagogisches Institut des Bundes, 7001 Eisenstadt, Wolfgarten. *Program:* In-Service Teacher Trng.

Pädagogisches Institut des Bundes, 6800 Feldkirch, Carinagasse 11. *Program:* In-Service Teacher Trng.

Pädagogisches Institut des Bundes, 8010 Graz, Theodor-Körner-Strasse 38. *Program:* In-Service Teacher Trng.

Pädagogisches Institut des Bundes, 9022 Klagenfurt, Hubertusstrasse 1. *Program:* In-Service Teacher Trng.

Pädagogisches Institut des Bundes, 1070 Wien, Neustiftgasse 95-99. *Program:* In-Service Teacher Trng.

Pädagogisches Institut des Landes, 6911 Lochau, Schloss Hofen. *Program:* In-Service Teacher Trng.

Religionspädagogische Akademie der Diözese, 8026 Graz-Eggenberg, Georgigasse 85. *Program:* Roman Catholic Religion Teacher Trng.

Religionspädagogische Akademie der Diözese, 4020 Linz, Salesianumweg 3. *Program:* Roman Catholic Religion Teacher Trng.

Religionspädagogische Akademie der Diözese Innsbruck, 6130 Schwaz, Gilmstrasse 1. *Program:* Roman Catholic Religion Teacher Trng.

Religionspädagogische Akademie der Erzdiözese, 1070 Wien, Burggasse 37. *Program:* Roman Catholic Religion Teacher Trng.

Stiftung Pädagogische Akademie Burgenland, 7001 Eisenstadt, Wolfgarten. *Program:* Compulsory School Teacher Trng.

THERESIAN MILITARY ACADEMY (CHAPTER IV)
Theresianische Militärakademie, 2700 Wiener Neustadt, Burgplatz 1.

Glossary

The German term for each educational credential, type of school, or significant component of an educational program appears with the first occurrence of the English translation in the text. For translations of Austrian vocational school programs, see Tabie 4.1, Chapter IV.

Many long German nouns are compound nouns and, thus, consist of two or more constituent words. Primarily the constituent words are translated below. For example, the compound noun, *Reifeprüfungszeugnis* (maturity examination certificate), does not appear in the list; but its parts, *Reife* (maturity), *Prüfung* (examination), and *Zeugnis* (certificate), do appear. Although words may be used in different contexts and, thus, translated differently, the translation provided below is that which usually applies in an educational context.

The following notes are intended for those unfamiliar with the German language:

- The umlaut, a diacritical mark over some German vowels, may be written in two ways. Either the umlaut (¨) appears over the vowel or an "e" is added after the vowel. For example, *Prüfung* also may be written *Pruefung*.
- The symbol "β" sometimes replaces a double "s." For example, *Abschluss* (leaving) also may be written *Abschluβ*.
- German adjectives may have different endings (e.g., -e, -en, -er, -es, -em) depending upon their position within a sentence, but the ending does not change the meaning of the word. For example, the adjective *erst* (first) may appear as *erste, ersten, erster, erstes, or erstem*.
- Nouns are always capitalized regardless of their position within a sentence.
- The following are examples of singular and plural nouns. The singular nouns, *Fach* (subject), *Institut* (institute), *Akademie* (academy), *Kurs* (course), and *Lehrgang* (program), become, as plural nouns, *Fächer, Institute, Akademien, Kurse*, and *Lehrgänge*, respectively.
- A noun which refers to a person may have a male and a female version. For example, *Lehrer* is a male teacher (though this term also is used in a generic sense) and *Lehrerin* is a female teacher.

Abiturientenlehrgang	Program for secondary school graduates
Abschluss	Leaving, final, conclusion
Abschnitt (-e)	Segment (-s), section (-s)
Abteilung (-en)	Department (-s)
Akademie (-n)	Academy (-ies)
Allgemein	General
Allgemeinbildende	General educational
Angewandt	Applied
Anstalt	Institution (usually secondary level)
Aufnahme	Entry, admission
Ausgezeichnet	Outstanding, first-class, excellent
Ausserordentlich	Special
Ausweis	Identity card, certification

Befähigung	Qualification
Befriedigend	Satisfactory
Beruf	Vocation, occupation, profession
Berufstätige	Employed person
Bestanden	Passed
Bestätigung	Confirmation, attestation
Beurteilung	Grade, judgement, rating
Bezeichnung	Title, designation
Bildung	Education, formation, development, growth
Bund	Public, federal
Bundesministerium	Federal ministry
Dauer	Duration, length (of time)
Diplom	Diploma
Diplomarbeit	Thesis required for first university degree
Dissertation	Thesis (dissertation) required for *Doktor* degree
Doktor	Highest university degree
Dolmetschen	Interpret
Eignung	Aptitude, qualification
Erfolg	Result, success
Erste	First
Erweiterung	Extension, enlargement
Ergänzung	Supplementary
Erwachsene	Adult
Erzieher	Educational assistant, trainer
Erziehung	Training, education, up-bringing
Fach (Fächer)	Subject (-s)
Fernstudien	Correspondence studies
Forschung	Research
Frei	Free
Gasthörer	"Guest" student or auditor
Gebiet	Area
Gegenstand (-stände)	Subject, topic
Genügend	Sufficient
Gesetz	Law
Gesamt	Comprehensive, total
Gewerblich	Industrial
Grad	Academic degree
Grundschule	Primary or elementary school
Gruppe	Group
Gut	Good
Gymnasium (Gymnasien)	General secondary school (-s); also translated as grammar school (in a British context) or top-level secondary general school
Handel	Business, commerce
Haupt	Main
Hochschule (-n)	College (-s), university (literally, higher school)
Höher	Higher (describes senior-level secondary institutions)
Hörer	Student (literally, listener)
Hort (-e)	Day care center

Humanistisch	Classical (as applied to education), humanistic
Ingenieur	Engineer
Internatsschule	Boarding school
Jahr (-e)	Year (-s)
Kind (-er)	Child (-ren)
Kindergarten (-gärten)	Preschool (-s) for children 3 to 6 years old
Kinderkrippe (-n)	Preschool (-s) for children 1 to 3 years old
Klausur	Written examination
Kolleg	Vocational institute (for graduates of general secondary schools)
Kolloquium (-ien)	Class examination (-s)
Konversatorium (-ien)	Dialogue (-s) (a type of class)
Krankenpflege	Nursing
Krankenpfleger	(Male) nurse
Krankenpflegerin	(Female) nurse
Krankenschwester	(Female) nurse
Kunst	Art
Kunsthochschule	Fine arts college (university-level)
Kurs (-e)	Course (-s)
Kurz	Short
Langform	Long-form
Lehranstalt	Institution (usually secondary level)
Lehramt	Teachership
Lehrer	Teacher
Lehrgang (-gänge)	Program (-s)
Lehrkanzeln	Classes in fine art colleges which are supplementary to artistic classes
Lehrveranstaltung (-en)	Course (-s)
Leibeserziehung	Physical education
Leistung	Achievement, accomplishment, performance
Magister	First university-level academic degree (awarded in non-engineering fields)
Matura	Maturity certificate (Latin term for *Reifeprüfungszeugnis)*
Meisterlehre	Instruction by artistic masters
Meister	Master (craftsman, artist, etc.)
Mindest	Minimum, lowest
Mittler	Middle, intermediate
Nachweis	Certificate
Neusprachlich	Relating to modern languages
Nicht	Not
Nicht-Maturanten	Persons who do not have the maturity certificate required for entering higher education
Nostrifikation	A process by which foreign educational credentials are considered for recognition by the Austrian government
Nostrifiziert	Recognized
Note (-n)	Mark (-s), grade (-s)
Oberstufe	Upper cycle or level
Öffentlichkeitsrecht	Official recognition by the Austrian government

Ordentlich	Regular, ordinary
Österreich	Austria
Pflichtfach	Compulsory subject
Pflichtschule	Compulsory school
Privatissimum (-ma)	Special research seminar (-s)
Proseminar	Introductory seminar
Prüfung (-en)	Examination (-s)
Realgymnasium (-ien)	Mathematics and science-oriented general secondary school (-s)
Reife	Maturity
Repetitorium (-ien)	Review class (-es)
Rigorosen	Final examinations in the doctoral program
Säuglingskrippe (-n)	Preschool (-s) for children less than one year of age
Schule	School
Sehr gut	Very good
Sommersemester	Summer semester (lasts from March to June)
Sonderkindergarten	Preschool for physically or mentally handicapped children 3 to 6 years of age
Sonderschule	School for physically or mentally handicapped children
Studienplan (-pläne)	Study plan (-s)
Studienrichtung	Major
Studium (-ien)	Study (-ies)
Stufe	Level (i.e., grade level), rank
Stunde (-n)	Hour, lesson
Technisch	Technical
Teil	Part, portion
Tierartz	Veterinarian
Übersetzen	Translate
Übung	Type of class, exercise
Umweltschutz	Environmental protection
Unterstufe	Lower cycle or level
Veterinär	Veterinary
Volkshochschule	Adult education college (literally, people's college)
Volksschule	Primary school
Volksschuloberstufe	Upper-cycle primary school
Vorlesung (-en)	Lecture
Vorprüfung	Preliminary examination
Wahl	Elective, choice
Wien	Vienna
Wintersemester	Winter semester (lasts from October to January)
Wirtschaft	Economy, housekeeping, domestic science, economics
Wissenschaft	Science and scholarship, knowledge
Wissenschaftlich	Scientific and scholarly
Woche (-n)	Week (-s)
Zeugnis	Certificate
Zweite	Second
Zusatz	Addition

Selected References

A. Publications Available in English

Bodenman, Paul S. *The Educational System of Austria*. No. E-80-14011. Washington, D.C.: U.S. Government Printing Office, 1980.

Bundesministerium für Unterricht und Kunst. *Austria: Organization of Education 1981-84*. Wein: Bundesministerium für Unterricht und Kunst, 1984.

Federal Press Service. *The Austrian Educational System*. Vienna: Federal Press Service, 1984.

International Association of Universities. *International Handbook of Universities*. 9th ed. Berlin: DeGruyter, 1983.

Organisation for Economic Co-Operation and Development. *Austria: Higher Education and Research*. Paris: Organisation for Economic Co-Operation and Development, 1976.

Stassen, Manfred, ed. *Higher Education and Research: Student Handbook*. Bonn and Strasbourg: Deutscher Akademischer Austauschdienst, and Council of Europe, 1980.

Steiner, Kurt, ed. *Modern Austria*. Palo Alto, California: The Society for the Promotion of Science and Scholarship, Inc. (SPOSS, Inc.), 1981.

von Klemperer, Lily. *Austria: A Survey of Austrian Education and Guide to the Academic Placement of Students from Austria in Educational Institutions in the United States of America*. World Education Series. Washington, D.C.: American Association of Collegiate Registrars and Admissions Officers, 1961.

B. Publications Available in German

Benedikt, Erich; Dobrozemsky, H.; Klaus, W.; Leitner, L.; Wimmer, J. *Die AHS-Reifeprüfung*. Wien: Österreichischer Bundesverlag, 1981.

Bundesministerium für Unterricht und Kunst. *Bildungsbericht 1975 an die OECD*. Wien: Bundesministerium für Unterricht und Kunst, 1975.

Bundesministerium für Unterricht und Kunst unter Mitwirkung des österreichischen Statistischen Zentralamtes. *Österreichische Schulstatistik: Schuljahr 1984-85*. Wien: Österreichischer Bundesverlag, 1985.

Bundesministerium für Unterricht, Kunst und Sport. *ABC des Berufsbildenden Schulwesens*. Wien: Herold Druck- und Verlagsgesellschaft m.b.H., 1985.

Bundesministerium für Wissenschaft und Forschung. *Statistisches Taschenbuch*. Wien: Bundesministerium für Wissenschaft und Forschung, 1985.

_____. *Weiterbildung an der Universität*. Wien: Bundesministerium für Wissenschaft und Forschung, 1983; reprint ed., Wien: Bundesministerium für Wissenschaft und Forschung, 1985.

_____. *Hochschul Bericht*. Wien: Bundesministerium für Wissenschaft und Forschung, 1981; reprint ed., Wien: Bundesministerium für Wissenschaft und Forschung, 1984.

_____. *Die Hochschulen in Österreich, OECD-Bericht 1975*. Band 1. Wien: Bundesministerium für Wissenschaft und Forschung, 1976.

_____. *Das Österreichische Hochschulsystem*. Wien: Bundesministerium für Wissenschaft und Forschung, 1986.

Bundesministerium für Wissenschaft und Forschung, Bundesministerium für soziale Verwaltung und Österreichische Hochschülerschaft. *Universitäten, Hochschulen: Studium und Beruf*. Wien: Jugend und Volk Verlagsgesellschaft m.b.H, 1985.

Deutscher Akademischer Austauschdienst (DAAD). *Studienführer Österreich*. Bonn: Deutscher Akademischer Austauschdienst, 1985.

Firnberg, Hertha. *Studieren in Österreich: Ein Leitfaden für den Universitäts- und Hochschulbesuch*. Wien: Molden Schulbuch-Verlag, 1981.

Kövesi, Leo, und Jonak, Felix. *Das Österreichische Schulrecht*. Wien: Österreichischer Bundesverlag, 1983.

Österreichisches Statistisches Zentralamt. *Österreichische Hochschulstatistik: Studienjahr 1982-83*. Wien: Österreichische Staatsdruckerei, 1985.

Useful Addresses

Austrian Institute
11 East 52nd Street
New York, NY 10022

Austrian-American Educational Commission (Fulbright Commission)
1082 Wien
Schmidgasse 14
Austria

Center for Austrian Studies
University of Minnesota
712 Social Sciences Building
Minneapolis, MN 55455

Education, Arts and Sports Ministry, formerly Education and Arts Ministry (Bundesministerium für Unterricht, Kunst und Sport, formerly Bundesministerium für Unterricht und Kunst)
A-1014 Wien
Minoritenplatz 5
Austria

Science and Research Ministry (Bundesministerium für Wissenshaft und Forschung)
A-1014 Wien
Freyung 1
Austria

Index

NATIONAL COUNCIL ON THE EVALUATION OF FOREIGN EDUCATIONAL CREDENTIALS

The Council is an interassociational group that serves as a forum for developing consensus on the evaluation and recognition of certificates, diplomas, and degrees awarded throughout the world. It also assists in establishing priorities for research and publication of country, regional, or topical studies. One of its main purposes is to review and modify admissions and placement recommendations drafted by World Education Series authors or others who might ask for such review. (The practices followed in fulfilling this purpose are explained on page 130.)

Chairperson—Stan Berry, Director of Admissions, Washington State University, Pullman, WA 99163.

Vice-Chairperson/Secretary—Andrew J. Hein, Assistant Dean, The Graduate School, University of Minnesota, Minneapolis, MN 55455.

MEMBER ORGANIZATIONS AND THEIR REPRESENTATIVES

American Association of Collegiate Registrars and Admissions Officers—Chairperson of the World Education Series Committee, Kitty M. Villa, Assistant Director, University of Texas, Austin, TX 78716; Virginia Gross, Assistant Director, Admissions, University of Iowa, Iowa City, IA 52242; June Hirano, Award Service Officer, East-West Center, Honolulu, HI 96848.

American Association of Community and Junior Colleges—Philip J. Gannon, President, Lansing Community College, Lansing, MI 48901.

American Council on Education—Joan Schwartz, Director, Registries, Center for Adult Learning & Educational Credentials, ACE, Washington, DC 20036.

College Entrance Examination Board—Sanford C. Jameson, Director, Office of International Education, CEEB, Washington, DC 20036.

Council of Graduate Schools—Ann Fletcher, Assistant Dean, Graduate Studies, Stanford University, Stanford, CA 94305.

Institute of International Education—Martha Renaud, Director, Placement & Special Services Division, IIE, New York, NY 10017.

National Association for Foreign Student Affairs—Robert Brashear, Associate Director of Admissions, University of Houston-University Park, Houston, TX 77004; William H. Smart, Assistant Director, International Education, Oregon State University, Corvallis, OR 97331-2122; Valerie Woolston, Director, International Education Services, University of Maryland, College Park, MD 20742.

OBSERVER ORGANIZATIONS AND THEIR REPRESENTATIVES:

USIA—Joseph Bruns, Chief, Student Support Services Division, Office of Academic Programs, USIA, Washington, DC 20547.

AID—Hattie Jarmon, Education Specialist, Office of International Training, U.S. Department of State/AID, Washington, DC 20523.

New York Education Department—Mary Jane Ewart, Associate in Comparative Education, State Education Department, The University of the State of New York, Albany, NY 12230.